KING
ARTHUR'S
ROUND TABLE

KING
ARTHUR'S
ROUND TABLE

How Collaborative Conversations
Create Smart Organizations

David Perkins

JOHN WILEY & SONS, INC.

To Ann
The Lady of our Castle

Contents

Acknowledgments   xi

CHAPTER 1   KING ARTHUR'S DREAM   1
A Smarter Table   1
Putting Our Heads Together   2
Power to the People   5
Cooling Down Conflict   7
Team Intelligence   9
From Camelot to Reality   12

CHAPTER 2   ORGANIZATIONS ARE MADE OF CONVERSATIONS   17
Ernesto's Truth   17
ImageTech and VisionTech   18
How Round Is Your Table?   20
Process Smart and Deciding Smart   22
People Smart and the Language of Actions   26
The Usual Suspects   29
Two Archetypes of Negotiation   33
Contact Architecture   36

CHAPTER 3   YAKETY YAK AND FEEDBACK   39
Yakety Yak, 1958   39
The Dilemma of Feedback   40
Three Faces of Feedback   42
Which Style When?   45
A Feedback Camelot   46
Four Brands of Better Feedback   51

Findings from the Feedback Front   57
Who to Whom   61
Here There Be Dragons   64

CHAPTER 4   THE DIFFICULTIES OF BEING OF ONE MIND   69
Mind Melds   69
What Is Intelligence?   70
Difficulty 1: The Five-Brain Backlash   75
Difficulty 2: Cognitive Oversimplification   77
Difficulty 3: Emotional Oversimplification   79
Difficulty 4: Regression in the Face of Stress   81
Difficulty 5: The Domino Effect   82
Difficulty 6: The Power Advantage   83
Are We Ready to Give Up Yet?   85

CHAPTER 5   FROM LORDSHIP TO LEADERSHIP   89
Policy 113   89
What Leaders Do   91
Four Forms of Leadership   95
Leadership for Intelligence   103
Man with a Horn   106
Streetwise Street by Street   108
Here There Be Dragons   113

CHAPTER 6   ANTS, WEATHER, AND ORGANIZATIONAL INTELLIGENCE 119
King Arthur's Ants   119
Common Scents   121
Knowledge Weather   126
Why Should I Buy This?   133
Yes, But, Rebut   136
The Asian Executive's Question   140
Making the Weather   143

CHAPTER 7   COLLABORATION, NOT COBLABORATION   147
One of Seven   147
Three Faces of Coblaboration   149

What Facilitation Does and Why It Is Not Enough 152
The Good: What Collaboration Means, How It Helps,
 and When It Helps 154
The Bad: The Pitfalls of Problem Sharing 158
The Rules of Which 162
The Ugly: The Challenge of Collaborative Citizenship 166
The Art of Citizenship 168
Here There Be Dragons 171

CHAPTER 8 CREATIVE CONFLICT, TRAGIC TRUST 177
A Tragedy of Trust 177
Calm as a Clam 178
Three Ways of Settling Conflict 180
Regressive and Progressive Conflict 183
How Trust Works 185
Trust in the Land of Lear 188
Better Conflict through Trust 192
Here There Be Superdragons 200

CHAPTER 9 CLIMBING TOWARD CAMELOT 209
Presto Change-o 209
Poetry in Motion 212
The One-Eyed Woman 215
Pocket Change 219
How Change Takes Flight 223
The Dragon Unlearning 225
The Three Arts of Unlearning 230
The Road to Camelot 240

EPILOG: ROUNDING THE WORLD 245

NOTES 251

INDEX 265

Acknowledgments

Have you ever noticed how odd it is to do work alone? Poets and students and day traders may take that path, but it's not how things generally get done in the world. Mostly, we work together, sometimes for better, sometimes for worse.

Working together is what this book is about, and, appropriately, this book reflects the fruits of working together with many people. Don't get me wrong—I'm happy to take full blame for the words on these pages, but along the way I benefited from a range of collaborations that energized and informed this inquiry.

For several years, some colleagues and I conducted an action research initiative in organizational development at the Universidad Jorge Tadeo Lozano in Bogotá, Colombia, focusing on the business side of the university and working with administrators in areas such as accounting, law, purchasing, and building and grounds management. Rector Evaristo Obregon, who suggested the project, was a steadfast champion of our efforts, as were other key members of the university community, including Fanny Mestre and Juan Sastoque. The principal researchers from Harvard were Chris Unger, Daniel Wilson, Veronica Boix-Mansilla, and me, and, from Jorge Tadeo Lozano, Dora Bonnet and Cecilia Miani. Although this book is not a straightforward report of that experience, many of the ideas originated there. I learned much from the members of the university and my partners in the project.

Several colleagues and I initiated at Harvard a forum about organizational development for a few corporate and governmental groups. Called LILA for Learning Innovations Laboratory, the program addresses organizational intelligence, learning, leadership, knowledge management, and related matters. Project manager Daniel Wilson, along with Deborah Sole, Teresa Whitehurst, and several other members of the Harvard community, have provided lively and thoughtful friendship, guidance, and analyses of pertinent literatures. Members from major corporate and governmental settings bring their wisdom and experiences to the table four times a year for intensive meetings examining such themes as the role of technology in knowledge management, new forms of leadership, and the place of trust in organizational culture. I believe LILA has been a forum of learning for all the participants, and certainly has been for me in many ways that have informed this book. I thank the members for their insights.

The Bogotá and LILA initiatives aside, several individuals figured importantly in the evolution of the notions expressed here. Carlos Vasco of Colombia, a partner in inquiry for many years, joined me in various conversations around these ideas. Ernesto Gore, an Argentine business scholar, spent several months at the Harvard Graduate School of Education as a visiting scholar, and we examined how knowledge spreads within organizations. Beatriz Capdevielle of Venezuela has a keen interest in organizational matters and has developed a large-scale educational reform. Our discussions of this and related matters have been valuable.

London business consultant Alan Robertson and I have sustained a lively and illuminating pattern of communication for several years on ambiguity and complexity in organizations. John Edwards, Australian educator and business consultant, introduced me to provocative ideas about professional knowledge. Israeli educator Gavriel Salomon and I talked about the sociology of organizations and wrote together about knowledge networking in organizations and society. Yesha Sivan, an Israeli educator and entrepreneur, sat with me many times to exchange ideas about organizations and the role of technology.

Lisa Frontado has worked with me for several years. She read and synthesized notes on a number of the sources cited in this book, and we sat and discussed them together, exploring what the ideas imply and where they might fit into a bigger picture. She has also been enormously helpful with details on references and editorial corrections. Her colleagueship is very much appreciated.

My editor at Wiley, Airié Stuart, offered astute counsel about the tone and audience of the book and specific editorial suggestions, as well as shepherding the book through the production process at a good pace. Faith Hamlin, my agent of several years, not only encouraged this particular writing project over alternatives but provided important advice at several points along the way. Their contributions were essential.

I have drawn ideas and experiences from several corporate, governmental, and university settings encountered over the years, where I have participated in projects or as a consultant. Some of the stories in the pages that follow reflect these experiences, and I'm grateful for them all. In the interests of confidentially, I have usually changed features of key figures, products, and services. However, I have tried to maintain the essential characteristics that made the experiences illuminating.

Working together in organizations small and large is an amazingly complex undertaking, often difficult to do and very challenging to analyze. No doubt I've neglected important matters and have gotten some of it wrong. Nonetheless, I hope that most readers will discover in this book ways of thinking about our collective activities that are both enlightening and empowering. After all, that's where things get done, so let's make the doing as smart and engaging as possible.

I

King Arthur's Dream

A Smarter Table

It's probably the last thing you'd think of, recalling the glories of Camelot, the magic of Merlin, and the attractions of Guinevere. It's probably not very romantic compared with the legend of Excalibur. But there it is: King Arthur was a social theorist.

Maybe he wasn't up there with Aristotle or Thomas Paine or Karl Marx, but he was in there trying. King Arthur wanted a lot more than a Camelot of dreams, soaring out of the morning mist with a banner on every spire. He wanted a *smart* Camelot, a collective enterprise that functioned intelligently.

Central to the legendary Arthur's agenda of unifying England and fostering peace and prosperity were the Knights of the Round Table. And that round table was anything but the aesthetic whim of a monarch oh so deeply into interior decor. The traditional kingly table swept down the length of a grand reception hall, the king seated in his divine position at the head. After all, the king was the king, and that ought to be worth a place at the head of the table. But who would sit at his right hand, who on his left, who nearby, who so far down the table you'd have to shout to be heard by the king? (And you don't shout at kings.) And what would those well down the table

say about the privileged up-table positions that they would have pre-
ferred for themselves? More to the point, what would they do about
it? What they *did* do about it in other courts was plot, form coali-
tions, seed dissension, and fight duels over status.

King Arthur knew that such a restless and fuming group could
not help keep a kingdom in order, so he exercised a very simple idea:
His table would be round. His knights would sit around a round
table. No position would be greater than any other.

But Arthur had more in mind than avoiding the downside of a
bickering mob of knights. He wanted the upside of a thoughtful community. His knights would converse as equals—proposing, challenging, debating, reaching accords, and solving the problems of the
kingdom. The round table not only symbolized this collaborative commitment but made it easier: At a round table, each knight sat within
reasonable speaking distance of all the others. Of course, Arthur himself would have to sit somewhere at the table. But who happened to sit
closer to him on that occasion would not be important.

It was a beautiful and practical thought. It still is. The symbolism
of place at the table is something we all feel, whether we're sitting in
a boardroom, jury room, ready room, team room, or an ad hoc let's-
solve-this-problem meeting in the corner of the corporate cafeteria.
We may not be ready to challenge our colleagues to duels, but long
tables with the boss at one end still and inevitably provoke uneasy
thoughts about status, as well as posing practical problems of shouting in order to be heard. Round tables—or, if not round, then square
or squarish—still and inevitably serve people well, symbolically and
functionally, when they gather together in a mutual spirit to puzzle
out a problem or construct a vision.

PUTTING OUR HEADS TOGETHER

I take my hands from the keyboard, pull my eyes from the monitor,
and look down from my second-story home office on the June lawn.
After a rainy weekend, it needs mowing. But I'd rather think about
lawn mowing than mow the lawn, so I think about lawn mowing and
King Arthur.

What if we had King Arthur's estate, with a veritable Camelot of a lawn? It would take days and days to mow that lawn. But get 10 of the Knights of the Round Table out there with power mowers, and together they'd have the Camelot lawn done 10 times as fast as one. Well, maybe not quite 10 times as fast. Social scientists have identified a phenomenon called *social loafing:* In many circumstances, when you add more people to a team, each individual works a little less hard. Okay, so eight times as fast.★

Fine for the lawn. Now imagine those 10 knights of industry putting their heads together to design a new power mower. You can be sure that they wouldn't get that job done 10 or 8 times as fast. It might even take them longer than a concentrated effort by a single person. It's so much easier to mow the lawn together than to design a lawn mower together. Call this:

☞ *The lawnmower paradox:* Pooling physical effort is usually rather easy. Pooling mental effort is usually rather hard.

It's not difficult to understand why the Lawnmower Paradox occurs. We can usually divide up physical tasks by assigning people to different physical parts of the task—different sectors of the Camelot lawn for instance. For mental tasks, it's typically harder to find conceptual parts that make for an efficient division of labor. Moreover, often we do not so much want to divide up a mental task as to bring the power of multiple minds to bear on the core problem. Even with the best will in the world, pooling mental effort is not so easy.

King Arthur's idea about the round table is a small step toward dealing with the lawnmower paradox. A round table makes it a little easier to pool mental effort. A round table makes a group a little more intelligent. Given all the brain power in a product development lab, a policy team, a programming team, a marketing task force, a planning committee, or any similar gathering in corporations, governments, or universities, the potential intellectual power would seem to be enormous. But how do we realize that power? Not easily, as Arthur recognized.

★*Note:* Citations regarding social loafing and other concepts, themes, and sources appear in the notes, organized by chapter and section.

I've spent most of my professional life as a cognitive scientist and educator interested in learning, understanding, thinking, and intelligence. Much of my work has concerned the individual thinker and learner, child or adult. In *Outsmarting IQ* (New York: Free Press, 1995) and other places I've written about the nature of intelligence—how intelligence is more than a matter of neurological efficiency; how intelligence involves not just the ability to think well but the sensitivity to read situations; how people can learn to be more intelligent. But individual intelligence is only one part of a more complex cognitive system. We are a social species. We almost always do what we do together. Much of what we do requires pooling not just physical effort but intelligence, especially in the modern world. In many ways, this interactive, collective, group, or *organizational intelligence* (the term I'll usually use) is much more important than individual intelligence. That's why it has captured a portion of my attention in recent years.

Cognitive science and related disciplines speak to the intelligence of groups, teams, communities, and organizations as they do to individual intelligence. They can help us to untangle the lawnmower paradox. Information processing is a concept that applies to groups as well as to individual minds. Basic demands of problem solving and decision making identified by researchers figure in group as well as individual thinking. Scholars have identified important elements of organizational intelligence, for instance, facilitative leadership styles that foster thoughtful collaboration. Notions from the business world such as communities of practice and knowledge management illuminate how information can flow well within organizations face-to-face and digitally, informing practical action. Such ideas help to show us how many individuals' intellectual efforts might merge into organizational intelligence.

The mission of this book is to advance King Arthur's dream. The aim is to look hard at the lawnmower paradox and offer an illuminating theoretical and practical account of organizational intelligence. An important starting point is to recognize that King Arthur is certainly not the only dreamer. Throughout human history people have wondered how to put their heads together without simply bumping skulls. Before we mow Camelot's lawn any further, it's worth recognizing a few more of these dreams.

POWER TO THE PEOPLE

Democracy was born of its opposite in Athens in the last years of the sixth century B.C. Democracy was not the enlightened conception of Athenian philosophers. It was the practical construction of Kleisthenes, a political figure embroiled in a power struggle between his extended family and a rival clan, who had the upper hand.

Kleisthenes adopted an almost paradoxical tactic to resolve his problem. He proposed a new constitution that would give dramatic powers to the people of Athens and the surrounding region, Attica. The people liked the package he was selling and eventually pushed his rivals out of their positions of power. The form of government that emerged from Kleisthenes' constitution and later refinements was called *democracy,* from the Greek *démos,* the people, and *kratia,* power—power in the hands of the people.

Athenian democracy was not exactly equitable by modern standards. Male adult citizens of Athens participated; but women, slaves, and foreign residents, even long-term ones, did not, although in many respects these groups fared better than in other cultures of the era. Athenian democracy was not exactly a lean mean machine, either. A huge popular assembly, the Ekklesia, met about every 10 days to represent the collective will and ratify decrees. Decrees to be ratified were generated by the Boule, a kind of senate consisting of 500 members that met almost every day. The Prytaneis, a rotating executive committee of 50 members, organized the work of the Boule. Legislation aside, a court system heard numerous legal cases as well as ruling on the interpretation of legislation, not unlike the U.S. Supreme Court. Each gathering involved at least 201 jurors and as many as 2,500.

Although these numbers clearly pose problems of efficiency, they demonstrate a striking commitment to one aspect of organizational intelligence: pooling people's judgment in ways that avoid bias from special interests. Thus, decisions would benefit the people of Athens generally. This principle played out in several notable ways. On the largest scale, the government introduced by Kleisthenes divided the citizens of Athens into 10 large groups called *phylae* (singular *phyle*). The composition of the phylae deliberately cut across old family power blocks and also geographical interests: Each phyle included members from three geographical areas of Attica that traditionally had been rivals—plains, coast, and hills. To allow participation even of the poor, citizens received a small stipend for attending the large meetings of the Ekklesia.

Representation in the Boule, the Athenian senate, was balanced by phylae. Moreover, members of the Boule were chosen by lot for a period of one year, rather than by the popularity contest of an elective process. The Prytaneis, the executive committee of the Boule, rotated among the 10 tribes every month or so. Ordinary citizens, members chosen by lot for the Boule who happened that month to be part of the Prytaneis, guided the state.

Jurors were chosen by lot so as to achieve a balance among the phylae. They were also a large group—at least 201 for each session, as mentioned earlier—selected just before the court convened. This made it virtually impossible to bribe jurors. The jurors were paid for participation to ensure that even the poor could contribute their judgment. The juries voted by public ballot, a practice that later evolved into secret ballots.

Athenian democracy was a marvelous invention, but not an unalloyed one by any means. Socrates, who was sentenced to death for impiety and corrupting Athenian youth in 399 B.C. by one of those huge Athenian juries, held that democracy turned the government over to people of no particular enlightenment and counted all voices as equal, though they might differ in wisdom. The makers of the U.S. constitution examined both Athenian and Roman democratic institutions and leaned toward the Roman model. They judged that appeals to passion rather than reason too easily captured the enthusiasm of the large Athenian groups, creating a kind of mob rule. They felt that the brief terms of office fostered inconsistency and undermined personal accountability.

Modern democratic institutions diverge from the Athenian model, particularly in the number, expertise, and continuity of individuals involved in various roles. However, they preserve a serious effort—sometimes more successful, sometimes less successful—to tap the judgment of diverse participants in ways that keep the bias of special interests to a minimum. As in Athens of two and a half millennia ago, unbiased collective judgment remains a guiding principle today, a principle at work in jury selection, state and national elections, and boardroom, stockholder, and union votes.

COOLING DOWN CONFLICT

Mr. Kealoha, not involved in the original incident, facilitates the conversation with serene detachment. He asks his teenage daughter Kili to explain more about the shouting episode. Kili does and Mr. Kealoha paraphrases Kili's account for the rest of the family. He asks Kili whether she thinks perhaps her timing was not so good. Kili acknowledges that probably it wasn't. Mr. Kealoha again paraphrases. He continues probing Kili's account for a while. Kili speaks to him, while the other family members listen.

Mr. Kealoha then turns to Mrs. Kealoha, who was also present at the incident. He wants to corroborate Kili's account. Is this what Mrs. Kealoha saw? Mrs. Kealoha agrees broadly but offers a few adjustments. Mr. Kealoha checks with Kili: Is this what happened? Yes, Kili acknowledges.

Kalau, their other teenage daughter, now has a turn. What was Kalau's account of events?

If we didn't notice all those names starting with K, such a dialog could happen in many places and cultures around the world, untangling conflicts by a kind of collective cognitive choreography in which people report and reflect and evaluate. But this particular dialog has a context in time and place: an account from 1985 by E. Victoria Shook of an indigenous practice of the Hawaiian people called *ho'oponopono*.

The traditions of ho'oponopono, a pre-European feature of Hawaiian culture, had almost vanished by the 1950s. In the early 1960s, efforts began to revive the craft, as clinicians working on social problems sought ways to respect and draw upon the rich particularities of Hawaiian culture. Part of that culture was a robust commitment to collaboration and harmony. Pukui, Haertig, and Lee, writing in 1972, lauded the Hawaiian extended family for its sense of unity, shared involvement and shared responsibility. It is mutual interdependence and mutual help. It is emotional support given and received. It is solidarity and cohesiveness. It is love—often; it is loyalty—always. It is all this, encompassed by the joined links of blood relationship.

Ho'oponopono is one mirror of this tradition. Ho'oponopono begins with difficulties in a group, where people experience something for which the Hawaiian language has a very special name, *hihia*, a relationship of negative entanglement. Hihia grows like a weed when one person transgresses against another, as with the shouting episode that Kili launched. Hihia points not just to a single offence, but to the way aggravations escalate. I snipe at you, you gouge back; I bide my time and strike again. Pretty soon we have a feud going, our lives entangled in a negative way rather than interwoven in productive harmony. Negative entanglements may begin with substantive issues, but they expand out of all proportion, so the real problem becomes the history of reciprocal transgressions as much as the initiating incident.

Shook emphasizes the highly structured character of ho'oponopono. The practice begins with a prayer to Christian or traditional gods, invoking their aid and support. The kind of probing conversation previously illustrated follows. The aim is to identify the original transgression and how it escalated and perhaps spun off side-entanglements. The process, in a single session or several, seeks to address all of these.

A facilitating figure—Mr. Kealoha in our example—plays a catalytic role. The facilitator draws out participants, paraphrases for the group to underscore points, probes for corroboration, and strives to sort out discrepancies. The facilitator offers a serene focus, the eye of the hurricane. Participants address the facilitator rather than the other individuals, with whom they may be at odds. As negative entanglements are identified and examined, the facilitator leads the participants into a phase of confession of wrongdoing and seeking of forgiveness, characteristically in both directions between two parties, since it would be rare that a negative entanglement reflects only one party's actions. If the circumstances demand, the facilitator helps to work out reparations beyond confession and forgiveness.

King Arthur's vision of the round table concerned people working together on a common cause. So does ho'oponopono, in the
critical case of resolving family tensions. But the style of ho'oponopono is not just for families. Tensions are likely to occur in policy initiatives, planning sessions, budget allocations, promotion decisions,
and endless other circumstances. Rounds of complaint and accusa-
tion are likely to escalate. The leader who guides concrete and reflective discussion, allowing for divergent points of view, can foster
insight and practical action by pooling the thoughts and perspectives
of the participants. The calm and deliberative process of ho'oponopono is just one example of how cultures across time and space have
reached for ways to combine human intelligence to solve human
problems.

TEAM INTELLIGENCE

Cars, trucks, and trains have brakes. Ships do not. Large oceangoing
vessels cannot stop on a dime. The closest that ships come to braking
is to reverse their propellers. Otherwise, the enormous momentum
of the vessel can carry it forward for miles before the friction of water
on the hull eventually beings it to a halt.

So it was a real problem when the U.S.S. *Palau,* a large transport
vessel for marine troops and helicopters, lost steam pressure and all
propulsion as it sailed at about 10 knots along a narrow dredged
channel approaching San Diego harbor. Besides turning the propellers, steam power operated the ship's electrical generators. The
power from the generators fed a system of electrical motors for shifting the rudder. No brakes, and no steering either! Nonetheless, 25
minutes later the *Palau* rested safely at anchor, a little off to one side
of the channel, a couple of miles further along from where the failure occurred.

The story of this incident and many others less dramatic but just
as illuminating is told by Edwin Hutchins in his 1995 book, *Cognition in the Wild* (Cambridge, MA: MIT Press). Hutchins explains that
by "the wild" he does not mean jungles or savannahs but the everyday world of work. Psychologists' laboratories have been the classic
and in many ways revealing setting for the examination of human

memory, perception, reasoning, learning, and other fundamental processes of mind. However, Hutchins insists that we do not really understand cognition until we examine closely what happens when people undertake complex collaborative endeavors in realistic situations. A civilian researcher for the U.S. Navy, Hutchins undertook an extended in-person investigation of the coordinated cognitive processes among individuals of various rank and role that allow a naval vessel to function at sea, with particular attention to navigation. Hutchins was there when the *Palau* couldn't put on its brakes.

How did the crew of the *Palau* handle the emergency? A few seconds after first warning to the bridge that steam pressure was failing, the engineer of the watch came back on the intercom with the final news: "Bridge, Main Control. I'm going to secure number two boiler at this time. Recommend you drop the anchor!" The captain notified the bosun to have his crew ready for such an action. But dropping anchor right away simply would not work when the *Palau* still had substantial momentum. The ship moved on.

A junior officer had the conn (that is, was steering the vessel by directing the helmsman, who handled the wheel itself). The captain ordered the navigator, the most experienced conn officer, to take over. Meanwhile, the helm was not responding for lack of electrical power. However, there was another backup mechanism for moving the rudder: Crewmembers could manually operate a worm-gear mechanism in an area in the stern called the *aftersteering,* slowly shifting the rudder position. The navigator called for them to get going.

Within three minutes, other crewmembers brought on line a diesel-powered emergency generator system, providing power for critical systems. The helm became somewhat more responsive, although erratic. The navigator still lacked clear position and bearing information. Because the helm responded slowly, the navigator tended to overcompensate, steering too far one way, then too far another, leading the *Palau* in a wavering course down the channel— but *in* the channel. Meanwhile, it was possible to project about how long the ship would take to slow down enough to drop anchor. The navigator selected a likely anchorage a couple of miles ahead.

The nearest call occurred just a little short of the anchor point, when a sailboat blithely took a course that would pass close in front of the *Palau*. Normally, five loud blasts from the *Palau*'s horn would have warned the boat off, but the horn, like so much else, depended on steam pressure. The navigator commanded the keeper of the deck log to fetch a portable battery-operated horn and get down to the bow to sound the warning. Meanwhile, the captain turned on the flight deck's public address system, powered by backup generators, checked that at least the crew on the deck of the *Palau* could hear it, and spoke out, "Sailboat crossing Palau's bow be advised that . . . I have no power. You cross at your own risk. I have no power." In parallel with this, the keeper of the deck log had made it to the deck with the portable horn, but clearly would not reach the bow in time. The navigator relayed through a junior officer the instruction to use the horn where he was. The five feeble blasts sounded.

The officers and crew had no way of knowing whether either of these strategies alerted the crew of the sailboat, by now almost completely out of sight beneath the huge hull of the *Palau,* to make course adjustments, but in any case the sailboat slipped by to one side without collision. Minutes afterward, the *Palau* dropped anchor at the chosen location. Hutchins sums up the drama as follows:

> The safe arrival of the *Palau* at anchor was due in large part to the exceptional seamanship of the bridge crew, especially the navigator. But no single individual in the bridge acting alone—neither the caption nor the navigator nor the quartermaster chief supervising the navigation team—could have kept control of the ship and brought it safely to anchor. Many kinds of thinking were required to perform this task. Some of them were happening in parallel, some in coordination with others, some inside the heads of individuals, and some quite clearly both inside and outside the heads of the participants.

The incident of the *Palau* illustrates one of the most familiar ways of putting minds together—a command hierarchy, a fundamental organizational structure found in corporate, governmental, military, and many other settings. A simpleminded view of a command hierarchy would picture a kind of brain-with-body—the boss as brain, making the decisions, while the rest provide the arms and legs to do the boss's bidding. However, as the story of the Palau shows, an effective command hierarchy functions quite differently. Far from being just arms and legs, the many subordinate officers and crewmembers involved in the *Palau* incident had to know their jobs and exercise discretion within their scope. Far from insisting on making all the decisions, the captain ceded fine-grained control of the situation to the navigator at the conn, as the person in the best position to guide the process. Far from one solution dictated by the captain, multiple solutions proceeded in parallel, as when some crewmembers operated the manual steering device in aftersteering while others brought the diesel backup system on line, or when the captain warned off the sailboat using the public address system while the navigator ordered the keeper of the deck log to try the portable horn. Rather than a brain with body, a command hierarchy with skill and discretion at multiple levels and multiple ways of responding to the same situation marked the organizational intelligence of the officers and crew of the *Palau*.

For some commentators on the worlds of business and government, hierarchy has a bad name these days—too old fashioned, inflexible, and undemocratic to be smart. But smart is as smart does. A line manager may be a cog between the mainspring and the minute hand or an intelligent and responsive agent. A division head may govern by decree or listen, decide, and guide. A CEO may issue the Ten Commandments from the mountaintop or balance a personal sense of things with the perceptions of others while accepting responsibility for critical decisions. Hierarchies can be smart, and democracies can be dumb. It's not just the structures that matter, but the people and operating styles within them.

FROM CAMELOT TO REALITY

The round table, Athenian democracy, ho'oponopono, effective command hierarchies—it's all a beautiful dream, King Arthur, but how often is it a reality? Indeed, you're a bit of a dream yourself. Historians can't figure out who the historical King Arthur was, or whether he was a nice guy (in some of the Arthurian tales he wasn't), or whether there even was a King Arthur, much less whether he favored round tables. And as to the round table and other solutions for the lawnmower paradox (remember: *Pooling physical effort is usually rather easy, pooling mental effort is usually rather hard*), how far do those dreams really take us?

Everyday experience suggests that the ideals overreach the reality. All too often, a group does not seem to function as intelligently as even its average member! Chaos, rivalry, and inefficiency rule instead. Most groups, teams, organizations, and communities do not seem to be either very *process smart* or very *people smart*—they neither exercise effective processes of information gathering, problem solving, and decision making nor foster a collaborative mindset and commitment to collective goals and visions.

At the level of nations and governments, Barbara Tuchman, in *The March of Folly* (New York: Knopf, 1984), recites the history of collective nonintelligence. Her cases in point include how Montezuma and the entire Aztec nation managed to let Cortez and 600 Spanish soldiers conquer them; how King George and his government, despite clear warning signs, bungled relationships with the American colonies to the point of triggering a revolution that England had no chance of suppressing; and how the United States gradually sank into the swamp of another unwinable war, the Vietnam conflict. Tuchman's formula for historical folly includes an explicit collective requirement. The disastrous policies and decisions could not reflect the mind and voice of a single person. Several had to be involved, including dissenting voices warning against the calamity.

Writers covering the corporate world record many instances of unwise collective behavior. Chris Argyris and Donald Schön, at the beginning of their book *Organizational Learning* (Reading, MA: Addison-Wesley, 1978), relate how a major corporation lost several hundred million dollars by abandoning a product too late. Several people within the company had known at least six years earlier that continuing to manufacture the product with sufficient quality control in a cost-effective way would be difficult. However, the corporate culture in question worked against organizational intelligence. Those lower down in the hierarchy and closer to the problems knew that the top executives would not want to hear about serious problems without good solutions, which they lacked. So they reported softened versions of the problems up the corporate ladder. The executives, noting the difficulties but not realizing how deep and intransigent they were, maintained their energetic support of the product. Noticing the commitment of upper management to see things through, those lower down relaxed. Finally the problems spiraled to the point where they could not be ignored. Everyone faced reality, but years late and many millions of dollars in the hole.

We have all encountered the shortcomings of organizational intelligence, at least on a small scale—family tiffs without any ho'oponopono to help, tedious meetings that go in circles, partnerships that begin with friendship and energy and end in sour rivalry. It's hard not to remember the familiar saying that a camel is a horse designed by a committee. And it's hard not to see camels all around us.

The history of collective folly, large scale and small scale, others' and our own, leads to the fundamental question of this book, really three questions in one:

☞ What is organizational intelligence, why is it so hard to come by, and how can we get more of it?

The what-why-how question defines the grail of this book's Arthurian quest. The point of departure is simple but rich in implications: How smart an organization or community is reflects the kinds of conversations that people have with one another, taking conversations in a broad sense to include all sorts of interactions. Without those conversations, you just have a bunch of people doing things in parallel. With those conversations, you have—well, depending on the quality of the conversations, you have a group smart or not so smart, flexible or rigid, innovative or hidebound, systematic or chaotic, enjoyable or depressing.

And can we attain more of this organizational intelligence that we cherish? Sure, *but*. The "but" reflects the fact that ineffective and even destructive patterns of interaction often dominate. Conversations commonly gravitate toward counterproductive patterns of autocracy, secrecy, rivalry, narrowness, confusion, and more. However, with thought and effort, better patterns can take their place, building a smarter collective.

The details of the story unfold in a kind of dialog between ideas and practical examples. Chapter 2 explores the notion that organizations are made of conversations, along with some brief examples. Chapter 3 focuses on a specific but particularly important hot spot in community and organizational life: feedback in its sometimes positive but often very destructive forms. The remaining chapters build further ideas and visit such other organizational hot spots as leadership, collaboration, the building of trust, the management of conflict, the nature of change, and one's role as an agent of change toward smarter collective endeavor.

2

ORGANIZATIONS ARE MADE OF CONVERSATIONS

ERNESTO'S TRUTH

Ernesto Gore, an Argentinean friend, colleague, and scholar of the business world, shared with me a provocative characterization of organizations a while ago. He said, "Organizations are made of conversations."

It was what I'd been looking for: a simple phrase to capture a basic truth. Remember the Greek senate, or the captain and crew of the *Palau,* or the Hawaiian family practice of ho'oponopono—conversations. Think of John F. Kennedy, Secretary of State Dean Rusk, Secretary of Defense Robert McNamara, and several others huddled in October 1962, tobogganing down a slope toward nuclear war unless they could figure out a safer way to deal with Russian missiles in Cuba—conversations. Consider *nemawashi,* the informal, friendly Japanese process of building and testing a consensus through a number of small side meetings among various interested parties, so that in a full formal meeting an idea can be approved smoothly without embarrassing conflict—conversations. Consider the tradition of *majlis* in Saudi Arabia, where people can hold challenging discussions with members of government—conversations. Think of the Greek Senate, the Roman Senate, the British Parliament, the U.S. Congress, the Israeli Knesset. Ponder the medieval craft guilds, ancestors of today's unions, and the medieval merchant guides, presaging today's Chamber of Commerce, agreeing on practices to protect their interests—conversations. Consider the corporate world today: the board meetings, sales meetings, strategic planning processes, focus groups, task forces, and due diligence inquiries—conversations.

Gore's idea makes a lot of sense. Biologist and cybernetician Humberto Maturana, business scholar and consultant Fernando Flores, and many others have made the same point. Contemporary concepts such as knowledge management and communities of practice picture community and organizational life in terms of reservoirs of knowledge and expertise shared through conversations of various kinds via various media. In an analysis of change processes in organizations—successful or unsuccessful—John and Laurie Ford focus on how key conversations unfold to initiate change, build understanding, move to performance, and achieve closure.

And King Arthur, of course. King Arthur's dream has people coming together to coordinate their thoughts and efforts smoothly, effectively, intelligently. But, when such collectivities work, what wires them together? As neurons connect one part of the brain to another, conversations connect the different parts of communities and organizations. Conversations are the virtual neurons of a collective mind.

IMAGETECH AND VISIONTECH

Gore's idea about conversations reminds me of some consulting on educational design I did a few years ago for two well-known companies interested in technology and learning, companies I'll call ImageTech and VisionTech. In both cases, I met several times with a design team, sometimes including the head of the division, who was keenly interested in the progress of the initiatives. From early on, I was struck by the different quality of conversations in the ImageTech and VisionTech groups.

At ImageTech, when head-of-division Ian (let's call him) was present, people didn't seem to have much to say at first. After Ian had said enough to show which way the wind was blowing, other people participated more. Sometimes someone would even challenge Ian a bit, raising a concern or a puzzle, but only after the trend in his thinking was plain. When Ian was absent, conversations were livelier. However, even modest conclusions required vetting. "Yeah, I think the way to go is such-and-such," a member of the design team might say. "So let's just check with Ian and probably that will be fine."

The VisionTech design group had a very different conversational style. When head-of-division Vernon (let's call him) was present, no one waited around for his opinion. People shared their judgments freely. Vernon mixed into the conversation along with everyone else, but if anything, he held back a bit until some other ideas had emerged. Of course, Vernon was the chief. If something proved difficult to decide, he heard people's input and then made the decision.

Regardless of whether Vernon was present, the conversation generally resulted in plans for action. When Vernon wasn't there, no one mentioned checking with him before moving ahead unless the action was pretty high level. "We'll let Vernon know what we're up to," someone might say. "If it doesn't sit right with him, he can let us know and we'll rethink it. Meanwhile, let's get going."

Gore proposed that organizations are made of conversations. Yes, and the quality of the conversations makes all the difference.

Of course, whether organizations are made of conversations depends on how broadly you construe conversations. The real topic here is *distributed cognition,* cognition shared across a collective, and its technical tools such as telephones and computers, as in Edwin Hutchins's analysis of the crew of the U.S.S. *Palau* during its emergency (see Chapter 1). Gore didn't just mean team meetings. He would want to include feedback sessions, giving and taking orders, exchanging memos, and issuing policies, some of it face to face and some of it by telephone, on paper, or by e-mail. To use a more general and formal term than *conversations:*

Organizations are made of interactions, the virtual neurons that tie an organization together.

HOW ROUND IS YOUR TABLE?

Imagine King Arthur reincarnated as an organizational consultant. He takes on all kinds and sizes—schools, universities, corporations, divisions of government, clubs, what have you. All the time he's asking, "How round is your table?" That's his way of probing the quality of conversations. Is this place a round-table kind of place, or a long-imperial-table kind of place, or what kind of place?

It's useful to have a somewhat more technical way of characterizing how well conversations hold a collective together and help people to think and work together. The contrast between *progressive interactions* and *regressive interactions* does this job. The metaphor packaged in this choice of words is simple: *progressive* makes progress; *regressive* slows things down or sends them back. Please don't mix up *progressive* as used here with the same word in a political context. Here, the word refers to the prospects of organizational intelligence.

☞ By definition, progressive interactions are process smart and people smart.

Process smart means that progressive interactions exchange information and ideas in ways that foster astute decisions, good solutions, and far-seeing plans. *People smart* means that progressive interactions foster the cohesiveness of the group, leaving people feeling good about working together and looking forward to doing more together. There may well be some conflict within the group, and indeed a certain measure of conflict is productive (see Chapter 8), but the forces of cohesion far outweigh the conflicts.

If King Arthur visited the division of VisionTech mentioned earlier, he would like what he saw. He would find a round table of ready discussion, thoughtfully formulated problems, creative explorations, sound decisions. He would find people who wanted to work together and move forward. In other words, he would encounter process-smart and people-smart conversations, progressive interactions, and organizational intelligence. He might even dub the VisionTech employees Knights of the New Round Table, especially Vernon, who creates that culture within the division.

In contrast:

🏴 By definition, regressive interactions are ineffective from the standpoints of process and people.

As to process, regressive interactions exchange information and ideas in narrow, confused, and cautious ways. Key information gets lost. Plans are less informed than they might be; decisions are lopsided. As to people, regressive interactions constitute a kind of centrifugal force, pushing people apart through dissatisfactions, rivalries, and lack of vision more than they pull people together.

If King Arthur visited the division of ImageTech mentioned earlier, he would find a very long imperial table. Even when Ian is not there, his shadow looms over the group. Explorations of possibilities are cautious; people are restrained, even a little suspicious of one another. They are hanging in for the time being, but in the long term they'd rather be doing something else. In other words, the conversations are not process smart and people smart, not so organizationally intelligent. Arthur would not want to welcome these folks into his New Round Table, and he might consider Ian a kind of black knight because of the negative culture Ian creates.

The distinction between progressive and regressive interactions is simply a handy tool. It gives us a more focused way of asking and answering, "How round is your table?" Here's how.

First of all, it's easy to use. Remember the last serious conversation you had with a son or daughter, or a parent, or a life partner, or a boss, or an employee. Recall the last meeting in which you participated. Recollect how you feel about the way you interact with the administration of any organization of which you are a part—the finance office, the personnel office, the purchasing department. It's not hard to judge, "Yes, that was pretty progressive," or "not so progressive" or "downright regressive." Social creatures that we are, we all have a sense of these things.

Second, as the range of cases from child–parent conversations to purchasing departments illustrates, the progressive-regressive dimension applies to virtually any context of interaction. Use it wherever you want and it's likely to yield pointed distinctions.

Third, what it gets at is important. Just imagine an organization where, when you meet someone in the hall, when you chat in the lunch room, when you attend a meeting, when you team up with a colleague, when you give advice to someone new, when you work out an innovative procedure with the office down the hall, the conversations—the explorations, the decision making, the planning, the speculations, the critiques, the debates, the proposals—mostly proceed in a progressive manner. Wouldn't that be a pretty good place to be? Wouldn't that be a pretty *smart* place to be?

PROCESS SMART AND DECIDING SMART

Information processing is the versatile clay of contemporary cognitive science. From sensory input to the outputs of speech and action, the human organism can be modeled as a complex and sophisticated information-processing system. How well we process information— the acuity of our ears and eyes, the reliability of our memories, the perspicacity with which we foresee what is likely to happen in various circumstances, the imaginativeness with which we devise alternative plans and products—adds up to intelligent or not-so-intelligent behavior.

Illuminating individual cognition, information processing also applies to pairwise and group interactions. However, *information* is too thin and dry a word. Neurons connect parts of our brains with one another, but no cables made of neurons drape from person to person. We talk about ideas. We share insights. We pool recollections.

So instead of information processing, I'll say *knowledge processing.* Not a lot hangs on referring to knowledge processing instead of information processing. The same logical points can be made either way. It's just that *knowledge processing* seems to have better poetry. It expresses more fully the rich, meaningful, and human character of conversations.

Progressive interactions among people involve good knowledge processing. However, what do we mean by *good?* The notion of good knowledge processing could be a hopelessly murky bouillabaisse of an idea. But it's not, providing we take knowledge processing case by case rather than expecting some generalized recipe for cordon bleu cognition.

To argue this, let's examine briefly a case in point, practical high-stakes decision making, about as fundamental and important a kind of thinking as you can name, and certainly a hot spot in the lives of organizations and communities. Recall again President Kennedy and the Cuban Missile Crisis. Whether it's my decision, your decision, or that of the two of us together, or a few other people are added to the mix, the basic knowledge-processing demands of decision making are pretty clear. The principles can be organized in different ways, but they distill down to much the same thing.

A few years ago, I organized several informal studies of the kinds of practical procedural knowledge adults tap to make good decisions. I asked people to explain as much as they could about how they labor through difficult decisions and gave them cues to remind them of practices that they might not recall in the moment. People had a great deal to say—not just one or two hot tips but a depth of practical savvy and long lists of strategies that spoke to the struggles that people inevitably have with important decisions in their lives.

What they said included familiar guidelines: List pros and cons, ask yourself what you really want, toss a coin, trust your gut, sleep on it, talk it over with a friend, talk it over with someone who's been there, combine options, defer the decision until you can get more information, remember your past mistakes and don't make them again, and so on. Some of these ideas conflicted with others logically—for instance, listing pros and cons versus trusting your gut—but practically, this didn't seem to bother people much. The same person might mention both ideas, because in practical situations what you do varies according to what the situation invites.

What they said also included some less common ideas. There were a couple of catty strategies, for instance: "Take a walk, stroke my cat . . . some turning-away behavior to clear my head." And "I talk it over with my cat." Idiosyncratic as these may sound, they have real virtues: They provide comfort, detachment, and a sympathetic listener—and one who charges a lot less than a therapist! For a different kind of strategy, there were people who emphasized imaginative exploration. "Try to envision the ideal—if you could control everything, what would you do?" "Pretend you've made the decision and live with your choice for a day. How does it feel?" But no one stopped short with only one or two points.

Organizing their practical lore yielded two big categories—four *general moves* that could be applied more or less in order, and four *general needs* that called for attention throughout. The general moves and general needs taken together write a broad recipe for good knowledge processing in decision making (Table 2.1).

All that for individuals, but what about groups? The general moves and general needs apply very well to knowledge processing in interactive contexts with multiple stakeholders. King Arthur and the Knights of the Round Table need to explore creative options, predict short-term and long-term consequences, look at a range of positive and negative factors, and synthesize a range of factors in a balanced way to choose a course of action. Groups have to find information, avoid narrow perspectives, manage the many factors in complex situations, and take care of the emotional turmoil of group members. In other words, the general moves and general needs define the kinds of knowledge processing needed for good decision making in a group.

Of course, the right thing to do depends somewhat on context. When people have time to think, which they usually do, the preceding decision-making practices make sense. However, in crisis situations some of these good practices become luxuries, and sensible shortcuts take their place.

The moral of this story looks not just to decision making but to any thinking enterprise that makes sense for groups. There are many other kinds of collective thinking—negotiation (which we'll look at later in this chapter), group planning, formulation of policies, coordinating collaborations, and so on, and all of them present opportunities for better knowledge processing:

↦ Taking kinds of thinking case by case, we can recognize patterns of knowledge processing that handle them well and put those patterns to work.

Consider design processes. James Brian Quinn, in his book *Intelligent Enterprise* (New York: Free Press, 1992), writes of the typical

TABLE 2.1   Four General Moves and Four General Needs

Four General Moves

Move	Why Important
Finding options beyond the obvious ones—creative options, hybrid options	It's all too easy to fixate on the given choices and miss hidden options. An old proverb says, "Between two options, choose the third."
Predicting short-term and long-term consequences of promising options	It's all too easy to be dominated by the short-term, missing long-term factors.
Evaluating options and their consequences in light of important factors, both positive and negative	It's all too easy to miss the downside of options you favor and the upside of options you don't; it's easy to look at just one or two factors when there are many.
Reaching a resolution that serves one's priorities in an appropriately balanced way, systematically or through a holistic intuitive sense of what's right to do	It's all too easy to get kidnapped by one particular factor that seems important at the moment.

Four General Needs

Need	Why Important
The need for information—from friends, technical sources, knowledge-sharing systems, etc.	Life commonly presents us with situations we don't know that much about.
The need for multiple perspectives— you, bystanders, rivals, etc.	It's all too easy to be blinded by one's own initial perspective.
The need to deal with complexity— managing a perhaps bewildering range of possibilities and consequences with a mix of systematicity and intuition	It's all too easy to lose one's way in a complex decision, and even end up making an impulsive decision simply to escape from the frustrating complexity and uncertainty.
The need to deal with negative emotions, finding and sustaining needed distance	It's all too easy for negative emotions to blind us, paralyze us, and push us to impulsive decisions.

five- to six-year product design cycle involved in developing a totally new car "as the design moved sequentially through product design, process design, plant engineering, manufacturing, environmental, regulatory, financial approval, marketing, sales, and distribution staff interfaces." Inevitable as such a sequence might seem, it commonly led to rounds of reworking the design to address problems not anticipated at earlier stages.

In the early 1980s, Ford Motor Company adopted a revised *simultaneous design* process that led to the Taurus/Sable line. A development group with full-time representatives from all the interests just mentioned and more drove the initiative. This helped to avoid the turf wars and costly reworking generated by the old system. Indeed, some of the gain can be understood in terms of the good decision-making factors identified earlier, because the simultaneous design process tapped a far greater range of perspectives early on, with richer knowledge and better prediction and evaluation of long-term consequences of choices.

Any team, any organization, any community can aspire to good knowledge processing and advance its practice. That's process smart. But what about people smart?

PEOPLE SMART AND THE LANGUAGE OF ACTIONS

The young film prodigy Orson Welles produced, directed, and cowrote the masterpiece *Citizen Kane* at the age of 25, acting the part of media mogul Kane himself. In one well-known scene, Kane and his wife dine at opposite ends of a long elegant table with no one between them. The table, about as far as you can get from King Arthur's round table, says it all. The two live totally different lives, communicating only at the most superficial level.

Kane's action amounts to a gesture of distance and authority. Such gestures are hardly limited to the movies. On a small scale, they figure in family life, in the familiar tradition that the paterfamilias sits at the head of the table, and in corporate life, where the same tradition applies in the boardroom to the CEO or the chairperson of the board.

If authority comes with its characteristic language of action, so does rebellion against authority. Revisiting that same boardroom with the chairperson at the head, we might find halfway along one side of the table the restless young Turk, up and coming, slumped just a little bit, looking as though he can hardly be bothered to attend to the so-very-conservative discourse of his older peers, although you can be sure that not a word passes him by, since it's something that he might be able to use.

Or, to turn to the positive side of all this, the firm handshake; the calm voice; the steady eye in times of stress; the commitment made today and kept tomorrow; the consultation with others before making a decision, even though in the end it's one's role to make the decision; attention to mentoring others—all these and many more ways of speaking and acting figure importantly in any context, from family gatherings to the floor of the workshop to faculty meetings at universities.

All such circumstances illustrate *symbolic conduct.*

☞ Symbolic conduct is made of the side messages sent by our words and behavior.

What I say right now and do right now has results right now. But beyond that, what I say and do right now will be read by you for what it says about me as a person—my commitments, my fears, my attitude toward you, my style of getting things done, and many other things.

We all inevitably and often inadvertently send messages by way of our immediate words and behavior that reach far beyond the moment. We all read the symbolic conduct of others, and, through our words and actions, "write" symbolic conduct for others to read.

Even a few actions from a figure in authority can create a positive or negative culture through symbolic conduct. I remember consulting for a division head of a computer manufacturer a number of years ago on the development of creativity in the division's personnel. During side conversations, I learned that the division head had declared an accountability policy: Every group leader should be ready at any time to give a full account of progress on fronts for which he or she was responsible. The division head indeed summoned people to his office at random moments for this purpose. The problem wasn't the mechanics of reporting in. People could do that. The problem was the message of distrust and the mood of vulnerability that his policy communicated.

I did a workshop for the division to introduce some creativity techniques, but afterward I very politely explained to the division head that he needed to think about the culture he was generating if he wanted to cultivate a creative group around him. He didn't invite me back. So it goes.

What applies to interactions in groups applies with a vengeance as corporations and nations face the public eye. A supremely sensitive and economically significant category concerns product recalls. Consumers look beyond the practical handling of the immediate crisis. They read the company's actions as standing for the company's values and predicting future conduct. The classic positive case is perhaps Johnson & Johnson's reaction to the Tylenol incident in the fall of 1982. Several people in Chicago were poisoned by cyanide-laced Tylenol. Johnson & Johnson moved immediately to announce the problem, asked everyone everywhere not to take Tylenol, and initiated a massive recall. The action was seen as highly responsible, and a follow-up marketing campaign with secure bottles of Tylenol restored the product's market position. In contrast, the Firestone tire debacle of August 2000, when Bridgestone/Firestone was pressured into a massive tire recall after mounting complaints, warns how the symbolic conduct of a collective can send profoundly negative messages that undermine trust.

It's largely through symbolic conduct that the culture of a group is expressed and reinforced. The organizational theorist Edgar Schein writes about the culture of organizations as a matter of the tacit belief systems that people hold and that underlie their behavior. Such beliefs are usually not articulated. They do not appear in mission statements or policies. But they surface in the way people say things and in how people behave. They manifest themselves through symbolic conduct.

To sum up, the concepts of knowledge processing and symbolic conduct sharpen the contrast between progressive and regressive interactions.

🍃 Progressive interactions involve effective knowledge processing and positive symbolic conduct, the kind of symbolic
conduct that builds cohesiveness, trust, and commitment.
Regressive interactions involve poor knowledge processing
and negative symbolic conduct.

Kane, at the other end of that nowhere-near-round table, sits too
far from his wife for effective knowledge processing—they can barely
hear one another. And he certainly sits too far away for his position
to be read as positive symbolic conduct in any way. Kane, indeed, is
almost an archetype of regressive interaction, not only at this moment but throughout the film.

THE USUAL SUSPECTS

ImageTech and VisionTech are specific places that show us general
patterns. There is a familiar feel to ImageTech's head of division to
whom all bowed down and a recognizable style in VisionTech's head
of division, who participated, facilitated, and made the decisions
when appropriate. Most of us can say to ourselves, "Oh yes, I know
the ImageTech situation. I've lived through that a few times." And,
regrettably less often, "Yes, I was part of that VisionTech."
    Scenarios like those at ImageTech and VisionTech transcend the
particular, pointing to *archetypes of interaction:*

🍃 An archetype of interaction (less formally, of conversation)
is a general recognizable pattern of interaction that emerges
over and over again in different settings.

To put this another way, archetypes of interaction are the usual suspects of collective life. Consider decision making again. Remember
Ian, head of division at ImageTech? Recall how Ian's staff members
watched to see which way he was leaning and felt unable to move forward when he wasn't around to sign off. ImageTech illustrates a broad
pattern that might be called the *autocratic decision making* archetype.
    In contrast, recall how Vernon of VisionTech hung back and lis-
tened to folks and how his staff, while respectful of his authority,

exercised common sense about minor decisions. VisionTech illustrates an archetype that might be called *participative decision making* (note that the participative archetype does not necessarily entail a democratic vote, just a participative process—Vernon was clearly boss).

The autocratic archetype surfaces over and over again in communities and organizations. The participative archetype shows up less often. ImageTechs are more common than VisionTechs. But paradoxically, the participative archetype is more progressive than the autocratic archetype, delivering better knowledge processing and more positive symbolic conduct. The tension between the autocratic and participative archetypes turns decision making in communities and organizations into a hot spot, like feedback, leadership, collaboration, and other hot spots to be considered later.

Let me make the case that the participative form indeed is more progressive, using the analysis of decision making developed earlier. We can grade the two archetypes with the eight aspects of knowledge processing for decision making introduced in Table 2.1. The participative archetype outscores the autocratic archetype on most of them—but not all of them!

+ *Finding options beyond the obvious.* The general and open sharing of ideas in the participative archetype yields a richer exploration of possibilities than usually happens in the autocratic archetype, where the boss dominates.

+ *Predicting short-term and long-term consequences.* The participative archetype brings to bear more minds and a greater range of experience in predicting short-term and long-term consequences.

+ *Evaluating options and their consequences.* The participative archetype pools diverse perspectives, helping to avoid one-sidedness and bias.

− *Reaching a resolution.* The participative archetype introduces more information, ideas, and opinions to be integrated, so reaching a resolution can be harder. Even if it's the leader's role to decide (remember, participative decision making doesn't necessarily mean a democracy), the leader has much more to think through toward the final decision.

+ *The need for information.*   The participative archetype provides a far richer range of information, although of course further information from outside the group may be needed.

+ *The need for multiple perspectives.*   The participative archetype builds in multiple perspectives, although further perspectives outside the group may be valuable, too.

− *The need to deal with complexity.*   The participative archetype makes things more complicated all the way along, because it increases the range of information, ideas, and opinions on the table.

? *The need to deal with negative emotions.*   The participative archetype can provide emotional support. However, if there are deep conflicts in the group, the general and open participation can escalate negative emotions.

In summary, the participative archetype yields superior knowledge processing in most respects. However, it can make dealing with complexity and reaching a final resolution more challenging.

Some people have a negative view of participative decision making because of bad experiences. They remember confusing meetings full of many voices, hours spent before arriving at a simple decision that should have taken minutes, and adjourning until next week to try again, and they conclude that the participative archetype cannot work efficiently.

They are mistaken. If they are bosses, they may be forgetting that it's their responsibility to decide, having listened attentively. Whether they are bosses or simply participants, they may lack basic skills and strategies needed for handling complexity and reaching a resolution with reasonable efficiency. Strategies for handling complexity include charting possibilities and pros and cons, prioritizing to isolate the really important factors, and so on. Strategies for reaching a collective resolution include, of course, voting, but, much better, effective consensus building through synthesizing seemingly different options and securing buy-in, as in nemawashi, the Japanese process of side conversations mentioned earlier, or through artful conduct of group interactions (see Chapter 7).

Now consider symbolic conduct. The participative archetype of decision making sends more positive, trusting, affirming messages, as follows:

+ The participative archetype sends positive messages about the ability, knowledge, and judgment of the others besides the leader. The autocratic archetype is dismissive.

+ The participative archetype declares trust in the others to act in the collective interest. The autocratic archetype is mistrustful.

+ The participative archetype respects the multiple enriching perspectives of the others. The autocratic archetype neglects them.

+ The participative archetype acknowledges the legitimate individual interests of the others. The autocratic archetype ignores them.

+ The participative archetype views positively the strength of the collective effort and the potential to work together effectively. The autocratic archetype assumes collective chaos or conflict or both.

So the participative archetype is more progressive. That's nice, but it's not just nice—it's smart. The progressive archetype serves knowledge processing better and holds the group together better.

Yet, as mentioned earlier, in many situations the regressive archetype dominates. Worse, what's true for autocratic and participative decision making holds for many other archetypes of interaction. Earlier, we had the lawnmower paradox about pooling mental effort being harder than pooling physical effort. Let's add:

℞ *The dinosaur paradox:* Regressive archetypes of interaction tend to dominate in community and organizational contexts, driving out progressive archetypes.

Why a dinosaur? Because the regressive archetypes are less sophisticated, but they're tougher. The questions of where archetypes come from and what makes the regressive ones tougher pervade this book, and Chapter 6 sums up the analysis. For now, we can turn to a further example involving collective decision making—negotiation.

TWO ARCHETYPES OF NEGOTIATION

For us alone it's easy. For us and them it's hard. We deciding what's best for us to do is one thing. We and those other people deciding what's best for us and them is another thing entirely. For us—say, John F. Kennedy and compatriots—deciding whether we'd like to see Russian missiles in Cuba is easy: No! For us and them—Castro, Khrushchev, and their compatriots in the Soviet Union—deciding the disposition of missiles is hard.

In general, we and they—that other nation, that other company, that other division, that other office, that other neighbor—is a tricky proposition. Decision making for just us may present some puzzles, but the kind of decision making involved in negotiating with them, by definition, involves at least somewhat conflicting interests. Talk about hot spots! What we want clashes with what they want, and at the worst, we're all likely to end up like two *T. rexes* vying for the same territory.

In their well-known book *Getting to Yes* (New York: Penguin, 1981), Roger Fisher and William Ury offer a vision of negotiation designed to get beyond the dinosaurs. They contrast two archetypes of negotiation: *negotiating from positions* and *negotiating from interests.* (*Archetype* is not a term Fisher and Ury use, but the idea fits what they say.)

Negotiation from positions is the *T. rex* version. People declare and defend their positions like territories. Rex X says, "My position is this: I want A, B, and C." Rex Y says, "Well, that may be what you want, and you can have A, but I absolutely have to have B and C, and I also must have D." Rex X sees Rex Y's demands as a territorial assault, and vice versa. Positions may become deeply entrenched, leading to a stalemate. More typically, concessions are made and a compromise results, a compromise that neither side feels good about. So, if they are anything as powerful as *T. rexes*, watch out later!

Negotiating from interests is altogether less Cretaceous. Instead of taking a position, a kinder, gentler Rex X says, "My interests, concerns, needs, are such and such. What are yours?" Rex Y responds in kind. After putting interests on the table and clarifying them, Rex X and Rex Y together try to solve the mutual problem of satisfying all the interests as well as possible. They try for what's commonly, tritely, but usefully called a *win-win solution*. In some cases, this can transform a negotiation into a collaborative rather than an adversarial experience and yield a much more fruitful resolution.

A compelling historical example is the Camp David treaty of 1978 between Israel and Egypt. Israel had taken possession of the Egyptian Sinai Peninsula in the 1967 Six-Day War. Egypt wanted it back, all of it. Negotiations bogged down over different ways of dividing up the Sinai, none of which pleased Egypt. The break-through came when the negotiators considered interests rather than positions. Israel wanted security, not the Sinai itself. Egypt wanted sovereignty over the land. The solution was a Sinai back in Egypt's hands but with large parts demilitarized.

The contrast between negotiation from positions and negotiation from interests illustrates all over again regressive versus progressive interactions. In fact, the knowledge processing and symbolic conduct of negotiation from positions versus negotiation from interests resemble remarkably well the knowledge processing and symbolic conduct of autocratic versus participatory decision making. This makes sense, because negotiation is a kind of decision making about how two individuals or groups in a potentially adversarial relationship will move forward. From the perspective of knowledge processing, negotiating from positions is likely to explore fewer and less creative options, miss important short-term and long-term consequences because the negotiators are playing their cards close to their chests, limit available information, narrow people's perspectives, and so on. From the perspective of symbolic conduct, negotiating from positions sends the message, "I'm a hard-liner, I don't trust you an inch, and I'm not going to give an inch," hardly a basis for present and future cohesiveness on anything.

The archetype of negotiation from interests may be more progressive, but is it the archetype we want? Can we have so very round a table? Maybe one *T. rex* at the end of a long table and another *T. rex* at the other end, staring each other down—if not leaping onto the table to try their best to make rexburgers out of one another—is about as good as it's going to get, realistically. That is—yes, let's face it—the progressive archetype is not always superior.

Remember that under conditions of time pressure or high risk, regressive decision-making practices may serve best. In the same spirit, the utility of negotiating from interests depends on the likely existence of win-win solutions or something in that direction. When the question is whether to go with Team A's or Team B's product design or who gets to manage European sales, win-win solutions may be thin on the ground, although one can look. In cases from a nasty divorce to longstanding international enmities, the parties involved not only deeply distrust one another but want to hurt one another, making a mutual effort to share interests and identify opportunities for win-win solutions extremely difficult, although skilled and neutral third-party facilitators can help.

Fisher and Ury acknowledge this with another interesting concept, the *BATNA* (best alternative to a negotiated agreement). As the two *T. rex*es sit down to give negotiating from interests a try, they should both have in mind their respective BATNAs—what they will do if progressive negotiation proves impossible.

℞ The real point and promise of progressive archetypes is not that they always serve better but that they serve better much more often than people recognize or act upon.

Negotiations often fall into the regressive archetype of negotiation from positions unnecessarily. It's natural to take positions. It's natural to defend territory. It's natural to react protectively and aggressively toward another's demands. That's why the word *archetype* suits so many regressive practices: The pattern tends to emerge over and over again. We are looking at tendencies deeply ingrained in the human condition, culture, and history—problems recognized in the tales of King Arthur, dilemmas addressed by the Greeks.

Fortunately, there are progressive archetypes of interaction, too. Progressive archetypes also have a basis in human history. They also show up again and again, although less often. The challenge is how to keep them in ascendancy.

CONTACT ARCHITECTURE

Most of us have played the game commonly called *telephone*. You may remember playing this yourself as a child, sitting in a row with other children. The neighbor to your left whispers a one-sentence message into your ear. You may not fully catch it, but you do the best you can, and lean toward your other neighbor, quietly relaying the message. It's fun along the way, since you often find yourself hearing and passing on strange messages indeed, but especially fun at the end, where the first and last people in line compare. Typically, the final message has taken on some mutant form that bears little discernable resemblance to the first.

All that fun comes from the fact that the game of telephone has a terrible contact architecture, one bound to mangle information. The *contact architecture* of a collective means simply the occasions and roles through which people connect. In telephone, people connect one to one in a row as peers. However, any substantial group, team, or organization involves a maze of connections between peer and peer, boss and subordinate, newbie and old hand, in styles formal and informal, in venues from boardrooms to mail rooms to bars after hours, by means from e-mails to meetings to conversations, and on topics from broad vision to why so-and-so is a jerk to how to keep the floors clean. *Contact architecture* is a name for this web of roles and communications.

Contact architecture is an important partner concept to archetypes of interaction. Archetypes illuminate how interactions occur when they do—but when do they? What if the people who need to be in touch are not in touch?

One broad but compelling view of this comes from organizational scholar Rosabeth Moss Kanter. In her book *The Change Masters* (New York: Simon & Schuster, 1983), she distinguishes between the segmentalism characteristic of so many organizations—hierarchies and sharply delineated responsibilities—and the integrative action that more permeable boundaries and loosely defined responsibilities allow. She argues that segmentalism provides a pleasing sense of order and control but profoundly limits adaptability because of the lack of communicative and collaborative relationships. In other

words, *segmentalism* describes an organization with a highly compartmentalized contact architecture that limits the opportunities for
effective knowledge processing and for community-building symbolic conduct.

An earlier example mentioned how Ford Motor Company
adopted a *simultaneous design* process for the Taurus/Sable line. The
key move was to bring together from the beginning representatives of
groups that typically were segmented, coming into play one after
another. Simultaneous design changed the normal contact architecture of the product development process, enabling conversations that
otherwise would not have occurred at all, or not soon enough.

In general, the idea that organizations are made of conversations
asks us to examine how well conversations occur, but also which ones
can occur at all. The contact architecture sets the stage, defines the
roles, and puts certain people and groups side by side, literally or
electronically. It determines what interactions can occur and how
often, leaving open the question of whether they unfold in progressive or regressive ways.

To sum up the message of this entire chapter, communities,
organizations and human collectives of all sorts are "made of conversations," if we mean conversations in the general sense of interactions. Metaphorically, conversations are the virtual neurons that
bind individuals into a larger-scale cognitive collective. Conversations can be progressive (good knowledge processing, positive symbolic conduct) or regressive (poor knowledge processing, negative
symbolic conduct). Within the opportunities provided by a collective's contact architecture, archetypes of interaction, progressive and
regressive, shape its character for more or less organizational intelligence.

As such, archetypes have a double importance. First, looking for
the archetypes helps us read the cultures of organizations and communities. Second, the archetypes define a path toward change,
toward shifting from regressive practices to progressive practices. We
can explore these ideas at finer grain by examining an especially sensitive area—feedback. Who gives it, how do they give it, what right
do they have to give it, and what does that have to do with how smart
an organization is?

TOOLBOX

While examining fundamentals of organizational intelligence, this book also mentions many concepts and frameworks that can serve as practical tools that address hot spots of community and organizational life like decision making, negotiation, feedback, leadership, and so on. Chapter by chapter, I'll sum them up in "toolboxes."

✳ For an overall take on a group or organizational culture, ask: *How round is this table?* Ask: Are these interactions more progressive or regressive? Ask: Is this effective knowledge processing? Is this positive symbolic conduct?

✳ *Cultivate seeing in archetypes.* Notice the patterns of interaction, the "usual suspects," progressive and regressive, that occur over and over again. Think what you would do to shift them in progressive directions.

✳ *Examine the contact architecture.* Is there good contact up and down and side to side, face to face and electronic? Can those who need to know find out? Can collaborations arise easily? What can be done to make it better?

✳ *Foster good collective decision making.* Be attentive to the four general moves and four general needs discussed earlier.

✳ *Avoid the regressive archetype of autocratic group decision making.* Favor the progressive archetype of participative decision making (without surrendering your power of decision if that's your role).

✳ *Avoid the regressive archetype of negotiation from positions.* Favor the progressive archetype of negotiation from interests.

3

YAKETY YAK AND FEEDBACK

YAKETY YAK, 1958

The Coasters' "Yakety Yak" was a number-one hit in 1958, both on the pop list and the rhythm-and-blues list. The group scored with "Yakety Yak" on top of their previous singles "Young Blood" and "Searchin'," and went on to such hits as "Charlie Brown" and "Poison Ivy." The Coasters had a big black sound and a hip tongue-in-cheek style. They sang about the passions and angst of the teen world and mocked that world at the same time.

"Yakety Yak" was a send-up of the hypercritical parent and the indolent restless young male. Parent tries to get teen to do this or that chore, every command a criticism of laziness, slovenliness, or criminal tendencies, backed by threats to take away privileges. The rhymes come down hard, every stanza nailed down with the classic refrain "Yakety yak," followed by the deep bass "Don't talk back!"

"Yakety Yak" is fun, but it points to a serious social conundrum. It dramatizes a sweeping critical relationship. The parent has nothing nice to say, and the young teen hears all that negative stuff as—yakety yak!

Young teenagers are not the only magnets for overcritical stances. Henry, let's call him, was one of several young developers in a software start-up. It was Henry's job to come up with a new interface design, but other pressures led him to put it off until the last minute. Then he worked late into the night at home prototyping something to show. The next morning found him in the office at his workstation, still tinkering with the fine points.

Sergio, another member of the group, wandered by, commenting on Henry's bleary-eyed state.

"Yeah," confessed Henry. "I came close to pulling an all-nighter. But I'm also trying to pull a rabbit out of a hat with this thing. I have to show it to the whole group in an hour, but wanna take a look at my hat rabbit?"

Sergio said sure, got the five minute tour, and said, "Well, I don't know. To me, there are two big problems with this. . . ." And he started to explain what they were in rational detail.

Henry was not pleased. Henry began to explain to Sergio in rational detail how stupid he was to lay such a message out when Henry had stayed up practically all night working. After that, Henry and Sergio didn't get along so well. Yakety yak strikes again.

Both Sergio and Henry failed to display much organizational intelligence here. It wasn't very smart of Sergio to get critical about Henry's hat rabbit after his heroic labors, especially since Henry had to show the group his hat rabbit soon and there wasn't time to fix anything up. And it wasn't very smart of Henry to tell Sergio how stupid he was for doing so. They were both inept, but they were behaving in very natural ways.

Variants on this happen all the time. They happen at workstations, in boardrooms, within senate buildings, and around the dinner table. They happen with software prototypes, the texts of new governmental policies, vision statements, five-year plans, clothing styles, budget allocations, outlines for speeches, plans for family reunions, or performance reviews. Doesn't matter. Feedback is a true hot spot of intelligence in groups, teams, organizations, and committees. Yakety yak.

THE DILEMMA OF FEEDBACK

If Coasters-style yakety yak were just bad-mouthing, life would be simpler. We could edit it out of our lives along with such unseemly social practices as planting elbows on tables during mealtime. But it's not that simple. Even yakety yak is feedback of a sort, and a close look at feedback argues it to be both immensely productive and annoyingly vexed.

Feedback is fundamental to performance and learning in individual, community, and organizational situations. Psychological studies in both the behaviorist and the cognitive traditions have demonstrated repeatedly that improvements in performance depend on feedback loops. If you don't know what you're doing right and wrong, you're not likely to get much better. Imagine the simple collaborative activity of playing catch by tossing a ball back and forth over a shed. You can't see your partner on the other side, and your partner can't see you. Neither of you is very likely to learn to toss the ball accurately, because you have no idea how close you've come. But never mind tossing—you both might get much better at catching balls, because you get plenty of feedback. The balls come soaring over the shed in unexpected places, you try to catch them, and you discover how well you did. The two of you would end up poor throwers and good catchers, all because of the feedback available.

Much of the feedback we need in order to perform better solo or in groups gets generated automatically by the circumstances, without anyone providing feedback. When children learn to walk or ride a bicycle or play catch (without a shed in the way), they experience directly what goes wrong. But feedback from another person is often helpful. The other person may know more about what you need to do than you do, or the other person may simply be better able to see what's going on. This can happen for simple physical reasons. In many sports activities, because we act from the inside out, it's hard to discern what our bodies are doing. It can also happen for attitudinal reasons. We get so caught up in what we're doing and the way we're doing it that we lose perspective and objectivity.

In collective thinking—whether it's around a novel design for a space shuttle, a wide-scale advertising campaign, a fail-safe pension program, or a new economic policy for a nation—ideas are generated, scenarios are proposed, forecasts are made. People are bound to disagree sometimes and to let one another know about it. In the sustained collective activities of business and government, people develop views on whether you are making the contribution you should and how you could do better. You are likely to hear those views in various graceful or ungainly ways from time to time.

So feedback is an essential part of a group's intelligent or not-so-intelligent functioning. That would be fine if feedback were not so sensitive a matter. But it is. You don't like to hear that this is weak or that is shoddy or the other thing is misconceived, and especially not that you as a person are careless or lazy or inattentive or stupid. Yakety yak! All this generates the extremely inconvenient:

℞ *Dilemma of feedback:* The good news: Interactions that provide feedback are very important for individual, community, and organizational effectiveness and learning. The bad news: They often flop, yielding no meaningful exchange of information and driving people apart.

In other words, feedback conversations have high potential to be progressive, but often are regressive. This is what makes feedback a hot spot of organizational intelligence.

THREE FACES OF FEEDBACK

There's no question that feedback is important and inevitable. The question is, what style of feedback do we give and get? Like other common interactions, the ways we give and get feedback come in patterns—archetypes of interaction. Each archetype represents a different manner of resolving the dilemma of feedback. Looking across different contexts, three archetypes stand out—negative feedback; conciliatory feedback, which is a kind of social stroking; and communicative feedback, a better way.

Negative feedback. Tell people what's wrong. (People need to know what's wrong and will accept it and correct it. It's "honest.")

Conciliatory feedback. Be positive and vague. Avoid criticizing. (You want to be supportive and avoid conflict, and negative feedback will be rejected, and relationships will be spoiled.)

Communicative feedback. Clarify what's on the table; offer specific positive as well as negative feedback, focusing on ideas, products, or behaviors, not core character or abilities. (People gain most from fair, balanced, and depersonalized feedback carefully communicated in a context of clarity.)

Negative feedback is the most painful archetype. It's the Coasters' yakety yak. It's the lay-it-on-the-line archetype, the one that tells people straight out what's wrong. It's the most obvious kind of feedback to give, the one that follows the natural avalanche of impulse. When we look at a situation with an evaluative mind-set, we often fixate on what we see wrong. And we do the straightforward thing— let the people responsible know about it. This is the kind of feedback Henry got from Sergio—and the kind of feedback Henry gave him back.

While we usually fall into this archetype of feedback automatically, it has a rationale. People need to know what's wrong. Why not be honest and tell them? This is how we generally behave toward ourselves. When we are developing an idea or a product, we look at what we've done so far, size it up, detect the shortfalls, and try to make things better. If I treat myself that way, why shouldn't I treat you that way? The negative feedback archetype resolves the dilemma of feedback, or tries to, by ignoring the second horn of the dilemma, the one that emphasizes how alienating feedback can be. It recognizes that negative feedback carries potentially important information and simply gives it. In many situations this serves well enough.

However, people learn over time that negative feedback often provokes defensiveness and alienation. This is especially likely when the feedback is personal, addressing the person's core identity rather than the idea or product. It was bad enough for Sergio to tell Henry what was wrong with his hat rabbit, but even worse for Henry to tell Sergio how stupid he was to do so.

Reacting to such sour experiences, people develop another archetype that might be called *conciliatory feedback*. Far from yakety yak, conciliatory feedback is social stroking. You want someone to feel good about what they have done, so you say, "I really like how you put that together." You do not want to get into an argument over something, so you say, "I think the plan is basically fine; there may be a couple of puzzles, but we can work them out later." When Sergio viewed Henry's hat rabbit, he might have said, "Mmm, yeah, looks good. Hangs together. I'll look forward to the group discussion in an hour." In a way, conciliatory feedback is not feedback at all. It's encouragement and conflict avoidance in the guise of feedback.

Like negative feedback, conciliatory feedback has a tacit rationale. Relationships are so important and feedback is so difficult to receive seriously that it makes better tactical sense to favor relationships over information. The conciliatory archetype resolves the dilemma of feedback by spurning the first horn of the dilemma, the one that emphasizes the importance of the information. Indeed, sometimes the information isn't important. Henry had no time for serious revisions before the meeting, so serious feedback could do no immediate good.

Communicative feedback is a more sophisticated archetype that embraces both horns of the dilemma. Suppose Henry did have time to make adjustments in his hat rabbit, so feedback could be useful. Sergio knows that people often misunderstand the situation they are giving feedback about and offend the receiver with misguided feedback, so Sergio begins by asking a couple of questions to clarify the specs and goals of the interface. Then Sergio offers his sense of the prototype's positive features. Then Sergio moves on to puzzles and problems and recommendations in a helpful spirit. The conversation is more elaborate and less natural than either negative or conciliatory feedback, but it's much easier for Henry to take, and to take advantage of.

You wish. Remember the dinosaur paradox from the previous chapter—regressive archetypes tend to dominate and drive out progressive ones. In the immortal words of baseball great Yogi Berra, "It's déjà vu all over again." Communicative feedback, the most progressive, is the rarest archetype we encounter. All too often, negative feedback rules. Many communities and organizations have a culture of negativity, with negative feedback the norm, along with distrust and other regressive patterns. In other settings, conciliatory feedback is the norm. People are too wary of the disunifying impact of negative feedback to risk it much. Stroking wins out over yakety yak, to create cultures of conciliation. A culture of conciliation assuredly is more pleasant than a culture of negativity, but neither one is particularly intelligent!

WHICH STYLE WHEN?

Toddler has just toddled out into the street. Although it's not a major street, from time to time one of those enormous shiny metal things has been known to whoosh by. Never mind communicative feedback, forget conciliatory feedback—you tell Toddler *No! No! No!* (And you might tell yourself *No! No! No!* too, for leaving Toddler in a position to wander out onto the street.) Or recollect again Sergio looking at Henry's hat rabbit. Never mind negative or even communicative feedback. In that situation, he ought to have given conciliatory feedback.

☛ Negative and conciliatory feedback have their advantages in certain circumstances.

It's worth a moment to analyze all three archetypes of feedback from the standpoints of knowledge processing and symbolic conduct. First, knowledge processing (Table 3.1).

Table 3.1 discloses trade-offs among the three archetypes. Conciliatory feedback scores worst from the standpoint of knowledge processing, because it delivers no information and may even mislead. Directness about what is wrong is the advantage of negative feedback, and sometimes that can be paramount. However, communicative feedback with its emphasis on clarity and balanced evaluation provides better knowledge processing.

Table 3.2 shows how the three archetypes score from the perspective of symbolic conduct.

The directness of negative feedback is most likely to be appreciated when the feedback rescues you from a grievous mistake.

TABLE 3.1   Feedback Archetypes from the Standpoint of
Knowledge Processing

Archetype	Analysis
Negative feedback	+ Communicates what you think is wrong efficiently and in no uncertain terms. − Fails to clarify the idea or behavior, which is surprisingly often misinterpreted by the person doing the criticizing. − Fails to communicate positive features, which are important to preserve and build on.
Conciliatory feedback	− Communicates virtually no information. May mislead by conveying the impression that all is okay.
Communicative feedback	+ Clarifies the idea or behavior under consideration, so that you're both talking about the same thing. + Communicates positive features toward preserving and building on them. + Communicates concerns and suggestions toward improvement. − Consumes more time, requires more thought and effort.

Conciliatory feedback can serve some situations well by keeping the peace and demonstrating support and solidarity. On the whole, however, communicative feedback broadcasts the most positive messages through symbolic conduct.

A FEEDBACK CAMELOT

The Round Table meets every Tuesday to consider affairs of the nation. Today, Sir Galahad declaims with a passion, "Jousts are altogether too bloody. A lance can take off someone's head just as easily as you might snap the top off a carrot. I've been considering the challenges and have a notion to put forth. There is an esoteric substance called *rubber* imported from a country far across the ocean. What if we were to tip our lances with this rubber? Surely such an innovation would make jousts safer and more fun, better family entertainment for all!" (For collectors of anachronisms, rubber is native to Central and South America. It had little presence in England or Europe until the 1700s. Oh, well.)

TABLE 3.2 Feedback Archetypes from the Standpoint of
Symbolic Conduct

Archetype	Analysis
Negative feedback	+ Sometimes read as frank and honest. – Often read as careless and dehumanizing, treating the receiver like an object or servant, especially when it speaks directly or indirectly to character, abilities, or a person's core identity.
Conciliatory feedback	+ Usually read as pleasant, encouraging, not threatening core identity. – As receiver learns over multiple occasions that the feedback is empty, can be read as evasive or pandering.
Communicative feedback	+ Read as careful, respectful, and honest.

King Arthur mutters to himself, "Here we go with Galahad again. Holy Grails, rubber-tipped lances, and who knows what next week. I'm a modern man at heart, but people like at least the chance of a little blood at their jousts."

But Arthur has a commitment to the spirit of the Round Table. So he smiles graciously and says, "Let's talk it over among us." And he uses communicative feedback step by step. Sometimes my colleagues and I have called this tool (in several variants) the *ladder of feedback*.

COMMUNICATIVE FEEDBACK STEP BY STEP

Begin and end by creating a positive framing—for instance, by thanking people for their contribution, expressing a broadly positive view of what's on the table as moving forward. In between:

* *Step 1: Clarify.* Ask clarifying questions to be sure you understand the idea or matter on the table. *Avoid clarifying questions that are thinly disguised criticism.*
* *Step 2: Value.* Express what you like about the idea or matter at hand in specific terms. *Do not offer a perfunctory "good, but," and hurry on to the negatives.*

❋ *Step 3: Concerns and suggestions.* State your puzzles and concerns and, when possible, couple them with suggestions for improving what's on the table. *Avoid absolutes: "What's wrong is. . . ." Use qualified terms: "I wonder if. . . ." "It seems to me. . . ." Avoid criticizing personal character or ability and focus on ideas, products, or particular aspects of behavior.*

We have already seen something like this at work. The illustration of communicative feedback that recast the conversation between Sergio and Henry followed this pattern—first checking for clarity, then offering appreciation, then turning to concerns. In general, even when the idea on the table may not impress you that much, it's worth thinking of the table as round and employing communicative feedback. Let's see how this might sound.

ARTHUR: You've brought an ingenious idea to the table, one well worth thinking through. Thank you for that. Now, first of all, let's seek some clarity. This rubber material, what is it like?

GALAHAD: Behold, a sample. *(Passes a wad of rubber around the table.)* Note how the substance is soft and springy, an ideal material for protecting our knights.

LANCELOT: Hmmm. *(Fingers the rubber.)* I take your point. And you're proposing what—a full-scale conversion to rubber-tipped lances, an experiment for one tourney, a little R&D work to build a prototype?

GALAHAD: It's my thought that for the sake of God's mercy we should convene an entire tournament under this new dispensation.

(Other knights add further clarifying questions.)

ARTHUR: Well, you sought a reaction. On the positive side, now and again, despite our care and regulations, we do lose men in the tourney. And that's surely a waste when they could join us in defense of the kingdom.

LANCELOT: The wives and ladies do carry on when now and again their knights are injured badly, not to mention killed.

And some have said that tourneys hardly manifest the level of civilization to which we aspire. Too much of a blood sport. Sir Galahad's plan addresses these problems.

(Others mention some positive features.)

GALAHAD: Well, thank you, your grace and all.

ARTHUR: Of course, we need to examine the concerns here as well. Here's one. I know this may seem crass, but in point of fact knights are rarely seriously injured, and the tournaments generate an excellent income that supports the state. I wonder whether people will have the zest for a kinder, gentler joust?

LANCELOT: I too wonder. *(General murmur of assent.)* But perhaps there are ways to deal with the dilemma. What do you think?

GALAHAD: From my perspective, filling the governmental coffers, even for the good purpose of benign rule, is of less significance than playing out God's command of mercy.

LANCELOT: Still, we must recognize that the matter has practical dimensions. Possibly we could utilize the rubber tips solely for the elimination rounds. The big events, which are the real crowd pleasers, could still proceed in the customary fashion.

ARTHUR: Perhaps so. Here's another puzzle, though, and I wonder what our thoughts are about it. This rubber (*Fingers it again*) seems hardly firmer than a boiled egg. Would not the lance simply pierce it? Or, if you put a great wad of rubber on the tip of the lance, would it not throw the lance out of balance?

GALAHAD: Hmmm, a technical problem to be sure.

(The knights continue to discuss the puzzles for another couple of minutes.)

ARTHUR: So what are you thinking now.

GALAHAD: I confess that I was somewhat more enthusiastic initially. Still, this rubber does present the possibility of more humane jousts. Let me propose simply the development of a prototype, to ascertain whether our engineers can resolve the problems and arrive at a robust technical solution.

ARTHUR: That would be a step forward. I allow that I am quite cautious. Still, it's useful to know what you can do with a new technology.

LANCELOT: Perhaps we could use the rubber in training but not in real tournaments. Let us examine the opportunities on the basis of more information.

Here, communicative feedback organizes a civil and thoughtful conversation. Galahad does not attain what he originally wanted, but he feels respectfully treated. Arthur preserves good relationships around the table and initiates a technical exploration that might yield valuable results in several directions.

Contrast this with the archetypes of negative feedback and conciliatory feedback. For the first, Arthur might easily have said:

NEGATIVE ARTHUR: I have to say that this is not a good idea. Clearly it's the high stakes and a bit of blood that keep people coming to the tournaments. We can't invest our Round-Table time on such fanciful notions.

Of course, such a reaction from Arthur does not leave the table very round. On the other hand, Arthur might have said:

CONCILIATORY ARTHUR: Interesting idea. I want to thank you for bringing it to the table, and maybe we do need a kinder, gentler tournament. However, today the Round Table faces several burdensome affairs of state. Perhaps we can take this question up at a meeting in a few weeks, when other matters are less urgent. So, on to item 1.

Arthur is calculatedly vague about when the Round Table might return to the proposition. He's hoping never. Galahad might feel vexed that the matter has been put off—or quite angry, if he's sharp enough to read Arthur's real intent. Although communicative feedback requires more time, it clearly combines deeper knowledge processing with positive symbolic conduct.

FOUR BRANDS OF BETTER FEEDBACK

Act 2, scene 2, *Romeo and Juliet:* Juliet bewails Romeo's membership in the Montague clan with the famous words "That which we call a rose / By any other name would smell as sweet."

She has Romeo in mind, but we could say the same thing about communicative feedback. It can take the stepwise form illustrated previously. However, many have recognized the problems of feedback and named patterns of interaction with features of communicative feedback. Here are four from the worlds of business and government, each with some positive features and also some limitations.

ONE MINUTE PRAISINGS AND REPRIMANDS

The One Minute Manager (New York: Berkeley, 1982), the popular management guide by Kenneth Blanchard and Spencer Johnson, includes two feedback strategies, the *one-minute praising* and the *one-minute reprimand*. Both require expectations established in advance between you and your subordinates. This is written out in a few words, in a process that the authors call *one-minute goal setting.* It provides the basis for later praise and reprimands.

For a one-minute praising, you give praise immediately after a good performance, tell the subordinate directly that you are going to offer an assessment, identify the good aspects specifically, and express pleasure at what the person did and how it helps the community or organization. In short, short form, the praising might sound like this:

"Let me tell you how much I like the report you turned in yesterday afternoon. It was right on target. I appreciate the close analysis of the resource implications, the long-term projection, and the point-by-point attention to all the targets. This will help all of us to move the project ahead, which feels just great. Thanks!"

For a one-minute reprimand, you tell a subordinate person that you're going to offer some clear feedback, reprimand the person right away, and describe specifically what was wrong and how you feel about it. But then you switch gears, emphasizing how you think well of the person and support and value the person's contribution. Then you put the matter decisively behind you. In short, short form, the reprimand might sound like this:

"I want to give you a specific reaction to the report you turned in yesterday afternoon. I worry that the report lacks long-term projections. I'm disappointed that it doesn't take up all the targets point by point. In order to move the project ahead, we really need a finer-grained analysis. But look, you do fine work for the group. I remember the initiative last month, which moved forward really well. Let's take another pass on this one and we'll be there."

One-minute managing reflects *behaviorism,* a theory of human and animal behavior developed by John Watson of John Hopkins University in the first decades of the twentieth century and carried forward by B. F. Skinner of Harvard University and others. One of its key tenets is that behavior changes through positive and negative reinforcement— roughly, reward and punishment, although these terms do not capture the nuances of the behaviorist position well. While discredited as an explanatory theory for complex cognition, behaviorism remains a powerful guide to changing behavior in animals and humans. Anyone can see that one-minute praising and one-minute reprimands are designed to provide positive and negative reinforcement. The emphasis on clarity and prompt response ensures that the reinforcement applies specifically to the intended behavior, positive or negative.

Behaviorist techniques often seem manipulative. The authors take pains to parry this criticism. They encourage managers to be clear with their subordinates in advance about the purpose and practice of one-minute praisings, reprimands, and related tactics. With everyone in on the game, it loses some of its manipulative aura.

How well do these practices score by the measure of communicative feedback? Clear, specific, and immediate response certainly aids effective knowledge processing. The praising naturally carries positive symbolic value. In the one-minute reprimand, the careful separation of criticizing the behavior in question and valuing the person and the person's contribution is an important symbolic move.

There are some limitations as well. No specific attention to clarification is written into these strategies. In the preceding examples, the boss assumes that it is perfectly clear what the report needs to be like and moves on to judgment. Potentially, this is a shortfall of knowledge processing. Also, praising and reprimanding are treated as separate episodes. Often situations are mixed, and one wants to acknowledge the positive aspects while raising concerns. Again, this is a limit of knowledge processing.

For a third limitation, the giver of feedback assumes a posture of strong and rather closed authority—the judge and deliverer of judgment. This symbolic conduct may sometimes be appropriate, but it is certainly double-edged. Concerning behaviorism specifically, Karen Pryor, an astute writer on applications of behaviorism, notes that strong negative reinforcement is highly problematic for a number of reasons and often backfires. She views with reservations the prominence of the one-minute reprimand in the scheme.

THE AFTER-ACTION REVIEW

The U.S. Army uses an interesting strategy to take stock after an action, the after-action review (AAR). The practice has also been adopted by corporations, as discussed by Baird, Holland, and Deacon in an article in *Organizational Dynamics*. The aim of this group process is specifically not to attach blame for anything that may have gone wrong, but to learn and feed the learning back into further planning.

The AAR unfolds as a discussion among key participants in the action. It can be organized into four steps:

1. What was the intent?
2. What actually happened?
3. What have we learned?
4. What do we do now?

Such a discussion can yield insight not only after a military action but also after a heavy negotiating session, an important project presentation, or an intensive planning session. It can provide an end-of-day routine for a development team or a sales team.

The AAR shows many characteristics of communicative feedback. Turning to symbolic conduct first, a reflective discussion that eschews blame and focuses on lessons for the future signals commitment to the growth of the team.

As to knowledge processing, the four steps prescribe a thoughtful pattern of analysis. Because events often outrun intentions, reminding oneself of the initial plan is a good first step. Juxtaposing the initial intent with what actually happened sets the stage for understanding alignments and misalignments. Where did we do what we intended? Did it prove to be a good idea in action? When we didn't do what we intended, why not? Could we have done it if we had tried harder or tried a different way? Was what actually happened better or worse than what we intended? Questions such as these arise naturally and lead to conclusions that inform future actions.

Overall, the AAR serves the goals of positive symbolic conduct and effective knowledge processing well. One limitation is that it is designed for and suited to an episode of action. It applies less well to generating feedback on, for instance, a report, a slogan, a proposed invention, a policy, or, indeed, a plan before execution.

NEMAWASHI

Nemawashi is the Japanese consensus process mentioned at the beginning of Chapter 2. In its original sense, *nemawashi* is a gardening term, meaning to tend to the roots. Formal meetings in the nemawashi spirit rarely include serious confrontations of viewpoints and substantive feedback. It's all been settled beforehand, at the roots. In a weave of pairwise and small group meetings, different stakeholders meet in various combinations to work through conflicts and tune up an idea. Seriously contentious ideas don't come before a formal meeting with the risk of an out-in-the-open debate. Among other things, nemawashi avoids challenges in public and semipublic settings and the attendant risk of loss of face.

Nemawashi is much more than a process of feedback. However, considerable feedback occurs within the practice. Moreover, the basic idea behind nemawashi is certainly not limited to Japanese culture. Politically savvy managers and leaders everywhere know that it's often smart to debug an idea and build support for it through small conversations with key figures before a formal airing. With these points in mind, it's worth examining the broad idea behind nemawashi, no matter what culture it's located in, as it relates to symbolic conduct and knowledge processing.

To a first approximation, nemawashi scores a plus for symbolic conduct, because it avoids the awkwardness of public confrontations. The side conversations may be conflictive, but at least they don't expose people to losing rounds in public. However, the conversations may occur within a select circle, the old-boy network, leaving those not in the loop feeling disenfranchised. In the ideal nemawashi process, stakeholders shouldn't be left out of the loop, but the reality can easily be different.

As to knowledge processing, the web of interactions can be much richer as a series of small conversations than as one big conversation. Individuals have more time to dig deep and can feel safer offering individual perspectives. On the other hand, nemawashi can plainly use a lot of time, and some of those individual perspectives might get lost or buried. Like any social practice, nemawashi requires thoughtful rather than perfunctory use to draw out its best.

DECONSTRUCTIVE CRITICISM

We all want to offer constructive criticism. However, Robert Kegan and Lisa Laskow Lahey, in an insightful and immensely practical book titled *How the Way We Talk can Change the Way We Work* (San Francisco: Jossey-Bass, 2001), argue that constructive criticism is not enough. We need *deconstructive* criticism.

The authors note the usual hazards of destructive criticism and go on to argue that even constructive criticism has built in assumptions that limit its contribution. To give a sense of their critique, let us call on King Arthur again.

CONSTRUCTIVE ARTHUR: You offer a thoughtful idea, Sir Galahad, and we all appreciate your bringing it forward. Reducing the bloodletting at the jousts would almost certainly shrink our audiences, and we can't accept that. However, the idea has good potential applications in practice sessions. I will order the royal engineers to develop a prototype to test in that context. Let me ask you to advise them in their inquiries, lending your insights and reporting back to the Round Table when results are ready.

Certainly, Arthur's words are measured and appreciative. Certainly, positive actions result. Nonetheless, Kegan and Lahey would point to implicit assumptions: There is one truth about the matter at hand. The giver of feedback has special insight into the truth of the matter. The giver of feedback bears most of the responsibility for rendering judgment, making positive suggestions, and sustaining the relationships. Kegan and Lahey emphasize that these assumptions are not necessarily wrong; it's just that how right they are can vary a lot from situation to situation. If one communicates in a more open way that deconstructs the tacit assumptions, the character of the feedback changes considerably. Let's rewrite the Arthur role in this spirit:

> DECONSTRUCTIVE ARTHUR: You offer a thoughtful idea, Sir Galahad, and we all appreciate your bringing it forward. I myself suspect that reducing the bloodletting at the jousts would almost certainly shrink our audiences, and I feel that this is not an acceptable consequence. But I could be mistaken, and you and others around the table might have different judgments on these matters. We can explore those and even gather evidence. In any case, the idea would appear to have good potential applications in practice sessions. . . .

Kegan and Lahey argue that the deconstructive style creates more of a mutual context for problem solving and learning by opening up avenues that otherwise are closed.

Plainly, deconstructive feedback is much more communicative than destructive feedback or even constructive feedback. It offers positive symbolic conduct and opens up areas of discussion that otherwise could remain closed.

There are interesting puzzles, too. Some may feel that Deconstructive Arthur sounds like too much of a wimp. Maybe so, depending on the circumstances. Leaders like King Arthur need to worry not only about the quality of the particular interaction but about maintaining their status and others' confidence in them. (See Chapter 5.) Openness is not the only kind of symbolic conduct at issue. There is also the symbolic conduct of delivering reasonable judgment with a sense of authority.

Communicative feedback as described—the quest for clarity, serious attention to positive aspects, raising puzzles and concerns—does not require Deconstructive Arthur. Instead, Arthur can choose to handle those matters in a more authoritative (but not authoritarian) way. What Arthur should do on a particular occasion is very much a contextual judgment, just the kind of contextual judgment that effective leaders need to be good at. And remember, Kegan and Lahey do not assert that the assumptions are always wrong.

The larger moral here is that many patterns of interaction—one-minute praisings and reprimands, the after-action review, nemawashi, deconstructive feedback, and no doubt others—can step away from the hazards of negative and conciliatory feedback and show valuable features of communicative feedback in a variety of ways. They are not identical, not quite all roses by other names, but they are certainly the same sort of flora.

FINDINGS FROM THE FEEDBACK FRONT

Communicative feedback—nice idea, but what happens when you put it into practice? This question can be raised for deconstructive feedback, nemawashi, or any other variant, but my colleagues and I can share some direct experience with stepwise communicative feedback.

We've introduced communicative feedback into several settings with gratifying results, usually calling it the *ladder of feedback*—one rung for each step. In the most extensive example, we worked for several years on an action research project with the managers of a large university—the accountants, purchasing agents, lawyers, buildings and grounds administrators, and others. The ladder of feedback was one of several tools designed to support good knowledge processing and symbolic conduct. Although there is no way to isolate the impact of communicative feedback specifically, the managers told us that it was especially useful.

The overall initiative yielded a number of positive results. According to surveys, the office workers felt that their work became more collaborative and had more personal meaning. People experienced more autonomy. Reflective practices became more common, allowing for cycles of reflection on and improvement of administrative procedures.

However, this did not mean that the road forward was well-paved and trouble-free. Several potholes tripped up progress from time to time. Here are some lessons learned about communicative feedback.

People new to the practice often twisted it back into something like the negative archetype of feedback. They would phrase clarifying questions in ways that amounted to aggressive criticism. Imagine, for instance, that Arthur said to Galahad:

> NEWBIE ARTHUR: Let me ask a clarifying question. How can you possibly imagine that people would flock to jousts with all the sting taken out of them?

It's legitimate to bring up areas of concern as part of clarifying, but in a more open way:

> OLD-HAND ARTHUR: Let me ask a clarifying question. Have you thought about how a slightly less risky joust would influence audience enthusiasm, attendance, and related matters?

Although Arthur can ask at this point, if he really wants to avoid frontloading negative criticism, he should simply listen to Galahad's answer and defer airing specific concerns.

People new to communicative feedback also often treated valuing in a perfunctory rather than authentic way. Imagine if Arthur had said:

> NEWBIE ARTHUR: On the positive side, that's a really clever idea. But we have to respect reality. There's no way that we could. . . .

Such a response hardly honors the ingenuity of Galahad's idea—which displays poor symbolic conduct. Moreover, the response does not give information to Galahad about the idea's specific strengths—which displays poor knowledge processing. The previous section already illustrated a better response from Arthur.

Participants also proved agile in finding excuses not to use communicative feedback in various circumstances. Here are several of their excuses, along with reasons to think about the situation differently.

* *If the idea on the table is deeply flawed, shouldn't I be direct rather than deceptively nice?* Communicative feedback doesn't ask you to be indirect. It asks for more directness—including the negatives but also clarity and positive features. Maybe the idea on the table seems too close to a miracle drug, a matter transporter, or a perpetual motion machine. Maybe you're already totaling up the losses. But perhaps you don't fully understand the idea yet. It will certainly have a couple of positive features that deserve respect and that may prove to be stepping stones to better ideas now or later. Also, your symbolic conduct becomes especially important when you think an idea is deeply flawed. You can air your strong concerns as part of communicative feedback, but the proposer is likely to take a purely negative response personally, which won't do anyone any good.

* *If it's not basically a democratic decision, shouldn't I simply drop the pretense?* Communicative feedback isn't about democracy, it's about informativeness and cohesiveness. The king is the king, but even kings have to worry about informativeness and cohesiveness if they want to keep their kingdoms. Making the final call on Galahad's proposal, Arthur might respond this way:

  ARTHUR: I'm glad we've explored this thoroughly, and I think we all see the merits in the idea. However, let us set it aside, at least for the present. The potential benefits are real, but the risks and effort required outweigh them as it looks now. Thanks to all for thinking it through together.

* *If I'm really busy, can't I simply move to what needs correcting?*
  This is simply shortsighted. Without clarity, one doesn't
  know what needs correcting. Unless positive features
  receive recognition, they could get lost in the next round.
  Suppose an aide gives you a draft of a new policy that seems
  to have loopholes. You're tempted to order the aide off to
  produce a new draft, but maybe the aide has thought about
  this already, and the loopholes aren't there. Better ask for a
  clarification! Maybe you want to be sure that the next draft
  includes the good features of this one. Better say what they
  are! Also, communicative feedback need not be time
  consuming. Like most patterns of interaction, it has an
  accordion character—sometimes expanded and sometimes
  compact. A simple clarifying question, a couple of gen-
  uinely meant positive considerations, a couple of principal
  concerns, and you might be done.

* *So I should always use communicative feedback!*   No, this takes
  the vision too far. Recall that the negative and conciliatory
  archetypes fit certain circumstances better than the communicative archetype. Urgent situations that require emphatic
  correction may call for the negative archetype, as with the
  example of the toddler running into the street. Situations in
  which feedback will not be useful and may alienate people
  invite the conciliatory archetype, as with Sergio, who
  would have done better to comment on Henry's hat rabbit
  in a vaguely positive way. Usually the communicative
  archetype serves better, but not always.

All the way from clarifying questions that amounted to sharp
criticism to excuses like being really busy, our observations identified
a pattern of defensiveness. We found that people tended in various
ways to backslide into negative and conciliatory feedback, especially
negative. Interviews and other probes suggested that this was not a
matter of fundamental philosophical reservations about communicative feedback. On the contrary, people appreciated the practice. It
was more a matter of force of habit and the pseudoefficient fit of negative feedback into busy lives. We found that people needed to do

more than try to adopt the new practice of communicative feedback. They needed to actively restrain an old practice.

What holds true for communicative feedback applies across the range of regressive and progressive archetypes. In many situations, regressive archetypes are dominant and not easily dislodged, even when people recognize the advantage of dislodging them and want to do so.

☞ *Active inhibition.* Effective use of progressive archetypes calls for active inhibition of their regressive siblings, not just good intentions to use the progressive form.

Remember King Arthur's thoughts when Sir Galahad brought forward the idea of rubber-tipped lances? Arthur didn't like the idea, but he held himself back from a quick authoritarian reaction. That was round-table thinking. Any serious member of a round table needs to practice this sort of active inhibition when faced with the impulse to jump to the negatives in a feedback situation, to adopt a starkly adversarial position in a negotiation, to skip consulting with other stakeholders on an important decision, or to fall into any other regressive archetype.

WHO TO WHOM

Vernon of VisionTech was the enlightened leader of a division of a high-tech company for which I did some consulting. Vernon came on stage in Chapter 2, in illustration of a progressive style. Imagine that you were an employee who worked closely with Vernon. You might say to yourself, "Vernon's an open fellow. I like a lot about what he does. So when there's something I don't like, I should walk up and say so—using appropriately communicative feedback, of course."

Maybe not. Communicative feedback is a polite and informative way to deliver the message, but feedback is still a supremely sensitive matter in human relations and the reach for organizational intelligence.

☞ How welcome feedback is depends on who's doing the feed-
ing and who's doing the eating.

A convenient English phrase makes the point: "It's not your place
to. . . ." For instance, "It's not your place to give feedback to your
boss." Even if the boss is a white knight.

Giving uninvited critical feedback to someone in a position of
authority is not people smart. The message may be fair and useful,
but the symbolic conduct constitutes a challenge to authority. A
position of authority normally confers the right to give feedback, and
giving feedback other than conciliatory feedback in the opposite
direction amounts to questioning the person's status. Perhaps that status ought to be questioned, but you can hardly do so with the expectation of a level playing field.

To generalize, the giving and receiving of feedback is a more intricate social exchange than it may appear to be at first. It's not just a
matter of how (negative, conciliatory, communicative) but to whom.
Even conciliatory feedback may be offensive to the wrong "whom."

So who is in position to give feedback to whom? Looking across
the intricacies of human conduct, the tacit rules map out roughly as
follows:

* *Authority relationships.* People in positions of authority
  generally have the right and indeed the responsibility to
  give feedback within the scope of their authority—bosses
  to subordinates, parents to children, teachers to students,
  and so on. Uninvited feedback *to* an authority figure generally is out of place.

* *Exchange relationships.* Trading or purchasing services and
  products creates a reciprocal right to give feedback and seek
  redress, for instance, if a purchase turns out to be defective
  or the check bounces.

* *Stakeholder relationships.* When people share a stake in
  something, that confers the right to offer feedback around
  actions that might affect the stake. Stockholders have the
  right to comment on how a company is run, partners in a

business have the right to offer feedback on one another's plans, and so on.

* *Friendship and colleagueship.*   These relationships are complex. Mostly, they carry expectations for conciliatory feedback. As a friend or colleague, you are supposed to be supportive. Giving uninvited critical feedback is symbolic conduct that offensively suggests an authority relationship. However, critical feedback is appropriate if it's necessary to save a friend or colleague from a serious gaffe.

* *Requesting feedback.*   The right to give feedback can always be conferred by asking for it, whatever the relationship otherwise. A boss may ask subordinates for feedback about a plan or product or even how things are going in general. A parent may ask children for feedback about what would make a good summer vacation, whether the dinner is tasty, or even how they're getting along now. Friends can request feedback about relationship problems, investment opportunities, or personal appearance. It's especially important for authority figures to seek feedback around areas of concern, because otherwise they are not likely to get much.

As if all these tacit rules weren't enough in themselves, they can easily conflict with one another. When a boss or a friend asks for feedback, the person is still a boss or a friend, so it's particularly important to offer communicative rather than negative feedback. Otherwise, the symbolic conduct can appear to challenge the relationship. In the same spirit, subordinates may also be stakeholders, or the boss and a subordinate may be friends, or friends may be partners. The multiple roles invoke multiple rules, so which do you follow?

It's a balancing act. When we move forward to offer feedback, we walk through a minefield of social rules and risk setting one off with every step. Does this mean that we should always tread carefully and keep our feedback within the safe and proper social channels? No, of course not! Some situations are serious enough to warrant overriding normal decorum and offering feedback that probably will be taken as out of place.

Suppose you see someone doing something self-endangering, perhaps not even realizing that it's dangerous. It's none of your business, but, in the spirit of general humanity, you might intervene anyway. Or suppose you have reason to believe that a boss is about to make a horrendous mistake on a matter that doesn't concern you. You might point out the pitfall despite the apparent challenge to authority. People do such things all the time. In other words:

↪ The moral is not "Never break the rules." The moral is "Don't be naïve about it."

There are many occasions that warrant breaking the who-whom rules of feedback. We just need to be aware of our transgressions and brace ourselves for people's likely reactions.

HERE THERE BE DRAGONS

Ian of ImageTech was the authoritarian director of a division of a high-tech company. Ian came on stage in Chapter 2 to illustrate what regressive interactions look like. Suppose you work with Ian of ImageTech. You may pine for the grace of communicative feedback, but you are not likely to get it from Ian. Nor would you want to advise Ian about how he should give feedback to you and others. Ian would not appreciate it. Worse, Ian's style colors the style of the whole group, promoting a culture of negativity. So really, what can you do?

This is a dragon situation. *Dragon situations* are circumstances that make progressive interactions difficult. A variety of colorful dragons thrive in the land of feedback. Besides the Ians of the world, many groups have entrenched cultures either of negativity or of conciliation. Acrimony between individuals can give feedback an edge. Urgency and high stakes produce stress and anxiety that can tip conversations toward a kind of clipped negative style.

Certainly, circumstances arise in which the best one can do is keep one's head down, hope, and endure. However, some of the dragons are not as large or as fearsome as their initial snorts and roars suggest.

In a Challenging Climate

People aware of communicative feedback can always strive to give it, whatever else is going on. Imagine a kind of anti-Ian who works under Ian, called Ina. When Ina is in the role of giver of feedback, she can control the style. If Ian asks for her view on something, Ina can employ communicative feedback. If a culture of negativity prevails at a meeting, at least Ina can maintain a communicative style as she speaks. If everyone appears all too nice, sweeping the real problems under the comfortable rug of conciliation, Ina can come forward with clarifying questions, positive points, and then concerns, breaking a cycle of comfortable deception.

Ina's influence may extend beyond the immediate occasion. Some people, with persistence and good craft, function as *developmental leaders* within groups, whatever their political position, fostering the evolution of a more progressive group culture (see Chapter 9). This is all the more likely if Ina has a power position—for instance, head of a team. The investigation mentioned earlier provided evidence for what also is common sense: The official leader has enormous influence over the culture of a group. People tend to mold their styles of conversation to the leader. If you are in such a position and adopt a communicative style of feedback and persist in it, many others will soon pick up on that.

With a Negative Person

Receivers of feedback can often ask for the pattern of feedback they want. Imagine that Ina and others are sitting with the formidable Ian. Ina is just rounding out her proposal for a new initiative. Ina says, "I'm sure I haven't explained all of this clearly, so I'd really find it valuable if we can start the discussion with clarifying questions and put off the good stuff and the bad stuff. Then, if you can tell me what you really like, that would help me know what the strengths are. And then, of course, we'll turn to the difficulties and try to work them through."

So how would Ian respond? Who knows. He might override Ina's appeal and get right to it with what he doesn't like—or what he does like, if he happens to like it. But he might go along with the process. At least Ina has tried!

WHEN STRESS IS UP

Another dragon fires up under conditions of stress, when something is urgent, stakes are high, or many small and medium-sized tasks accumulate. In such situations, progressive practices tend to backslide into negative archetypes. Even Ina may succumb. It's worth striving to be alert to the contexts of stress and to actively inhibit the natural tendency to backslide—the principle of active inhibition mentioned earlier.

However, occasional backsliding is inevitable, and people often perceive backsliding as a sign that progressive practices are hopeless, that they don't work. It's important for Ina and those like her to frame this backsliding as a natural side effect of difficult circumstances, one that can be fought against and that will fade as the good practices become more integrated into the group culture. Recognize it, regret it, pick up the good practices again, and move on.

Dragons are dragons. They are not going to scuttle into the corner and hide their heads. Still, the quest for communicative feedback is not only worthy but possible in difficult circumstances. The dilemma of feedback—potentially very progressive but in reality often regressive—means that careful and committed work on feedback is one of the basics for building process-smart and people-smart communities and organizations.

TOOLBOX

✳ *Cultivate seeing in archetypes.* Notice the three archetypes of negative feedback, conciliatory feedback, and communicative feedback around you. Notice cultures of negativity or conciliation.

✳ *Resist the dinosaur paradox* that favors regressive interactions. Give and promote communicative feedback step by step: positive framing, clarification, valuing positive features, concerns and suggestions, and positive conclusion.

✳ *Value and foster other practices with features of communicative feedback,* such as one-minute praisings and reprimands; The after-action review (What was the intent, what happened, what have we learned, what do we do now?); the nemawashi process of consensus building through a network of small conversations; deconstructive criticism, with its sensitivity to the assumption of one truth, which the feedback giver has; and so on.

✳ *Exercise active inhibition* with respect to negative and conciliatory feedback (except in those circumstances where they're appropriate), avoiding such slips as asking clarifying questions that are obviously critical and offering perfunctory "that's good, but" acknowledgement of positive features, and setting aside such excuses as "I don't have time" or "It's too flawed an idea to bother."

✳ *Respect the tacit rules* for who can give feedback to whom. When you feel you need to break them, don't break them naïvely. Expect consequences.

✳ *Cope with the dragon situations* such as challenging climates, negative people, and stressful circumstances by giving and asking for communicative feedback. Try to function as a developmental leader, a model and guide for others, and a force to shift the group away from cultures of negativity and conciliation.

4

THE DIFFICULTIES OF BEING
OF ONE MIND

MIND MELDS

The savant of *Star Trek*, Commander Spock, a Vulcan from the planet Vulcan, first officer and science officer of the U.S.S. *Enterprise,* he of the pointy ears and pointedly dissective comments, included in his repertoire of mental resources the Vulcan mind meld. Placing his hands in an odd position on your head and muttering "My mind to your mind," Spock would meld his mind with yours, become one with your psyche, energetically poke around your most intimate mindscapes, and bring a ruinous situation around to a good end.

Star Trek may seem a long way from King Arthur, but *Star Trek* in its several versions is a futuristic Camelot. The typical captain across the several *Star Trek* series is an Arthurian figure, committed to ideals and leading dedicated officers and crew with authority but not authoritarianism, offering respect, seeking counsel while exercising command, and fashioning a potent collective. And *Star Trek* even has its Merlin, its wizard—Spock, of course.

My mind to your mind—if only we could! And maybe we can in a limited sense, by thinking together in the best ways. But it's not easy. Anyone who's been around the world of organizations knows that it's not—whether in business or government, universities or foundations, military programs or international trade alliances. Remember the grim examples from the end of Chapter 1—miscommunications up and down the corporate ladder that cost hundreds of millions of dollars and the many episodes of historical folly like King George's handling of the American revolution or the U.S. involvement in Vietnam. Remember the hot spots of organizational intelligence from previous chapters—autocratic rather than participative decision making, negotiation from positions rather than from interests, and negative and conciliatory feedback both sacrificing opportunities for richer learning and development. No, it's not easy.

So why is organizational intelligence so hard to come by? Recall that this is one of this book's central questions. To make a start on it, we need to clarify what intelligence means. After that, we'll look at six specific factors that tend to make interactions regressive rather than progressive, helping to explain why it's so hard for several smart people to add up to a smart group.

WHAT IS INTELLIGENCE?

If two heads are sometimes better than one, what is the one that two heads are better than?

Today's theories of intelligence mostly have to do with individual intelligence, one head at a time. Ideas about organizational intelligence gain their meaning through extrapolation from 1 head to 2, 7, 27, 207, thinking together in some reasonable sense. To define organizational intelligence sensibly, we need to understand just how it is an extension of ideas about solo intelligence.

All theories of individual intelligence begin with informal notions about what intelligent behavior looks like. As people deal with the complexities of life, some individuals behave in smarter ways than others. Clarissa makes thoughtful decisions, handles her complicated bank account with aplomb, doesn't get sucked into dead-end social relationships, takes care of her aging father and his medical complications systematically and with genuine feeling but not ruinous depression, manages the local office of an advertising firm sensibly and inventively, and even did well on her SATs. Clarissa behaves in a quite intelligent way consistently over time and circumstances.

Taking inspiration from Clarissa's consistently intelligent behavior, an especially concise and pointed characterization of intelligence comes down to this:

℘ *Definition 1:* Intelligence is a matter of knowing what to do when you don't know what to do.

Most of the time, we get along in life by deploying knowledge and know-how we already have. We already know how to drive to work, so we drive to work on Monday with little difficulty. We already know how to labor through tax forms, so, as the time comes around once more, we fill them out and file them with minimal pain. However, every so often the world throws us a curve, such as an aging parent or an erratic client. We don't know what to do—not exactly, at least. But perhaps we know what to do when we don't know what to do. Perhaps we know to persist, adopt a strategy, consult with a neighbor, try to reason backward from the outcomes we want, and so on. Displays of such general competence are signs of intelligence.

To put it another way, consistent and effective coping with intellectually challenging novelty reveals intelligence—the new employee, the new boss, the new technology, the new regulations, the new market, the new competitor, the new product, the new culture of foreign partners, the new reporting system. Whenever something new shows up, intelligence is at a premium. Here is another definition of intelligent behavior, a more technical version that adds some refinements:

℘ *Definition 2:* Intelligence is the somewhat general capability for and tendency toward complex adaptive knowledge processing in response to or in quest of novelty.

Coping with novelty still holds the spotlight, but this elaborated view of intelligence adds details. It looks for *somewhat* general capabilities, not necessarily intelligence that cuts across everything. According to

Definition 2, one person might prove capable in matters of science, mathematics, and engineering but not so capable in matters of human relations, which are important in the workplace, and another person's capabilities might be just the other way around. Although circumscribed, both their capabilities show intelligence of significant range.

Definition 2 looks not only for capabilities but also for tendencies, what philosophers and psychologists sometimes call *dispositions*, such as the tendency to seek evidence or be open minded or curious. This criterion says that people who have a capability in principle but show no tendency to use it are not really behaving intelligently. They may be intelligent in principle, but not in practice. Finally, Definition 2 asks that intelligent people not only respond well to novelty but even seek it out to some extent, as in such traits as creativity or inventiveness.

While theories of individual intelligence commence with informal notions about what intelligent behavior looks like, they go on to propose psychological mechanisms underlying the intelligent behavior. The classic account began with research reported by the great psychologist and statistician Charles Spearman in 1904. Examining the results of batteries of tests, Spearman found that people who performed well on one kind of test tended to perform well on others. He used a statistical technique to measure the strength of this trend. His work, along with the penetrating work of the French psychologist Alfred Binet, led to today's concept of IQ. Spearman argued that differences in intellectual ability corresponded to a physiological reality, a kind of pervasive energy in the human nervous system. People better supplied with this energy, a matter he thought to be largely genetically determined, behaved in more intelligent ways across diverse intellectually demanding situations.

Versions of Spearman's stance survive today and have their champions. However, I prefer a broader view of intelligence that includes semigeneral traits and dispositions and better explains intelligence as it plays out in practical contexts. Indeed, Binet's notion of intelligence was closer to this than it was to Spearman's. It's important to recognize that the question "What is intelligence, really?" cannot be answered as simply as "Where did I put my socks, in the drawer or the hamper?" It's not just a matter of looking at the world and finding out. Debates about what intelligence really is depend on choices of the *explanandum,* of the phenomenon to be explained. If you're trying to explain why some people tend to score better consistently on a range of intellectually challenging tests, it's hard not to end up with a notion of something like IQ. If you're trying to explain how people cope with diverse and challenging circumstances in the world, it's hard to be satisfied with IQ and natural to end up with a more complex and nuanced picture.

Many modern views of intelligence offer such pictures. One well-known example is Howard Gardner's theory of multiple intelligences. Gardner originally argued for some seven distinct intelligences, each supported by separate neurological functions, including linguistic, logical-mathematical, musical, spatial, bodily kinesthetic, interpersonal, and intrapersonal intelligences. In more recent writings, Gardner has found reason to add an eighth, even a ninth.

Still another model with somewhat different commitments was developed by Yale psychologist Robert Sternberg. His triarchic theory of intelligence identifies three principal dimensions of intelligence: analytical intelligence, akin to what typical intelligence tests test; practical intelligence, reflecting practical knowledge about particular areas such as management, engineering, or teaching; and creative intelligence, concerning creativity and innovation.

My book *Outsmarting IQ* (New York: Free Press, 1995) advances my own view of individual intelligence, one that recognizes three layers—neural intelligence, the contribution of effective neural functioning to intelligent behavior; experiential intelligence, the contribution of experience in various domains and areas of life to intelligent behavior; and reflective intelligence, the contribution of general strategies, dispositions, and mental management to intelligent behavior. And of course there are many other models. Although they sound different and grind somewhat different axes, they also overlap and complement one another in various illuminating ways.

All that is a quick sketch of ideas about individual intelligence. Now, what about the intelligence of a group—a team, a division, a sales force, a government task force, a product development unit, or indeed a whole organization? What matters most for organizational intelligence is not any one theory of individual intelligence but a trend across them: Almost all of them propose that intelligence depends on how well the mind-brain processes information. This basic idea lies behind my suggestion that knowledge processing is a key component of organizational intelligence. As with individuals, so groups, teams, organizations, and communities can *know what to do when they don't know what to do* and display the *somewhat general capability for and tendency toward complex adaptive knowledge processing in response to or in quest of novelty.* Human collectives can prove to be more or less able and energetic decision makers, problem solvers, and planners in novel situations. While in part this reflects the ingenuity of individual members of the group, it also reflects how effectively the members exchange and pool ideas and sift possibilities; how progressive their conversations are. The notion of archetypes of interaction provides a specific way of analyzing stronger and weaker patterns of interaction in terms well suited to community and organizational behavior.

While effective knowledge processing extrapolates directly from individual intelligence, symbolic conduct addresses a distinctive challenge of work with others. Individual thinking sometimes lacks committed cohesiveness, but this problem becomes acute in organizations, where the members may have individual interests and agendas, where rivalry for a position or a budget can disrupt collaboration, and where clusters of allies can form and re-form according to the political winds. For a group to display intelligence in a sustained way, the members have to value their interchanges and stick together to keep making them, and this depends on positive symbolic conduct around such matters as mutual respect, common mission, and collaboration. Here again, archetypes of interaction provide a way of analyzing recurrent patterns for their symbolic significance.

All this explains why one might think of organizational intelligence in terms of archetypes of interaction, the knowledge processing they accomplish, and the symbolic conduct they express. But it leaves unaddressed the two fundamental puzzles of organizational intelligence introduced in earlier chapters, the lawnmower paradox (pooling physical effort is usually rather easy, pooling mental effort is usually rather hard) and the dinosaur paradox (regressive archetypes of interaction tend to dominate). As we pass from one head to two or more, what goes wrong? Why is organizational intelligence so hard to come by?

Discouragingly, at least six factors stand in the way of greater organizational intelligence: (1) *the five-brain backlash,* too many voices making things unproductively complicated; (2) *cognitive oversimplifica-tion,* the human tendency to oversimplify cognitive processing; (3) *emotional oversimplification,* the equally human tendency to oversim-plify emotions; (4) *regression in the face of stress;* (5) *the domino effect* in which one person's regressive behavior tips others in the same direc-tion; and (6) *the power advantage,* the fact that power figures sometimes take advantage of regressive interactions. It's important to understand all six factors, because, if we recognize when they threaten, we can often avoid or reduce them. So let's take them one at a time.

DIFFICULTY I: THE FIVE-BRAIN BACKLASH

Being of one mind when you are only one mind usually goes splen-didly, but being of one mind when you are 2 or 7 or 27, or 227 is no picnic. Say you're planning a picnic. Say most of your extended family has shown up for a holiday weekend, and you're planning a picnic for the entire motley crew. You start alone, at your desk in the living room, wielding pencil and pad. Your brother gets in on the planning, and right away there's an organizational intelligence bonus—more ideas, pitfalls avoided. Then a cousin joins the chat. Two or three refinements result. Then another cousin sits down, and matters begin to get complicated. A couple of aunts show up, and pretty soon it's conversational chaos: Let's go to the beach; let's go to the mountains; get beer; no, get wine; buy sandwiches; no, make sandwiches. You should have hidden in a closet and figured it out by yourself.

Often two heads are better than one, but seven? Twenty-seven? Everyday experience provides a heads-up here: Adding a few more heads does not always make a team smarter, even when the heads are on friendly terms. It may just make matters more complicated and even reduce the effective intelligence of the collective—the lawn-mower paradox with a vengeance!

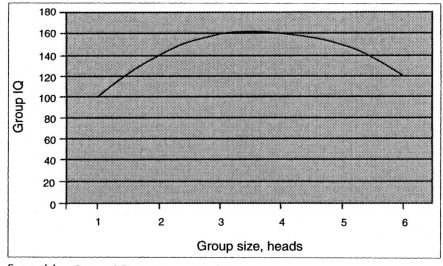

FIGURE 4.1   Group IQ versus group size.

To have a little fun with this, we could graph the typical intelligence of a group against the number of people in the group. The result might look something like Figure 4.1. The graph says that two heads are somewhat better than one, and three are better than two. However, the added value peaks around three or four. After that, more heads drive down the intelligence of the group.

☞ Above about four people, the added value of another head often does not compensate for the added complication introduced by an extra head.

Your sense of the matter might put the turning point at a four-brain backlash or a six-brain backlash instead. Whatever.

The five-brain backlash does not trash all hopes of large-scale organizational intelligence. As simple a solution as really good group facilitation can help a dozen or more participants to function with added rather than subtracted value. Organizational structures of various kinds—hierarchies, linked teams, and matrix structures—can coordinate the work of many more minds than that. The five-brain backlash is a difficulty, not a disaster. But there it is, and it's only the beginning.

DIFFICULTY 2: COGNITIVE OVERSIMPLIFICATION

The world rubs our nose in complexity—complicated environments full of VCRs, income tax forms, and malfunctioning mufflers; several threads of activity in progress, from having a baby to making a will; people with very mixed motives; social and political mazes to run; technical and legal conundrums to resolve. We have to simplify to keep up with it all, and sometimes we oversimplify. The renowned cognitive psychologist Herbert Simon has characterized human beings as of *limited rationality*. At the conscious level particularly, we are low-capacity information processors who cannot deal with complexity in an ideal way. Instead, we automatically take cognitive shortcuts. We stereotype—for instance, Sarah is just a secretary and won't understand the numbers here; Ezra is just an engineer and might not handle the human dimension well; Maude is just a manager and won't understand the technicalities of the production process. And maybe they won't. Stereotyping is useful up to a point, giving us quick, convenient ways of categorizing people and events, but we pay for its convenience with mistakes, sometimes more mistakes than we can afford to make.

Oversimplification figures not only in human cognition generally but in thinking processes specifically. In *Outsmarting IQ*, I identify four broad intelligence traps in human thought. Thinking tends to be:

* *Hasty* (for instance, impulsive decision making)
* *Narrow* (for instance, closed-mindedness; tacit assumptions that blind)
* *Fuzzy* (for instance, confusing different concepts; missing crucial subtleties)
* *Sprawling* (general disorganization in thinking; failing to move toward a conclusion)

The first three are varieties of oversimplification. The fourth is a failure to organize the complex factors in a situation, which instead bounce one's thinking this way and that way haphazardly.

Harvard psychologist Ellen Langer documents another aspect of cognitive oversimplification. Her experiments demonstrate how people tend to function mindlessly. Not only laboratory studies but everyday experiences demonstrate mindlessness, and recently a waiter in a local bistro gave me the perfect example. Delivering the group's orders, he firmly announced, "Watch out for this plate—it's very hot!" as waiters do, but he was carrying the plate comfortably in the palms of his hands. In mindlessness, people respond to familiar surface cues and fall into routines without really thinking about what they are doing. The waiter said what he was in the habit of saying while serving a dish, hot or not.

It's important not to stereotype oversimplification as seamlessly negative, because oversimplification can serve certain purposes. Mindlessness in driving to work lets us be mindful of what we're going to do when we get there, assuming a safe route. Stereotypes about secretaries, engineers, managers, and other roles aid in sizing up the likelihoods of situations rapidly, when we can afford mistakes. Executive decisions that might count as impulsive when there's plenty of time might count as quick thinking in an emergency. The problem with cognitive oversimplification is not that it has nothing to contribute but that it does serious harm from time to time.

So far, all this refers to individual intelligence, but what about interactive intelligence? Oversimplification is at least as likely to impair thinking when individuals think together as when individuals think solo. The struggle to meet complex situations on their own terms and do them justice is a continual challenge for thinking, solo or collective. However, a much deeper problem appears when we compare progressive and regressive archetypes of interaction.

⮡ **Cognitive oversimplification favors regressive archetypes, which are usually less complex than progressive ones.**

Recall the regressive archetype of autocratic decision making and compare it with the progressive archetype of participative decision making. The regressive archetype is much simpler: The boss doesn't consult, but simply *decides*—no worrying about probing other people's views, drawing out their experiences, or reckoning with their interests. The same point applies to the regressive archetype of negotiation from positions and the progressive archetype of negotiation from interests. Negotiation from interests involves such annoying complications as trusting one another, laboring to articulate specific interests, and trying to fashion nuanced win-win resolutions. Negotiation from positions may lead to stalemates or to compromises that no one really likes, but, hey, it's simpler. Negative feedback offers the pristine simplicity of just mentioning the bad stuff, which is the stuff most likely to be on the mind of the critic, and conciliatory feedback is even simpler—just be vaguely positive. In contrast, communicative feedback involves a careful weave of clarification, affirmation, and advice.

DIFFICULTY 3: EMOTIONAL OVERSIMPLIFICATION

When your spouse calls you *egocentric,* you know what the message is: You are fatheaded, or, in the root Latinate sense of the word, centered on your own ego, attending lavishly to your own interests and not enough to those of others.

When the great Swiss psychologist Jean Piaget calls you egocentric, he has something a little different in mind. He is letting you know (although he probably would not do so, because he wants to keep observing your natural behavior) that you are acting without taking full account of what others understand or the standpoint from which others perceive. You might not be behaving in a particularly selfish way at all—just in a way oblivious to how others see things differently.

Egocentricity in this technical sense is a pervasive problem in human relations and human society. The psychologist Lawrence Kohlberg, analyzing people's moral development, recognized the need for *perspective taking*—broadly, putting yourself in others' shoes—as an essential part of living a principled life. Carol Gilligan proposed that the relational style of many women represents a different pattern of living a moral life, less oriented toward principles and more toward caring for others. Although disagreeing with Kohlberg in many ways, she also underscored the role of perspective taking. Challenges of perspective taking appear in many other ways. For instance, when youngsters write their first essays or stories in classrooms around the world, they tend not to take into account what their imagined audiences are likely to know or not know. They write as though their readers share their own background knowledge. All this includes more than strictly emotional aspects of others, but emotional oversimplification expresses the spirit pretty well.

Emotional oversimplification is not just a sin we commit against others. We oversimplify our own emotional lives. Sometimes we fail to recognize our own mixed feelings about something because we believe we should be decisive. Sometimes we are not honest with ourselves about why we do what we do. Emotional oversimplification cuts both ways, outward toward others and inward toward the hidden core of the self.

As with cognitive oversimplification, emotional oversimplification undermines progressive interactions. Autocratic decision making is emotionally more simple-minded than participative decision making. The autocrat in question need not reckon into the equation how slighted Doris over there feels or whether Lenny will get a chance to undertake the project he's been developing for so long. Participative decision making asks the participants, and especially leader figures, to be attentive to all this. Likewise, negotiation from positions simple-mindedly says: Never mind the others' felt interests—take a position and defend it. Likewise, negative feedback treats the other person simply as an object to be corrected, and conciliatory feedback treats the other person simply as an ally to be cultivated.

One recent champion of the role of handling emotions well in organizational contexts is Daniel Goleman. In his book *Working with Emotional Intelligence* (New York: Bantam Books, 1998), Goleman makes empathy a key dimension of emotional competence, including such features as awareness of others' feelings and perspectives, perceptiveness about developmental needs, alertness to political relationships, and the adoption of a service orientation. Clearly, these traits have a progressive character. Unfortunately, they are not so easily attained. In their absence, regressive patterns are likely to thrive.

〰 The trend toward emotional oversimplification favors regressive archetypes of interaction.

DIFFICULTY 4: REGRESSION IN THE FACE OF STRESS

Max is three problems from the end of the exam, and the clock is ticking. Max spent far too long on problem 12, telling himself twice a microsecond that he should move along, but somehow he was unable to let go, and still he didn't solve it. And now, as he reads problem 13, unlucky 13, he has to read it three times, pleading with the words to make sense, which finally they sort of do— although, last night when he was studying, problems like 13 were totally his.

This is regression in the face of stress. Under stressful conditions, cognition tends to revert to old patterns. Recent learning gets blurry, and buried habits surge out of the mental underground like vampires at midnight, killing off newer and better practices.

One interpretation of this phenomenon goes back to a 1908 psychological result called the *Yerkes-Dodson law* for its discoverers. They found an inverted-U-shaped relationship between arousal and performance: Up to a point, performance improves with factors that boost arousal, but beyond that it begins to deteriorate.

An inverted-U-shaped curve reassures us that stress is not all bad. Some stress stimulates performance, goading, provoking, inspiring, invigorating. Some stress makes things more interesting. Stress comes in a range of flavors—noise, fear, time pressure, anger. Any of these at a moderate level might boost performance. Sometimes, for some people, it's just right to work in a café amidst the noise of strangers, but as stress rises to very high levels, people begin to clutch, lose it, fall apart, seize up, get stressed out—there seem to be as many phrases to describe reactions to stress as Eskimos proverbially have for varieties of snow.

Regression in the face of stress is bad news for organizational intelligence. Progressive interactions are needed most when the going gets tough, you need to decide now, there's a lot at stake, conflict threatens, or deadlines loom. Unfortunately:

☞ Unusual stress is likely to reawaken regressive archetypes, just when progressive archetypes are most needed.

DIFFICULTY 5: THE DOMINO EFFECT

You may be a very saint of communal effort, but it's difficult to sustain progressive interactions alone. The other party needs to cooperate. Imagine again the archetypes of autocratic and participatory decision making. Say you cherish participatory decision making but your boss has the opposite mind-set. Well, good luck! You can make certain moves—press to be heard, offer your vision and cautions—but only up to a point and by putting your own status at risk. Or say you yourself are the boss. Even then, it's not easy in certain organizational cultures. Sometimes people expect you to decide. They want the Word from Above. Collaborative gestures could be seen as a sign of weakness, read as symbolic conduct sending the message that you lack the confidence to lead.

Or say you cherish communicative feedback. Same story: It's hard to offer communicative feedback to others when they are treating your ideas like voodoo dolls, complete with pins. It can even be hard when others are offering conciliatory feedback. Your effort to pack some substance into your comments breaks the tacit social norm that we're not going to hassle one another with any serious learning here.

☞ Regressive practices provoke their kind, leading to even more regressive practices, like a row of dominoes falling over.

Progressive behavior also inspires response in kind. As a regressive domino knocks others over into regression, so progressive dominoes can almost magically lift others up. However, the knockdown is more powerful than the lift. If many people in a group start out in a regressive style, it can be difficult to turn the group around through individual action, although explicit training that helps everyone to get up to progressive speed may do the job.

DIFFICULTY 6: THE POWER ADVANTAGE

The temptations of power appear in human legend and history from Greek myths and politics all the way up to today's corporate scandals and international intrigues. They add up to a final factor standing in the way of progressive interactions.

One intriguing case in point is the Enron scandal of 2001 to 2002. Up until the summer of 2001, Enron appeared to be a tremendously successful company that used sophisticated methods—indeed, methods and associated balance sheets that at least some observers found hard to penetrate—to deal in the trading and marketing of natural gas, electricity, and other resources. Then things began to unravel. Gradually, it became apparent that Enron's impressive record was based on shady accounting practices that masked huge debts and created the illusion of a thriving company.

Although several Enron executives bore clear responsibility, former CEO Jeffrey Skilling was something of a shadow figure. Seen as both brilliant and arrogant by his colleagues, Skilling brought innovative practices in risk management to Enron, joining the company in 1990 and ascending in February 2001 from chief operating officer to a brief stint as chief executive officer. In mid-August 2001, Skilling abruptly and mysteriously resigned, citing personal reasons unrelated to health. Through prior and subsequent stock sales, he managed to extract nearly $90 million from Enron.

Skilling's management style showed all the earmarks of someone after a power advantage. Although Enron was putatively a flat company where smart voices were always heard, Skilling's voice was reportedly law. Although ostensibly everyone had opportunity, it was said that Skilling developed a set of cronies who received remarkable freedom to pursue freewheeling and questionable development initiatives, while others who were more cautious found themselves pushed aside. Most striking were the accounting practices that covered up where Enron really stood as a company. Highly placed individuals within Enron testified that Skilling certainly knew of and approved these practices. Skilling, although a financial whiz kid known for staying close to what was going on, repeatedly claimed ignorance of the wheeling and dealing.

We may never know the truth about what Skilling did and did not do, but the general picture suggested by the Enron case is all too familiar and not at all hard to analyze. Within organizations, people commonly strive to attain power, sustain power, and take advantage of power. They do so in the face of competition from other power seekers. They do so for the pleasure of power itself, the status and prestige it can bring, and the material benefits that power can often secure. They do so in ways that sometimes benefit the overall organization, but sometimes do not.

Regressive archetypes of interaction often serve the interests of such individuals better than do progressive archetypes. Whereas progressive interactions foster the ready flow of information as part of good knowledge processing, the power advantage often lies in restricting and obfuscating information. Whereas progressive interactions involve pooling multiple viewpoints and interests, the power advantage often lies in serving the interests of oneself and one's cronies over those of rivals, investors, and the group in general.

So far, this pictures power figures as strong and able, if short on scruples. However, weaker and less able individuals often follow the path of power advantage, too. For many reasons, people who are not all that competent sometimes end up in midlevel positions of power. They may be less interested in conquering the world than in simply holding on to what they have, but that, too, invites regressive patterns of interaction. The fundamentally weak person in a midlevel position of power is likely to view progressive archetypes as showing weak authority and likely to fear revealing ineptitude through frank, open, and flexible interactions. Regressive archetypes warn people against challenging the authority figure as well as concealing limited capabilities better.

Regressive patterns of interaction can work to the advantage of people bent on attaining, maintaining, and taking advantage of power positions, even though they serve the general interests of the group less well.

ARE WE READY TO GIVE UP YET?

King Arthur's dream of the Round Table could turn into King Arthur's nightmare. Although the concept of progressive interactions sets a direction toward being of one mind, and although something in this spirit certainly happens from time to time in groups, teams, organizations, and communities, and although people do a great deal of thinking together in spit-and-bailing-wire style, a discouraging list of difficulties stands in the way of really strong organizational intelligence. To review:

* *The five-brain backlash.* As the number of people in the conversation increases, even if there are no sharp rivalries in the group, the complexity of the conversations often swells to a point where it becomes counterproductive (although good facilitation can ameliorate this effect even with fairly large groups; and, of course, there are other reasons besides cognitive efficiency for thinking together—for instance, group solidarity).

* *Cognitive oversimplification.* The deep-rooted tendency to oversimplify knowledge processing and the fact that regressive interactions are usually simpler than progressive interactions favor the dominance of regressive interactions (although individuals and group cultures can develop attitudes and strategies for accommodating complexity).

* *Emotional oversimplification.* Egocentricity, in the sense of blindness to the emotional lives and perspectives of others and oversimplification of one's own view of oneself, favors regressive interactions, which treat people as emotionally simpler (although individuals and group cultures can strive toward more sensitive attitudes).

* *Regression in the face of stress.* High stress tends to trigger a kind of cognitive regression and resurrect behaviors and attitudes learned earlier, which in trend are regressive—just when progressive practices are most needed (although some

stress can improve performance, stress can be managed, and over time new practices can become habits).

* *The domino effect.*   It's difficult to sustain progressive inter-actions when others adopt regressive practices. Regressive elements, especially in leadership, tend to drag the whole group down (although persistent efforts toward progressive practices, especially on the part of leader figures, can help).

* *The power advantage.*   People who pursue, sustain, and take advantage of power positions within an organization often find that regressive styles of interaction better serve their interests (although a strong culture of progressive interac-tions can work against this and even eject such people).

These multiple challenges are daunting. The fundamental what-why-how question from Chapter 1 asks what organizational intelli-gence is, why it's so hard to come by, and how we can get more of it. The preceding ideas give so many reasons why it's hard to come by that perhaps the answer to how we can get more of it is that we usu-ally can't!

Perhaps. But each of the preceding challenges comes with a par-enthetical message that the difficulty is not absolute. Understanding them is a step toward surmounting them. So much is to be gained from King Arthur's dream of smarter groups, teams, communities, and organizations that it would be foolish to crumble now. Rather than giving up, let's undertake an examination of one of the knotti-est organizational problems, the nature of good leadership.

TOOLBOX

It might seem difficult to assemble a toolbox out of a chapter full of factors that work against interactive intelligence. But not so—the factors define hazards to watch out for, avoid when you can, and compensate for when you can't.

✳ *Beware the five-brain backlash.* Keep working groups small when you can—two, three, or four people. Divide up initiatives so that they can be pursued by smaller groups (see Chapter 7).

✳ *Use strong and artful facilitation* when there are good reasons for a larger group to convene.

✳ *Watch out for cognitive and emotional oversimplification.* Try to see in archetypes and notice the struggle between simpler regressive archetypes and more sophisticated progressive ones. Take the time to work things through in a full way with progressive archetypes of interaction.

✳ *Manage stress.* Spy it early, cut it off at the pass, use stress management techniques such as relaxation and time-outs to keep it short of the danger zone where it triggers regressive interactions.

✳ *Resist the domino effect.* When others behave in regressive ways, do your best to initiate and sustain progressive interactions.

5

FROM LORDSHIP TO LEADERSHIP

POLICY 113

Once upon a time, a considerably younger, discernibly thinner, and immensely greener me began work as a researcher at the Harvard Graduate School of Education and soon experienced several baptisms into the professional life of large institutions. One concerned two high-level administrators, both long since retired. As someone running research projects, I had to consult with them on occasion. Which administrator to approach depended on the nature of the problem. Every time I went to see one of these administrators, she would say something like, "We can't do that, because of Policy 113."

Many other people had similarly shaped encounters with this administrator. Sometimes by talking things over with her you could find a way to get what you needed, but she always seemed to send a significant message through her behavior: "The organization and its policies are more important than your problem. You are here for the organization; the organization is not here for you." I came to think of her as the Inhibitor.

I counted myself lucky when my problem called for a visit to the other administrator. The typical response to a problem brought to her desk was something like, "Well that's tricky to take care of because of Policy 113, but maybe we can figure out a way to do it." So we would sit and talk it through—How about this; how about that; okay, let's do it that way.

Not that the second administrator was a pushover. Every now and then, she would declare, "We have to handle this one strictly by the book, and here's why." However, usually she and I could find a way forward. Her conduct sent a message very different from that of the Inhibitor, seeming to say, "The organization is here for you." Other people had similar experiences with this administrator, and I came to think of her as the Facilitator.

I do not know how the Inhibitor and the Facilitator developed into who they were—whether it was personality, training, or prior experiences in different institutions—but I learned to recognize their kind. Since then, I've rediscovered both types many times. What a nuisance to encounter the Inhibitor! What a pleasure to encounter the Facilitator!

The concept of regressive versus progressive interactions maps neatly into the styles of the Inhibitor and the Facilitator. The Inhibitor interacted in regressive ways. She did not engage in effective knowledge processing, because she tended to stereotype situations under one or another policy. She did not broadcast positive symbolic conduct; on the contrary, she suggested that people were simply servants of the organization. She was an icon of lordship, not leadership. In contrast, the Facilitator interacted in progressive ways. She engaged in joint problem solving with me and others and projected the message that the organization aimed to serve its members. She was a round-table kind of person, leader rather than lord. The juxtaposition of the two dramatizes why leadership is such a hot spot of organizational intelligence.

The Inhibitor and the Facilitator might seem odd dramatis personae with which to populate an exploration of leadership. These were middle managers. But who's to say that leaders have to stand on top of the mountain? To understand where leaders can stand, it's useful to understand better what leaders do.

WHAT LEADERS DO

The important thing about King Arthur is not that he was king but the kind of king he was. Most kings aren't remembered for much at all, and others are remembered for awful slaughter, lawful robbery, or laughable incompetence. King Arthur—seemingly behind the eight ball for regal fame, because, as noted in Chapter 1, he didn't even exist—is remembered positively for the kind of king he was, for, in fact, the way he led.

So what do true leaders do? One way to pick apart this puzzle is to clarify the circumstances that call for routine management versus leadership roles. Inevitably, this is not a categorical distinction—a manager may be a leader or not, and a leader a manager or not. That acknowledged, the broad story can be told this way.

Within organizations, the need for management begins with what might be called:

The Deal: You provide your committed effort in specified directions in return for certain rewards.

In King Arthur's day, the standard Deal between a knight and a squire was that the knight would support the squire and teach him to become a knight, while the squire would take care of the knight's armor, dress him, fight beside him, and such. The standard Deal in organizations today involves salary, bonuses, and status contingent on effort and performance. Other versions include the ancient practice of exchanging subsistence, status, and spoils of conflict for military service, or governance and defense for shares of crops. In any individual case, one can debate whether the Deal is a good deal, but good versions of the Deal certainly get a good deal done in the world.

The Deal assumes routine management that organizes people and processes so that the work gets done well and efficiently. This can be a fairly straightforward matter. The manager specifies procedures and assigns roles. People know how to do their jobs, or there are standard ways of teaching them. People are willing because of the system of rewards. Ideally, everyone feels good about the Deal and clear about what's to be done. Everything moves forward smoothly.

But the Deal doesn't always do it. Sometimes an unexpected competitor appears, a program needs to be rescued, a new and challenging direction emerges, or a problem proves much more difficult than expected. In other words, sometimes the circumstances call for a sense of direction or flexibility in the face of exigencies that fall outside the defined routines of the Deal. Sometimes the situation demands extra commitment, energy, endurance, individual and collective creativity. All this leads to:

> *The whither and why questions of leadership:* What can I do when people don't see the way forward, despite the Deal (the whither question)? What can I do when people aren't motivated enough to take the way forward, despite the Deal (the why question)?

Leadership amounts to interacting with the group in a way that answers the whither and why questions. However, resolving the whither and why questions does not necessarily mean figuring out the answers yourself and telling people directly whither to proceed and why. Artful leadership is full of indirection.

Still less does effective leadership mean superstar leadership. Business scholar James Collins and a research team conducted a five-year historical analysis of companies that over time had made a sustained transition from good to great. Provocatively, the study revealed that the leaders were mostly anonymous. Their style was self-effacing rather than self-aggrandizing, but fiercely dedicated to the success of the enterprise. In contrast, the leadership of companies in a comparison group displayed much more of the celebrity syndrome. Celebrity leaders may produce success during their tenure, but the organization does not function well without them, and they tend not to arrange for able successors. Collins writes, "In over three quarters of the comparison companies, we found executives who set their successors up for failure or chose weak successors, or both."

Many styles of leadership have been recognized, and they answer the whither and why questions in different ways. Bernard Bass of the Center for Leadership Studies, State University of New York at Binghamton, introduced an insightful contrast between transactional leadership and transformational leadership. In *transactional leadership,* the transaction is the Deal—effort and fealty are traded for the benefits—and if the Deal as it stands does not generate the needed direction and motivation, the transactional leader can provide clearer direction within the present Deal or work out a new Deal with revised directions and stronger incentives.

Transformational leadership calls for more than tinkering with the Deal. As usually understood (there is some variation across sources), it involves projecting a vision that helps people develop commitment and showing a path forward to fulfill that vision, as with Moses, Joan of Arc in thirteenth-century France, Gandhi, Winston Churchill in England during World War II, and Lee Iacocca at Chrysler Motor Company during the early 1980s. Leadership in this style speaks to the whither and why questions by inspiring people with the compass direction of a powerful vision and its elaboration.

The rich literature on leadership identifies many other styles and substyles. *Command and control* is a familiar example, one that can, if it does not lapse into blind autocracy, serve well in military and some other circumstances. A less frequent but often more welcome style is *facilitative leadership,* in which the leader supports, nudges, elicits, mentors, empowers, and in other ways furthers the collaboration and development of a group. The facilitative leader does not stand on the mountain and offer a big vision, but rather answers the whither and why questions by helping people to help themselves. Still another is *charismatic leadership,* akin to visionary leadership, but in which, for one way of putting the contrast, the personal charisma of the individual induces astounding and sometimes blinding degrees of commitment. It's worth adding that the various labels—transformational, visionary, charismatic, and so on—are used in somewhat different ways by different authors.

The recognition of many styles of leadership in the current literature helps bring leadership down the mountain. Good leadership is not necessarily Olympian—Zeus on top with a commanding presence and lightning bolts to back it up. Middle managers can act as leaders, too. Individuals of experience and wisdom can function as leaders without any special political power. Small close-knit teams at any level from the executive office to the mailroom can often lead themselves collectively, even if there's a nominal leader, with practical leadership on particular matters shifting informally according to interest and expertise.

Organizational theorist Peter Senge and colleagues identify three particularly important loci of leadership. *Executive leaders* such as CEOs can contribute vision and broad policy. However, they do not directly touch the strata of the organization where the work gets done. *Local line leaders* are the most important leaders, because they supervise the productive heart of the organization, where, more than anywhere else, leadership makes a difference. A third and intriguing category is *network leaders:* advisors, coordinators, and internal or external consultants who cut across divisions of an organization, cross-fertilizing with ideas and provocative questions. Leaders of this sort usually lack political power; paradoxically, this can boost their influence. They plant seeds rather than issue mandates, and often the seeds generate more useful change.

Besides recognizing that leaders can function at many levels, we do well to recognize that leaders can function in many roles. There are political and managerial leaders; leaders such as chief knowledge officers, responsible for knowledge management within organizations; intellectual leaders among university professors; and senior researchers in government and industrial laboratories. There are community leaders of various sorts—elected public officials, union organizers, town managers, and ministers. There are the leadership roles of highly experienced people within communities of practice—those in the Peace Corps, the fire department, or the repair shop—who have seen it all and can share their savvy. There are the transient leadership roles of able people without any particular power, position, or deep expertise who step forward at the right moment with the right idea and the right passion and guide for awhile. No role in itself makes the person a leader of note. All depends on how well the leader answers the whither and why questions of leadership through concrete action in practical contexts.

With this broad map of leadership in mind, it's worth turning back to the Inhibitor and the Facilitator to ask where they stand on the map. One consequence of bringing leadership down from the mountain is that the two have places to stand. They need not be top-tier visionaries marshalling the hearts and minds of the whole organization. In the Facilitator, with her progressive conversational style, we can recognize one of the line managers that Peter Senge pointed to as functioning as a facilitative leader, an individual who in her dedicated and thoughtful way raised her administrative function beyond the routine to a genuine intellectual partnership with her office's clients. In the Inhibitor, with her regressive style, we can recognize a kind of antileader, attentive to her administrative function but in a manner that made things harder for her office's clients.

FOUR FORMS OF LEADERSHIP

The literature on leadership has all the effulgence and sometimes the exoticism of a coral reef. Species after species gets its distinctive niche in the fluid ecology of community and organizational life. Earlier and later appear such notions as transactional leadership, transformational leadership, command-and-control leadership, facilitative leadership, visionary leadership, charismatic leadership, servant leadership, and adaptive leadership—and there are plenty more to be found walking through office buildings, sport stadiums, and churches, yet to be described in books and journals. It will be helpful to boil things down in the same manner applied to feedback—by seeking out the most fundamental archetypes of interaction, the patterns that recur over and over again.

Looking across a number of conceptions of leadership, there seem to be four broad archetypes, whatever the nuanced variants. I'll call them *answer-centered leadership, vision-centered leadership, inquiry-centered leadership,* and *leadership by leaving alone.* This scheme is adapted from a somewhat similar analysis developed by my good friend and colleague Daniel Wilson.

Each archetype resolves the whither and why questions of leadership in a fundamentally different way. This is what puts the four archetypes in sharp contrast to one another, although of course many leaders combine them. The following list defines each archetype briefly and sketches how it addresses the whither and why questions. A discussion of each follows.

Answer-centered leadership.   Declares what's to be done and why. (This gives people the whither they need, leaving it mostly to the Deal to provide the why.)

Vision-centered leadership.   Offers a strong energizing vision about the general direction, along with great personal commitment. (The overall vision provides a broad whither, as well as an inspiring why.)

Inquiry-centered leadership.   Fosters inquiry at various levels through questions, facilitation, and establishing community and organizational structures supportive of inquiry. (By finding their own particular whither within the overall agenda, people will develop more individual and collective ability and a sense of why. Besides, the leader may need the group's help to find a good direction.)

Leadership by leaving alone.   Leaves people alone to find their way. (Because in the end people need to learn to find their own whithers and whys individually and collectively within the overall agenda, and this will also reveal who has what it takes, leading to more central roles.)

ANSWER-CENTERED LEADERSHIP

KING ARTHUR: Keep the portcullis down at night! That's the safe way!

You see, there's this puzzle about what to do with the portcullis (the imposing gate that slides up and down at the main entrance to the castle) between dusk and dawn. If Arthur had an answer-centered style, as in this example, he might simply decide the matter and almost everything else. Leadership through answers certainly is the most natural archetype of leadership. You know, and they may not, so tell them!

Looking to the whither and why questions, answer-centered leadership provides direction by articulating what's to be done and how and perhaps what purpose is served. As to motivation, answer-centered leadership does not go far beyond the Deal, but it may add a little by helping people feel more secure, which sometimes can be quite important. In other words, answer-centered leadership amounts to what some authors call *transactional leadership* as defined earlier and others call *command-and-control leadership*.

In many circumstances, answer-centered leadership is a very helpful interactive style, replacing the spinning compass of uncertainty with declared direction. It's also important to recognize that *answer-centered* does not mean *answers only*. A narrow leadership style that offered little else but answers hardly any questions, vision, or leaving alone would be absurdly inflexible.

Not that such things don't happen. Answer-centered leadership can easily slide into pathological forms. It carries two risks of lordship: micromanagement, the needless hovering over people who in fact do not need to be told what to do; and authoritarianism, the overbearing treatment of people who have minds of their own and soon enough will either passively or actively resist or leave. In the opening story of the two administrators, the Inhibitor is not only an answer-centered leader but one with the pathology of authoritarianism.

One common and unfortunate consequence of both pathologies is fear. A good answer-centered leader, like a strong but fair father, can create considerable psychological safety, but micromanagement or authoritarianism typically generates fear. Psychological safety is widely recognized as an important lubricant of collaboration. Amy Edmondson of the Harvard Business School and her colleagues have investigated the learning of cardiac surgery teams—about as high-stakes a collaboration as you could ask for—and found psychological safety versus fear created by the team leader to be a key factor in how well such teams learn and perform.

Besides risking these pathologies, answer-centered leadership suffers from three other limits. It does not address strongly the leadership goal of motivation, leaving that mostly to the Deal. It does nothing to promote the individual or collective growth of the participants, who become dependent on the leader. This can be unfortunate for the participants, but also for the leader, who can become trapped in a static role of providing answers, often the same answers time after time. Finally, the leader, who is supposed to have the answers, may have none, or not good enough ones. Such problems prompt many aspiring leaders to seek other archetypes, other fundamental ways of responding to the dilemma of leadership.

VISION-CENTERED LEADERSHIP

KING ARTHUR: What to do with the portcullis at night is but a particular case. The important matter is our message to the people inside the castle and outside—that we are there for them, to protect them. That is my passion and yours. Now, let us consider what that means in this case. . . .

Vision-centered leadership is a natural response to the whither and why questions and the limits of answer-centered leadership. Here the leader offers a vision of the group's mission and ideals, both displays and calls for high commitment, draws others into the vision, and helps relate the vision to immediate situations. The vision may be the leader's own or one the leader finds implicit and potential in the collective, drawing it out and bringing it to life. Sometimes it's hard to tell the difference! In *The Fifth Discipline* (New York: Doubleday/Currency, 1990), Peter Senge emphasizes that many leaders have visions, but not so many effectively cultivate a shared vision. It is the shared vision that mobilizes people's minds and hearts.

Answer-centered and vision-centered leadership have a certain structural kinship: Answer-centered leadership offers particular answers, whereas vision-centered leadership offers the Big Answer that gives an overall direction and informs immediate plans. Other concepts in the literature in the neighborhood of vision-centered leadership include *transformational leadership, visionary leadership,* and *charismatic leadership.*

Again, the *centered* part needs to be taken seriously. Effective vision-centered leadership does not rely entirely on the vision. The leader also makes measured use of questions and answers and leaving alone. In most cases, the leader depends on the Deal for further motivation.

Like the other archetypes, vision-centered leadership has its pathologies. Perhaps the most disturbing of these takes the form not of enlightening vision but of blinding vision, in the case of the charismatic leader who inspires entirely irrational and ultimately self-destructive commitment. Cautionary examples include those atypical religious leaders who lead their flocks to mass suicide or political leaders who build a vision of success-for-us on hatred of some rival ethnic group that presumably stands in the way.

The collapse of Enron, mentioned in the previous chapter, shows some of these signs. Chief operating officer and then short-term chief executive officer Jeffrey Skilling reportedly was a visionary leader, promoting a high-risk competitive culture that disdained concrete assets and valued the clever deal, all in a missionary spirit of opening up and loosening up stodgy markets. Surfing on such risky waves was likely to lead to a wipe-out sooner or later.

INQUIRY-CENTERED LEADERSHIP

KING ARTHUR: So, should we keep the portcullis down at night? Why? Why not? What is your counsel? Who will examine and assess the factors in play?

King Arthur starts with a good question for inquiry-centered leadership, but this archetype ranges well beyond the leader's direct queries. In the story of the two administrators that begins this chapter, the Facilitator was a inquiry-centered leader who engaged in joint problem solving with those who came to her. An inquiry-centered leader would also encourage others' questions, facilitate conversations, initiate investigations, welcome multiple viewpoints, and the like. Inquiry-centered leaders let others do a lot of the thinking and let them take the credit for it.

Beyond direct personal contact, an inquiry-centered leader fosters organizational structures that support inquiry, for instance small teams composed of diverse expertise, matrix structures that promote organizational crosstalk, or support for small-scale testing of risky innovations with high potential. In other words, an inquiry-centered leader attends to the contact architecture of an organization, promoting a rich mix of relationships.

Chapter 2 mentioned Rosabeth Moss Kanter's distinction between segmentalism in organizations—compartmentalization in the name of control and order—and integrative action. Kanter goes on to acknowledge that an organization needs compartmental structures to maintain routine operations. However, she recommends supplementing these structures with a parallel participative organization, a web of innovation that deliberately mixes people from different levels and divisions in ways that foster flexible problem finding and problem solving. This is just the sort of structure that an inquiry-centered leader might work to establish.

Inquiry-centered leadership means that inquiry is the center of gravity, not that nothing else ever happens. Where it's the leader's role to make certain decisions and issue certain kinds of commands, the leader does so, with appropriate consultation. If the leader has answers that seem to be needed, the leader puts them forward. And of course, the leader in this style will often leave things alone and may occasionally offer visions in the service of inquiry. Done right, all this can support rather than stifle inquiry. Artful inquiry-centered leaders often accomplish a kind of magic, contributing considerable substance to the conversation while letting people feel that the plans and decisions are a mutual accomplishment in a context of shared power.

For example, in a *Harvard Business Review* article, Ronald Heifetz and Donald Laurie explore how Colin Marshall, CEO of British Airways in the 1980s, led a reform initiative that emphasized inquiry processes. Marshall saw in British Airways a lackluster enterprise that provided poor service to its clients, who nicknamed it "Bloody Awful." Underneath the operational problems, Marshall suspected cultural problems: matters of trust, responsibility, and respect for clients. Rather than decree solutions, Marshall initiated an inquiry process involving the company's leadership. The group reached out to flight crews, passenger lounges, and flight reservation centers for ideas and perceptions.

Conflicts were seen not just as isolated matters to be fixed but as clues to the underlying problems of culture. The process included an examination by those at the higher echelons of their own conduct and how it contributed to the difficulties. Through this inquiry process, Marshall led the leadership of British Airways to the conclusion that the problems were not technical matters that could be adequately addressed by tweaking the system but cultural matters that required a large-scale cultural shift toward responsible collaboration and commitment to the performance of the airline. The ultimate result was a much improved British Airways. Heifetz and Laurie offer this as one example of *adaptive leadership,* the kind of leadership needed when organizations face not just technical difficulties but fundamental challenges of culture and direction.

In general, inquiry-centered leadership addresses the whither and why questions by helping participants to figure out the direction and by mobilizing people through what psychologists call *intrinsic motivation.* Although the Deal remains an important force, when people participate in finding and choosing a direction, they tend to increase their commitment beyond the Deal. Other concepts in the literature in broadly the same spirit as inquiry-centered leadership include *facilitative leadership, servant leadership,* and *stewardship.* Ronald Heifetz's notion of *adaptive leadership,* as described in the British Airlines example and his book *Leadership Without Easy Answers* (Cambridge, MA: Belknap Press, 1994), has a strong inquiry-centered character, even though it addresses situations in which organizations need to adapt substantially, the usual turf of vision-centered leadership.

Like answer-centered and vision-centered leadership, inquiry-centered leadership can slide into pathologies. One such pathology is *underfacilitation.* Fostering inquiry is considerably harder than giving answers and requires a set of skills all its own. When a would-be inquiry-centered leader lacks the art and craft, the community or organization may drift this way and that, wasting time and losing confidence and commitment. The leader may conclude that inquiry doesn't work. Another pathology of inquiry-centered leadership is *false openness,* an inquiring stance that simply disguises the leader's own answers waiting in the wings. Genuine inquiry-centered leadership requires following where the inquiry leads, rather than manipulating the process back toward answers the leader has already fixated on. Soon enough, false openness will be discovered, breaking the relationship of trust that inquiry-centered leadership cultivates.

LEADERSHIP BY LEAVING ALONE

(KING ARTHUR *says nothing at all about the portcullis. But he's watching to see what the castle administrative team does.*)

Leadership by leaving alone is a somewhat paradoxical and some-times even perverse resolution to the whither and why questions. Its philosophy is to let people alone to give them a chance to strive and cope unhindered—and to find out who has what it takes.

After finding out what people do, the leader may reconfigure groups, make promotions, and even fire people so that those who have what it takes—that is, those who can be left alone effectively—are in a position to guide the work. Leaving alone does not speak directly to the whither and why questions. It declines to provide direction beyond whatever broad assignments are part of the picture. It does nothing spe-cific to motivate people beyond the Deal. Indirectly, however, leader-ship by leaving alone can produce both direction and motivation, in the short term by throwing people on their own resources and letting them find their way and in the long term by reconfiguring the organi-zation to favor those who have what it takes.

As with the other archetypes of leadership, *leaving alone* simply identifies a center of gravity. Leadership by leaving alone makes judi-cious use of answers, questions, and vision. The contrast with the others lies in its central strategy, essentially a Darwinian strategy of establishing conditions for adaptation and selection.

Although it may seem an odd approach, leadership by leaving alone is quite normal in some settings. Junior professors, for example, are mostly left alone to develop their lines of research, with relatively little mentoring. When promotion time comes, their advancement depends on how much they have accomplished. Young lawyers in a firm or salespeople on a sales force will often face a fair amount of leaving alone, with the leadership mostly watching and selecting rather than directing.

Again like the other archetypes, leadership by leaving alone has its pathologies. What my colleague Daniel Wilson has called *leading through abandonment* is a pure version of leadership by leaving alone, with little leavening by the occasional answer or question or vision, a sink-or-swim version in which people feel not only unsupported but unfairly treated, unclear about basic expectations, resentful when the leader takes them to task later on grounds not previously aired, and distrustful of the leader's motives and commitments. Recalling the theme of psychological safety, leadership by leaving alone generally tends to be weak on psychological safety, and the pathology of abandonment generates fear.

LEADERSHIP FOR INTELLIGENCE

King Arthur is pretty mad by now. "Where's my Round Table?" he's roaring. "If all that you academics can essay is the construction of category systems," he's muttering, "I'm going to go falconing."

He's up in the turret now, taking the high ground, pacing around and around, north, south, east, west, growling, "Leadership for intelligence means more than just an intelligent leader. Any idiot wants an intelligent leader. But leadership for intelligence, the kind of leadership that draws my knights together into an effective deliberative force, that's my grail!"

He's worried about the what-why-how question from Chapter 1, especially the part about how we can get more organizational intelligence. He wonders what leaders can do. Although something of a celebrity himself, he recognizes James Collins's point that celebrity leaders often leave their organizations not so intelligent. He counts out on his fingers, "Answers, fine; questions, fine; vision, fine; leaving alone, fine. But where's my round table?"

Look at it this way, your grace. We know what your round table calls for—progressive interactions, process smart and people smart, interactions that involve good knowledge processing and positive symbolic conduct. So we know logically what leadership for intelligence has to mean—fostering those progressive interactions within the group.

So let's reexamine the four archetypes, scoring them as we did archetypes of feedback for knowledge processing and symbolic conduct. Tables 5.1 and 5.2 assume healthy forms of the archetypes, because the pathological forms uniformly bring ineffective knowledge processing and negative symbolic conduct.

The trade-offs among the four archetypes confirm a tendency from the exploration of feedback in Chapter 3. Any archetype has its strengths and its weaknesses, and even archetypes that show marked weaknesses can serve well in particular contexts.

TABLE 5.1   Leadership Archetypes from the Standpoint of Knowledge Processing

Archetype	Analysis
Answer-centered leadership	+ Speaks to the whither question directly, informing and guiding the group with your experience and knowledge. − Assumes you have good answers. You may not, or answers generated by the group collectively or members of it might be better. − Creates little incentive for the group members to develop good knowledge processing among themselves. A dependency can develop that limits the group and traps you.
Vision-centered leadership	+ Provides through the vision a general whither and why against which people can consider particular situations. − Masks, demotes, and excludes possibilities not consonant with the vision, even as it promotes others through the vision. − May create a dependency relationship between leader and followers. When the leader leaves, the followers may be lost. − Does not in itself facilitate fine-grained interactions to foster collective knowledge processing.
Inquiry-centered leadership	+ Facilitates the group's collective knowledge processing around whither and why, when handled well. + Models what facilitating knowledge processing looks like, informing and inspiring others. − Risks underutilizing your own knowledge and experience when you know much more than others.
Leadership by leaving alone	+ Makes room for people to rise to the occasion, figuring out whither and why as best they can. − Does nothing else to help with the complex challenges of collective knowledge processing.

104

TABLE 5.2 Leadership Archetypes from the Standpoint
of Symbolic Conduct

Archetype	Analysis
Answer-centered leadership	+ Leader's conduct can be read as secure and safe, in the hands of the master. The whither and why are settled, so let's move forward! − Can be read as condescending, distrustful.
Vision-centered leadership	+ Tends to be read as hopeful, forward looking, and inspirational—the Big Answer for whither and why. + Fosters trust in the leader's commitment. − If you don't buy the vision, can be read as arrogant, manipulative, or deluded.
Inquiry-centered leadership	+ Leader's conduct tends to be read as participative, respectful around whither and why. + Reinforces confidence in the capabilities of the collective. + Encourages and supports individuals and the collective in developing better knowledge processing. − If not well done, can be read not just as a problem with the leader but an incapacity in the group. − Sometimes can be read as a sign of the leader's weakness or lack of knowledge.
Leadership by leaving alone	+ Sometimes read as refreshing and liberating. − Often read as callous and risky.

From the perspective of knowledge processing, inquiry-centered leadership is the clear winner in trend, but in certain circumstances another archetype may serve the group's knowledge processing better. As Table 5.1 indicates, when the leader has far more experience with the situation at hand than the other members, the knowledge processing of the whole group may benefit from answer-centered leadership, with occasional questions and other inquiry moves to keep the group developing. Think of the practical wisdom that a veteran entrepreneur can bring to a group whose members have never attempted a start-up, or the seasoned counsel that you as a parent might bring to a son or daughter who has never purchased a used car.

With these points in mind, let's examine the four archetypes from the perspective of symbolic conduct (Table 5.2). Again the comparison shows a pattern of relative advantages, with each archetype possessing particular strengths. Again, inquiry-centered leadership displays the strongest progressive pattern, providing the leader can carry it off well. The symbolic conduct of inquiry-centered leadership tends to strengthen the confidence and cohesiveness of the group and motivates others to attempt similarly progressive interactions.

Arthur, we've found your round table. Most of the time, it's inquiry-centered leadership—with, remember, an appropriate mix of the others—that generates progressive interactions and spreads them throughout the group, creating a more intelligent collective.

MAN WITH A HORN

If inquiry-centered leadership is so adaptive, you'd think that we would see more of it. The shortfall is another manifestation of the dinosaur paradox from Chapter 2, in which less progressive archetypes tend to dominate more progressive archetypes. One reason is simply that answer-centered leadership is the most straightforward archetype—you have the answers, so give them—and an extension of this temptation is:

☞ *The leadership trap:* The smarter and more experienced the leader, the more alluring answer-centered and vision-centered leadership become, despite their less progressive interactive styles.

Smart leaders with abundant experience are likely to have answers to situations, including the Big Answer of a vision, and are likely to think that these are the right answers. If a leader has a confident answer, little or big, why not put it on the table?

From time to time the leader should, but the general reason why not was mapped earlier: The leader's answer, small or big, may be wrong, or not as right as it could be, and even if it's right, a barrage of answers or a dominating vision can subvert opportunities for individual and collective growth and can create dependencies that are entrapping for both the leader and those who are led. Unfortunately, this fact does not reduce the temptation of the leadership trap. It's just so utterly natural and compelling to give an answer when you have it!

So here's a story of leadership. It's about a single small act of answer-centered leadership leading into inquiry-centered leadership. *Streetwise* was a small magazine that had long occupied a secure and fairly successful niche, although subscriptions had been falling slowly for three years straight. Within the *Streetwise* staff, opinions differed about what to do, but considerable camaraderie took the edge off such controversies.

The *Streetwise* staff had a number of small traditions. One of them took physical form. In the coffee area was a hand-operated klaxon from an old Ford car, a klaxon that could still issue a healthy toot. The klaxon had belonged to the founder of *Streetwise,* for some years gone but fondly remembered. During coffee breaks, one or another person occasionally would toot the horn for good luck.

The current director of *Streetwise* retired, and a new director with plenty of experience elsewhere took over. On the first day, he announced emphatically his intent to listen hard and work collaboratively with the staff to reenergize and expand the magazine. However, before leaving work after his first day on the job, he committed a serious faux pas. Seeing the old klaxon lying around the coffee area, discerning no purpose to its decrepit presence, and annoyed about the impression it might make on visitors and clients, he tucked it away in the back of a closet. This was his confident little answer to a little situation.

But the situation was not as small as it appeared to be. The next day, someone noticed, and the question rippled idly through the office in the course of the morning: "By the way, where's the klaxon?" Eventually the buzz reached the new director. He was taken aback for a moment—the klaxon was just an ugly piece of junk. However, he rescued it from the closet and restored it to its honored place beside the coffee pot.

But he went beyond this. When the first and subsequent organizational meetings were held, he brought the klaxon in and set it on the conference table. "When anyone thinks I'm not listening, or other people aren't listening, or we need to think harder about something," he said, "toot the horn."

Sometimes they did. More often, they just said, "Here's where I need to toot the horn." Either way of tooting the horn helped people to stand back and think.

The story of the klaxon celebrates how artful leadership that resists the temptations of the leadership trap can braid knowledge processing and symbolic conduct together into highly progressive interactions. The history of the horn, and the new director's behavior around the horn, gave it strong symbolic significance in the culture of *Streetwise*. It also illustrates again the idea of developmental leaders from Chapter 3, a notion developed further in Chapter 9. This is not yet another type of leadership—four are enough!—but a name for the influence inquiry-centered leaders can have, creating and sustaining a progressive microculture around themselves through their example and influence.

STREETWISE STREET BY STREET

The man with the horn was streetwise for *Streetwise*. He did the right things in the right spirit for the occasion, and went on to establish a culture of thoughtfulness. One might think that a leader in this style could lead well anywhere, but a considerable body of experience and research on the nature of leadership points in a different direction. Leadership is tremendously context sensitive. What serves well in one situation to resolve the whither and why questions may not serve so well in another. It's a commonplace that leaders who are good at start-ups are not necessarily good at running an organization over the long haul, and vice versa. Somewhat different skill sets and mind-sets are involved. Understanding leadership requires understanding the different rules of different streets.

STRESS STREET

You'd think that a leader ought to be as smart and experienced as possible. Paradoxically, research on leadership has disclosed over and over again low correlations between leaders' experience and intelligence (as measured by IQ tests, a limited index of intelligence to be sure, or by similar methods) and the performance of teams. Why is it that two factors that ought to make a positive contribution do not?

The answer is that they do make a difference, but the difference they make depends on context and veers sometimes one way and sometimes another. Writing in the *Administrative Science Quarterly*, Fred Fiedler identifies the missing factor as interpersonal stress. When there is little interpersonal stress, intelligent leaders generate more effective group performance, but when interpersonal stress is high, the intelligence of the leader doesn't make much difference! According to Fiedler, leaders of high intelligence commonly become overreflective about relationships, fretting and worrying and failing to focus their intellect on moving things forward.

The influence of experience runs in exactly the opposite direction. When stress is low, leaders with extensive experience actually generate lower overall group performance than novice leaders. Fiedler explains that experienced leaders thrive on challenge. When they do not encounter it, they tend to go slack and cut corners.

The story so far suggests that different kinds of leaders are ideal for different levels of interpersonal stress, smart but not so experienced ones for low levels and not so smart but deeply experienced ones for high levels, but another twist is worth mentioning. In a study of army officer candidates, before training in stress reduction the less intelligent candidates secured better results than the more intelligent ones. After stress-reduction training, the trend reversed. Stress management allowed the brighter candidates to invest their intellect effectively. The straightforward implication is that stress management is a key enabling skill for leader figures.

STRUCTURE STREET

Badrinarayan Pawar and Kenneth Eastman, writing in the *Academy of Management Review*, analyze the complex fit between transformational leadership—close to what I've called here *vision-centered leadership*, so I'll use that term—and organizational structure. In general, vision-centered leadership fits best during periods when people in the organization recognize the need for adaptive shifts. This can happen when disruptive challenges from outside or within threaten the effectiveness and even survival of an organization, as when a vicious rivalry develops between two subgroups, a key product flops, cuts in government or military spending dry up a longstanding funding source, or a competing way of accomplishing the organization's mission emerges—say, e-publishing in contrast to conventional publishing, or the classic example of desktop computers in contrast to mainframes. It can also happen when tempting but challenging opportunities arise—a technological breakthrough or a major partnership. In such situations, a vision that can unify people behind a clear direction becomes especially attractive.

Organizational structure influences receptivity to vision-centered leadership. Pawar and Eastman adopt an insightful five-way analysis of structure developed by Henry Mintzberg of McGill University— *simple structure, adhocracy, machine bureaucracy, professional bureaucracy,* and *divisional structure.* They argue that vision-centered leadership suits simple structure (small centrist management, little hierarchy, little specialization) and adhocracy (small-scale, fluid, flexible, often temporary), because it's both easy to reach people and acceptable to push a vision.

However, vision-centered leadership finds less ready acceptance in a machine bureaucracy (complex well-oiled elaborately regulated machine), a professional bureaucracy (relatively autonomous agents grouped together, as in a law firm), or divisional structure (organization with several semiautonomous divisions), because these structures isolate people and groups from one another, often generate rivalries, and make following a particular vision less likely.

Finally, Pawar and Eastman argue that vision-centered leadership plays best in organizations with a *clan mode of governance.* This refers not to government in the structural sense but to one of three notions of organizational culture developed by Wilkins and Ouchi. In the clan model, people see an alignment between their self-interest and the interest of the overall organization and thus experience a kind of kinship. Trade unions and corporations with employee ownership strive for this feeling of affiliation. In contrast, forms of governance that emphasize the Deal almost entirely—this compensation for such-and-such services—do not so much generate alignment between self-interest and overall organizational interests and make the task of the vision-centered leader more difficult.

Although an organization's situation may not fit vision-centered leadership, Pawar and Eastman do not conclude that vision-centered leadership has little to contribute. It may be just what's needed, but the leader must somehow surmount the structural barriers in order to move the vision forward.

STREETS OF INQUIRY

While these dependencies are worth bearing in mind, our focus on organizational intelligence generates a particular interest in how inquiry-centered leadership gains or loses momentum depending on the context. Personal contextual factors such as cognitive ability, experience, and stress management seem important, as do aspects of organizational structure such as those Pawar and Eastman examined. The following plausible trends outline where inquiry-centered leadership is most pertinent and easiest to sustain:

* *Inquiry-centered leadership is likely to be more pertinent to a group when many members are relatively bright and experienced.* In such circumstances, the leader is less likely to come up with the best answers solo.

* *Inquiry-centered leadership is likely to be more pertinent when a group is together for the long haul.* If a group is together only briefly, and the leader has good answers, answer-centered leadership may be the best way forward. Inquiry-centered leadership is a long-term investment, building up the cognitive capabilities of the group and avoiding a relationship of dependency that is entrapping for both the leader and the participants.

* *Inquiry-centered leadership is likely to be easier during calmer times than periods of disruption and adaptation.* This principle is the flip side of Pawar and Eastman's point about vision-centered leadership. During periods of disruption and adaptation, many people feel threatened in different ways, and views about what to do can differ starkly. Inquiry-centered leaders will find that getting people to think coherently together can be difficult. People are looking for a savior,

and vision-centered leadership can help bring a group together. This does not mean that inquiry-centered leadership will fail in such circumstances, only that it becomes a more difficult path, and a leader in that style has to be particularly adroit, and probably needs to mix in some vision, as well.

❋ *Inquiry-centered leadership is likely to be more influential for a simple structure or adhocracy than for a machine bureaucracy, professional bureaucracy, or divisional structure.* This conclusion parallels Pawar and Eastman's conclusion for vision-centered leadership, and for essentially the same reasons. Both inquiry-centered and vision-centered leadership benefit when the organizational structure allows ready contact and minimizes interunit rivalries. In a machine bureaucracy, professional bureaucracy, or divisional structure, the inquiry-centered leader can exercise the archetype to good effect with immediate colleagues and try to promote it through organizational structures; even so, it is not as likely to percolate through the organization.

❋ *Inquiry-centered leadership is likely to be easier within a clan mode of governance than within one based almost entirely on the Deal.* This principle again parallels Pawar and Eastman's conclusion for vision-centered leadership. The alignment of self-interest and organizational interest in a clan mode of governance fosters more basic cooperativeness, a better foundation for getting people to think well together.

❋ *Inquiry-centered leadership is likely to be easier when there's a moderate power structure than when there's a strong hierarchical power structure.* This trend follows as a corollary of the leadership trap. In a strong power structure, leaders at the top will tend to get seduced by the power into answer-centered leadership. People below the top, who might provide leadership based on experience and wisdom, will tend to be overridden by the power above, and exercise their power toward those below them. With a moderate power structure, there is more elbow room.

What morals follow from this tangle of interdependencies? Really, there are two complementary morals. One acknowledges that although organizational intelligence built by inquiry-centered leadership is the adaptive priority in many circumstances, there are certainly situations better suited to other archetypes.

The second moral says that various factors make inquiry-centered leadership easier or more difficult. Leaders committed to inquiry-centered leadership need to be aware of these factors and know how to handle the challenges.

HERE THERE BE DRAGONS

Remember the man with the horn, the fellow who took over directorship of the magazine *Streetwise,* who ditched the old Ford klaxon that had great significance for the long-time employees, but who was savvy enough to bring it back and make it into a symbol of inquiry? He had it easy.

Recovering from the gaffe was not that much of a problem, given that he brought with him an initial commitment to inquiry-centered leadership, that he came to join a relatively small group of people, that *Streetwise* was not in a crisis situation despite gradually declining subscriptions, and that the people at *Streetwise* already worked together pretty well. But what if circumstances are antagonistic to progressive interactions? Dragon situations were worth discussing for the theme of communicative feedback, and they are worth discussing again here for the theme of inquiry-centered leadership. Imagine the man with the horn—Gabriel, let's call him—facing situations that fundamentally challenge inquiry-centered leadership.

AUTHORITARIAN CULTURE

Suppose that Gabriel works in an organization with a tradition of strong authority and an authoritarian boss with a regressive style of interaction. Gabriel has a commitment to inquiry-centered leadership, but no special power in an organization where power counts for a lot. What can he do to exercise inquiry-centered leadership?

Gabriel's options are limited, not only because of the authoritarian boss but also because the boss's symbolic conduct will tend to create a general culture of authority and submission. But there is one thing that Gabriel always can do: conduct himself in an inquiry-centered way insofar as possible, despite the cultural context. He can make inquiry-centered moves when the opportunity arises—for instance, in side conversations, in meetings by putting a key question on the table or suggesting processes to be followed, even in direct exchanges with the boss. Gabriel probably will not be able to shift the dominant culture, but he can fight the good fight, and he probably can create a culture of inquiry within small groups that work directly with him.

Chaotic Culture

The setting is not authoritarian, but it is chaotic. During meetings, the conversation caroms from one thing to another almost like free association. Gabriel can insert ideas like everyone else and make them as inquiry-centered as he pleases, but they are soon lost in the subsequent conversational clutter. Such chaos often occurs even when there is a facilitator—the boss or someone else—simply because the facilitator is not facilitating aggressively enough or artfully enough to keep things coherent.

Here the most helpful thing Gabriel can do is probably to make process suggestions rather than substantive suggestions—for instance, to recommend a facilitator if there is none, or to propose sticking to a topic until it's worked through or explicitly tabled. Most likely, others are aware of the chaotic culture, and a modicum of order will be welcomed.

Culture of Command

In the foregoing situations, Gabriel lacked specific authority, but authority in itself does not eliminate dragon situations. Suppose Gabriel has authority. A dilemma for the authority figure committed to inquiry-centered leadership arises when the structures and culture of the organization particularly favor command. In cultures of command, inquiry-centered moves can appear weak and undermine the confidence and commitment of the participants.

Gabriel, as the authority figure, can try to change the culture, but this may not be easy or even appropriate. A culture of command need not be authoritarian, the extreme pathological version. In some circumstances—although, in my view, not most—cultures of command carry clear advantages. Military structures, for example, require a culture of command to fulfill their functions well. Again, the result need not be authoritarian; witness the flexibility with which the captain of the *Palau* in Chapter 1 allocated responsibilities to deal with the engine crisis. Cultures of command also make sense in other high-stakes situations where clear responsibility and rapid response are at a premium, as with teams of surgeons, air traffic controllers, and emergency repair service personnel.

So what can Gabriel do to pursue inquiry-centered leadership as an authority figure in a culture of command? Rather than trying to change the culture quickly, even if it needs changing in the long term, a different path for Gabriel is to distinguish between command decisions and the processes that lead up to them. Gabriel can put questions on the table, initiate processes of inquiry, and consult with people toward a decision as time allows, but in the end make the decision crisply and firmly.

CULTURE OF CRISIS

Again imagine that Gabriel is in a position of authority. Another dilemma Gabriel could face is a period of crisis. In such circumstances, people often find no security in provocations to share views, investigate possibilities, synthesize perspectives, and so on. They want the Big Answer of vision-centered leadership. They want a savior.

Gabriel would do well to give people some of what they want, remembering that inquiry-centered does not mean inquiry only. However, Gabriel would also do well to resist the more seductive extremes of visionary leadership. He might engage people in a collective process of vision building, saying that what's needed is a vision everyone can get behind, putting ideas on the table if necessary, but drawing ideas from others, as well. Joint vision building not only can fulfill the need for vision but also can create a greater level of buy-in through the participatory process. Or, within a vision he offers, he might foster processes of inquiry about how to play it out.

By definition, dragon situations are difficult. Still, the picture sketched here is not so grim. Rarely is Gabriel or any other committed inquiry-centered leader helpless. Always there are personal moves such a figure can make to nudge interactions in the direction of inquiry. Always there is the potential to function as a developmental leader, creating small groups with progressive microcultures even when the larger setting is regressive. In the end, inquiry-centered leadership has more to do with the commitment, skill, and ingenuity of the leader than with the dangers of the dragon-infested wilderness.

TOOLBOX

* *Try to see in archetypes.* Watch for the four archetypes of leadership in others' behavior and your own: answer-centered leadership, inquiry-centered leadership, vision-centered leadership, and leadership by leaving alone.

* *Watch out for pathologies of leadership* in yourself and others—authoritarianism, micromanagement, underfacilitation, false openness, blinding vision, and abandonment.

* *Practice and foster inquiry-centered leadership* to build organizational intelligence, relating in ways that model and promote inquiry, and setting up structures and processes that foster and facilitate inquiry. In other words, function as a developmental leader, which creates a progressive culture.

* *Remember that inquiry-centered does not mean inquiry always.* Flexibly adopt leadership moves of answers, vision, and leaving alone as appropriate.

* *Be alert to the distinctive opportunities and challenges* of different organizational structures, cultures, levels of stress, and related factors.

* *Remember that tools from prior chapters serve leadership for inquiry well*—negotiation from interests, communicative feedback, and so on.

* *Watch out for the dragons* of authoritarian culture, chaotic culture, culture of command, and the savior syndrome, and deal with them in ways that foster inquiry-centered leadership despite the challenges.

6

ANTS, WEATHER, AND
ORGANIZATIONAL INTELLIGENCE

KING ARTHUR'S ANTS

I can't stall forever. Previous chapters rolled out the lawnmower paradox, which says that it's much harder to pool mental than physical effort; the conversational nature of communities and organizations; how progressive and regressive archetypes govern conversations; what these look like in such areas as decision making, feedback, and leadership; and why it's so hard to be of one mind. But the big picture of organizational intelligence remains in pieces, a puzzle waiting to be put together. I can't stall forever. This chapter is it. But let's start small. Let's start with ants.

Individual ants are not quite as dumb as bricks, but almost. Behind those compound eyes and mandibles that prove so deft at picnics and in 1950s science fiction films sits a minuscule brain that is not very good at going it alone. Put a single ant down most anywhere, and it doesn't do anything much but wander around aimlessly.

But when ants get together, it's a different matter. They show real antelligence. They build complex nests, forage for food, transport it from long distances, care for batches of eggs, farm fungi in their tunnels, and so on, the usual anthill of Amazing Facts about Ants. Similar lists celebrate the collective acumen of other hive insects, such as

119

termites and honeybees. Ants don't seem to be terribly warm and caring creatures, but they have something going with ant togetherness.

Clues about the nature of ant togetherness come from a provocative area of research into complex systems that looks at how relatively simple rules followed by relatively simple interacting units can yield complex and useful aggregate behavior. One champion of such inquiries is the cognitive scientist and educator Mitchel Resnick, who emphasizes how children and adults alike need to be cautious about what he calls a *centralized mind-set*.

How do the ants get their work done? Many people have a centralized theory. They tend to think it's the queen ant, equipped with some ant version of PERT charts and Project Planner software, that makes up the work roster and schedule. How the queen ant could pull this off is hard to say, because she is no more luxuriously endowed with neurons than the hoi polloi. The queen-ant theory of the colony's affairs reflects the natural assumption that complex actions involve a single guiding agent—the answer-centered leadership of Chapter 5. But they need not.

In one of his elegant demonstrations, Resnick shows how simple rules can generate complex foraging behavior. Here on your computer screen is a simulated ant colony in the middle of a field. Two or three piles of food are scattered around. The ants simply wander for a while. One discovers the food source and goes back to the nest. Soon a conveyer belt of ants is hauling the food from one locale, usually the closest one, back to the nest. Then the ants find and transport the next pocket of food, and then the last one.

This is supremely intelligent behavior for a bunch of simulated ants. However, it happens without a boss, through the interaction of a very simple set of rules that each virtual ant follows. Here's one set of rules that will do the job:

* *Rule 1.* If you find a chunk of food, take it back to the nest. And leave a scent trail (which slowly evaporates).

* *Rule 2.* If you find a scent trail, follow it in the direction that it fades, not gets stronger.

* *Rule 3.* If none of the above, wander around.

How does the rule set generate such intricate and adaptive results? When there's nothing else to do, the ants wander around (Rule 3), and an ant eventually stumbles across a pocket of food. This sends her back to the nest, leaving a scent trail (Rule 1). When other ants happen to cross her trail, they follow it backwards, in the direction of its fading scent (Rule 2), and therefore end up at the food, which sends them back toward the nest, reinforcing the scent trail further (Rule 1 again). After a while, the scent trail captures most of the ants, and, in the spirit of the old ant saying, "Many mandibles make light work," the patch of food is soon gone.

Naturally, ants still cruise along the scent path to where the food was. But, since they don't find a chunk of food, and since they've already followed the scent trail, Rules 1 and 2 don't apply. They default to Rule 3 and start wandering around. Eventually, a free-roaming ant finds another food source, and the process starts again.

No one says that Rules 1 to 3 are precisely the rules that real ants use. It's the idea that's important. Simple rules shared by interacting units can generate strikingly adaptive behavior, even when the units themselves are very stupid. Scholars studying complex systems call such behavior *emergent,* because the small-scale rules involved (for instance, our Rules 1 to 3) do not directly specify the larger-scale activity (for instance, collecting all the food in the neighborhood). Rather, they indirectly bring it about, because of the way the units interact.

King Arthur would be proud of ants. They are round-table arthropods all the way. The ants have got their collaborative act together. In fact, when not together, they have hardly any act at all.

COMMON SCENTS

We are not ants. We have two legs instead of six. We have leaders who exercise significant influence if they do not call all the shots. As individuals, we conduct ourselves more intelligently than the largest ant colony at least 50 percent of the time. So what does ant cooperation have to do with human organizational intelligence?

Here's the connection. Ants work together pretty well, even though interant communication is pretty sparse—no English, no Chinese, no Swahili, just a matter of leaving scents behind, touching feelers, and the like. Maybe the ants' style of forming larger-scale more intelligent units points to a deeper way to think about human organizational intelligence.

So what are the scents and feelers that keep human beings coordinated? Chapter 2 introduced archetypes of interaction, the virtual neurons that wire human minds together toward effective collective enterprise. Interactions at the human level are not unlike scents and feeler touches at the ant level. They do not have much bandwidth compared to the internal wiring of our brains, just as scents and feeler touches don't have much bandwidth, not even relative to the meager brains of ants. Nonetheless, just as the scents and feeler touches suffice to yield emergent large-scale ant behavior that is reasonably intelligent—for an ant—perhaps progressive archetypes of interaction suffice to yield emergent collective human behavior that is reasonably intelligent.

Recall Chapter 1's fundamental what-why-how question about organizational intelligence: "What is organizational intelligence, why is it so hard to come by, and how can we get more of it?" Here is an answer to the "what" part. The perspective of this entire book can be summed up in one sentence:

☞ Human organizational intelligence is an emergent consequence of the balance of progressive archetypes of interaction over regressive archetypes of interaction within a well-developed contact architecture.

This says that cognition in a collective is distributed—parceled out and combined in various ways. It says that when people interact in progressive styles, more intelligent group behavior emerges in the collective. It's not merely that the particular conversation is more intelligent. The larger-scale longer-term results are likely to be more intelligent, too.

Of course, there's more to this idea. Here is the entire theory in simple list form, the full what-why-how, drawing on ideas from the previous chapters. The general formulation just presented appears as item 10:

A ROUND-TABLE MODEL OF ORGANIZATIONAL INTELLIGENCE

1. *Organizations as conversations.*   Organizations and communities are made of *conversations*. The intelligence of a collective, strong or not so strong, comes from individual contributions combined by a multitude of interactions of various kinds at various levels.

2. *Hot spots of interaction.*   Especially important are interactions related to familiar *hot spots* such as feedback, group decision making, leadership, collaboration, conflict, and so on.

3. *Knowledge processing.*   The intelligence of a group depends on how well the collective knowledge processing goes— whether options are flexibly explored in decisions, plans anticipate pitfalls, and so on.

4. *Symbolic conduct.*   The intelligence of a group also reflects the symbolic conduct within a group—the implicit messages people read in one another's actions about intentions and expectations, messages that hold people together or drive them apart.

5. *Archetypes of interaction.*   Certain relatively simple patterns of feedback, leadership, negotiation, and other interactions occur again and again with characteristic styles of knowledge processing and symbolic conduct. These are *archetypes of interaction*. We learn them from others and constantly re-create them because they're common sense, a matter of responding in kind, basic reactions of dominance, submission, or reciprocity.

6. *Progressive versus regressive.*   Effective archetypes of interaction are usually *progressive*. They generate sound collective thinking and learning through good knowledge processing and through positive symbolic conduct that builds group cohesion and commitment. Ineffective archetypes are *regressive*.

They undermine a group's thinking and learning through poor knowledge processing or negative symbolic conduct or both.

7. *Like breeds like.*   Both regressive and progressive archetypes of interaction stimulate their own kind, making a higher or lower level of organizational intelligence fairly stable, part of the way typical hot spots are handled, and thereby part of group culture.

8. *Regressive dominates progressive.*   Regressive archetypes, simpler and more egocentric, often spread through a group better, especially under stressful conditions. Therefore, lower organizational intelligence is more stable in groups than higher organizational intelligence, the dinosaur paradox of Chapter 2.

9. *Contact architecture.*   Who has how much contact with whom in what roles is the *contact architecture* of a community or organization. It reflects not only long-term formal structures but informal groups, temporary teams and committees, deliberately cross-cutting task forces, social networking, and so on. It includes face-to-face and electronic contact. It determines when interactions can occur but not whether they are progressive or regressive.

10. *Intelligence as emergent.*   The overall intelligence of a community or organization reflects the balance of progressive over regressive archetypes of interaction within a well-developed contact architecture.

11. *Progressive within reach.*   Despite the threat of regressive archetypes, many groups, teams, organizations, and communities do maintain largely progressive cultures. The greater collective adaptiveness of progressive archetypes leads to their continuous reintroduction by developmental leaders, even in the face of *dragon situations*—that is, especially stubborn patterns of regression. With commitment, effort, and vigilance around organizational hot spots, progressive archetypes can be sustained.

To expand on the last item, the round-table model of organizational intelligence yields a broad approach to the "How can we get more of it?" part of the what-why-how question. If we want more of it—and we often do, although not always—the theory advises looking to the web of conversations within a community or organization and focusing on the basic recurrent patterns of interaction, the archetypes of interaction, good and bad. It recommends looking at these from the perspectives of both effective knowledge processing that gets the thinking done and positive symbolic conduct that sustains group cohesion and commitment. It urges developing a rich but not burdensome contact architecture within the collective so that needed interactions can occur, while remembering that just because people are in touch doesn't mean that the interactions happen progressively.

Progressive archetypes of interaction tend to be somewhat more complicated than regressive ones, but not vastly more. So progressive archetypes can be cultivated by familiar means—sharing strategies, championing, modeling, and training—especially by the influence of developmental leaders. However, because like breeds like, one will be dealing not just with technical challenges but with individual and cultural inertia and cultural change in meeting rooms, boardrooms, cafeterias, team settings, big presentations, corridor conversations, e-mail exchanges, and all the many contexts of interaction that make up an organization or a community. Also, because progressive archetypes are less stable than regressive ones, they require sustained deliberate commitment, effort, and vigilance on the part of leaders and participants. (For more on the challenges of change, see Chapter 9.) Of course, the master plan for organizational intelligence is no more than a broad agenda. It takes on concrete operational meaning as we examine particular relationships; specific hot spots of interaction such as collective decision making, feedback, and leadership; and the progressive and regressive archetypes that go with them. These explorations appear in the chapters dedicated to particular hot spots, so here let's center on the theory itself.

Any theory needs an argument. Earlier chapters gave some of the argument for the round-table model; more is upcoming. The following list itemizes where various parts of the argument appear.

BUILDING THE ARGUMENT

* *Chapter 2.*   Explains the basic idea of progressive and regressive archetypes; points 2 and 3 in the round-table model.

* *Chapter 4.*   Shows how archetypes stimulate their own kind and why groups are usually not so intelligent collectively; points 4 and 7 in the round-table model.

* *Chapters on particular hot spots.*   Show how specific regressive archetypes lie behind many organizational problems (feedback, leadership, etc.) and what progressive archetypes can replace them; point 8 in the round-table model.

* *Chapter 6 (present chapter).*   Explains the logic of small-scale progressive interactions adding up to large-scale organizational intelligence; points 1, 5, and 6 in the round-table model.

KNOWLEDGE WEATHER

On a very small scale, today's weather is a very simple matter. Examine a cubic millimeter of air with instruments, and you will find the Earth's atmosphere at a particular pressure, with a certain direction and speed of overall motion, and a precise humidity. That's about all of the weather worth describing in a cubic millimeter of air. Moreover, this cubic millimeter interacts with its neighboring cubic millimeters in very simple ways that scientists can easily model.

However, the large-scale effects of these local interactions include cumulus clouds and sunny days, thunderheads and thunderstorms, today's gentle rain, and tomorrow's downpour. When small-scale units of atmosphere interact in relatively simple ways to yield complex large-scale effects, scientists interested in the theory of complex systems speak of *emergence,* just as with the ants. Whether it's individual ants or individual cubic millimeters of air, the idea is the same.

Organizations and communities have weather too, metaphorical sunny and stormy days. The weather of a collective can be thought of as an emergent consequence of many interactions at various levels. As with real weather, the weather in a collective is more than a simple sum of the contributing interactions. People are not elementary units, and their interactions are not elementary, either, but the idea of emergence is still the same.

For an example of how small-scale interactions among people could generate large-scale effects, consider the production of a daily newspaper. No one person writes all the articles; no one person designs all the layout; no one person cranks up the presses and ensures that they run well; no one person delivers the papers. Yes, there are managers; yes, there's a CEO; but no one queen ant calls all the shots on a daily basis. Different people contribute different parts in coordinated ways, with the result materializing on your doorstep the next morning—a coherent, informative, and even thoughtful construction.

Of course, the production of a daily paper is mostly a matter of well-polished routine. What happens to the newspaper company when challenges surface and choices need to be made? The round-table model says that when progressive archetypes of interaction dominate to ensure smooth interchanges, good coordination, and sustained commitment (process smart and people smart), the overall result is likely to be intelligent, and the newspaper will thrive for years to come. When regressive archetypes dominate to generate confusion, obtuseness, and alienation (process inept and people inept), the overall result is likely not to be very intelligent, and the newspaper may go bottom up or get bought out by a competitor with more savvy.

The weather metaphor helps to build an argument for the notion of organizational intelligence as emergent, because it helps us to see how emergence comes about. Organizational weather is in large part knowledge weather, made of knowledge flows rather than winds at various temperatures and humidities. For a satellite view and to get a better sense of how small-scale conversations can yield large-scale effects, it's useful to examine:

℘ Five aspects of the flow of knowledge in communities and organizations:

* *Generating knowledge,* through examination, experimentation, and importation of it or people who have it

* *Communicating knowledge,* by coworking, coaching, formal training, manuals, and various media
* *Integrating knowledge* from diverse sources toward a particular decision, solution, plan, or vision
* *Acting on knowledge,* carrying out the plan, realizing the vision, and executing the decision
* *Hard (explicit) knowledge versus soft (tacit) knowledge,* and how they influence generating, communicating, integrating, and acting on knowledge

GENERATING KNOWLEDGE

Organizations and communities need to generate knowledge that they do not already have. Generating knowledge can signify a number of different things—conducting surveys, doing experiments, trying things out informally. It can also mean importing knowledge, as by subscribing to key journals, engaging consultants, or hiring full-time people with the needed expertise.

Knowledge generation, as with any other kind of interaction, can unfold in a progressive or regressive way. Progressive practices involve a creative and critical spirit, exploring for new ideas and information and subjecting them to the filters of evidence and critical analysis. Regressive practices discourage adventurous exploration and critical scrutiny.

COMMUNICATING KNOWLEDGE

However abundant generated knowledge may be, little happens unless the knowledge flows to those sites where it can be most useful. Knowledge travels through processes of communication—anything from informal conversations to formal reports, from tips of the week to elaborately articulated policies, from in-person demonstrations to online manuals. Progressive patterns of communication are clear and open. Where possible, they make room for dialog, which allows for error correction as well as problem solving. But one cannot always expect such sunny communicational weather, of course.

INTEGRATING KNOWLEDGE

When knowledge makes its way to where it needs to be—in the heads of an executive group or a design team, for example—the question remains: What happens to it then? Knowledge integration occurs through processes such as problem solving, decision making, and planning. When we plan in a business context we might draw on knowledge about budgets, available personnel, patents secured, potential markets, materials availability, and so on. When we plan in, say, the context of a political campaign, some of these factors continue while new ones emerge, such as political platforms, survey trends, election schedules, and so on. It's all about integrating knowledge to build imaginary pathways into the future, appraise their advantages and perils, and edit and select to arrive at a viable plan.

As with generating and communicating knowledge, archetypes of interaction that integrate knowledge can show progressive characteristics—such as rich exploration of possibilities, drawing information and insight from all the stakeholders—or regressive characteristics—such as one-track thinking and decisions taken by an authority figure who is out of touch with other stakeholders.

ACTING ON KNOWLEDGE

With a solution or decision or plan in place, the stage is set for action. But will the play proceed? Straightforward though this step may seem, follow-through turns out to be a major problem in collective (as well as personal) contexts. There is a complex and challenging phenomenon I like to call the *idea-action gap*. Organizational scholars Jeffrey Pfeffer and Robert Sutton refer to it as the *knowing-doing gap*.

Here is a snapshot of the basic dilemma. Sustaining momentum long enough to give a new direction a reasonable test is a progressive pattern. However, many regressive patterns confound acting on knowledge. How often does a new policy come to nothing because people pay no attention to it at all or only token attention? How often does a new initiative get lost amidst the pressing demands of five old initiatives? How often does a new strategy for relating to one another, exercising enlightened leadership, or conducting meetings evaporate in the heat of immediacies?

Larry Bossidy and Ram Charan's book *Execution* (New York: Crown Business, 2002) underscores the importance to organizations of a culture of getting things done reliably and well. Dell Computer Corporation is one case in point. The authors emphasize that Dell's success in the computer market depends on much more than its distinctive direct-to-customer sales. Only after a customer order comes in is a Dell computer assembled, and parts ordering is part of the process, too, so Dell avoids the costs of maintaining inventory and getting stuck with inventory during market dips. The ordering, assembly, and delivery procedures are fine tuned so that every step operates with great efficiency, typically getting machines to customers within a week. Although Dell deals with physical equipment, it depends critically on highly efficient knowledge processing—the acquisition of orders, specs relayed to the assembly process, tracking of assembly and delivery, and so on. This is high-precision execution.

Expeditious attention to translating knowledge into action cannot be counted on. Bossidy and Charan argue that many organizations may have reflective and informed leadership but lack a culture of getting things done. Such a culture involves a systematic combination of realism, clear goals and priorities, follow-through, a reward system that benefits the doers, and several other elements.

WHAT KIND OF KNOWLEDGE?

Hard knowledge—some scholars say *explicit knowledge*—is the sort of knowledge that can be posted in policies, written down in manuals, spelled out in guides to good practice, totaled up on spread sheets, itemized in inventories, tallied in reports, and arrayed in bullets. It allows reasonably precise expression. The contemporary attention to knowledge management began with efforts to organize and systematically share hard knowledge, typically with technological support.

Soft knowledge—some scholars say *tacit knowledge*—is what the folks in the office who've been around for 20 years know in their bones. It's the sense of judgment one develops that this will work and that won't. It's the unwritten and largely unwritable rules. It's the feel one gets for the way things work in the organization. It's the stories told around over coffee about how to get things done. As attention to knowledge management has expanded over the past several years, practitioners have recognized that soft knowledge constitutes a large part of the knowledge capital in organizations and have sought ways to surface and share it, again often using technology to capture stories and nuggets of wisdom or to put those new to a problem in touch with those who have been around the block a few times.

The U.S. Department of Defense (DOD) launched Project Exodus in response to the realization that more than 50 percent of its current midlevel and senior leadership would be retiring within five years. With them would go the wisdom of decades of experience. Project Exodus, conducted by the research and engineering firm SAIC in collaboration with the DOD's Change Management Center, harvests, organizes, and makes accessible some portion of this savvy. A systematic interview process leads participants to tell stories that disclose their practical sense of how to get things done and captures *knowledge nuggets* that are useful for others.

While Project Exodus depends on knowledge capture, British Petroleum's Virtual Teamwork Program helped to connect people to solve problems at a distance. The technical features included videoconferencing, video capture, shared electronic whiteboards, and like equipment. The program yielded dramatic savings of time and money. In one instance, an expert in Aberdeen solved an equipment failure problem on an oil-drilling ship in the North Sea over a video satellite link, avoiding the days of costly downtime that would be incurred if the ship returned to port or the expert flew out to the ship.

The knowledge weather of generating, communicating, integrating, and acting on knowledge applies to hard and soft knowledge and their yeasty mixes, but not quite in the same way. Although hard knowledge can be generated by investigation, soft knowledge is more likely to be generated through lived experience. While people often communicate hard knowledge by spelling it out, they generally communicate soft knowledge through demonstration—"Look, do it this way"—and through advising about particular cases—"If you do that, what's going to happen is this." While acting on hard knowledge is like taking systematic account of a fact or following a rule, acting on soft knowledge is often like following a hunch or seizing an opportunity in the moment.

Symbolic conduct is mostly soft. The commitments, the cautions, the ideals, and the indulgences expressed through symbolic conduct get generated through intuitive reactions, communicated tacitly through speech and behavior, integrated into decisions and plans that implicitly take them into account, and often passed into action with no more reflectiveness than a spinal reflex. Just as people tend to be less explicitly aware of soft knowledge in general, even though it surrounds us like an atmosphere, so do they tend to be less explicitly aware of the messages carried by symbolic conduct.

Yet the messages of symbolic conduct often shape a community more decisively than do exchanges of hard knowledge. In *The Change Masters* (New York: Simon & Schuster, 1983), Rosabeth Moss Kanter notes how an invitation to participate in employee task forces has a totally different meaning when it's spun as "we want all our people to feel included" versus "we need to use the talents of all our employees more fully" in order to meet a range of competitive challenges. The first smacks of condescension, the second of genuine need. She comments later on the power of symbolic actions that substantively may not matter that much; for example, Honeywell general manager Richard Boyle configured his schedule to join every meeting of a series of employee problem-solving task teams. What was most important was not how many ideas Boyle contributed to the meetings but that he made the time to show up and participate.

****

The foregoing discussion amounts to an argument that the organizational intelligence of organizations and communities reflects their knowledge weather, the intricate flows and counterflows through which knowledge, hard and soft, gets generated, communicated, integrated, and acted on. The intelligent behavior of a collective resides in no one thing, because too much is going on, but rather is the emergent consequence of the many knowledge transactions that make up the minutes, hours, and days of group life.

WHY SHOULD I BUY THIS?

Knowledge weather is a smooth phrase, and the facets of knowledge weather make a neat analysis, but what are the point-by-point arguments? What supports a view of organizational intelligence as an emergent consequence of progressive archetypes of interaction? Here are several arguments.

ARGUMENT 1: FROM WHERE ELSE COULD IT COME?

If organizational intelligence means anything cogent, it must have to do with the interactions between the participating individuals and groups. Without the links of collaborative effort, there would be nothing but a set of individuals functioning independently—or, worse, in ways at odds with one another. This harks back to the idea from Chapter 2 that organizations are made of conversations.

ARGUMENT 2: FROM THE DEFINITIONS OF INTELLIGENCE

Definition 1 from Chapter 4 proposed that *intelligence is a matter of knowing what to do when you don't know what to do.* The rich connectivity provided by progressive archetypes of interaction makes it more likely that a collective faced with a situation in which it does not know what to do will find among its members a way forward, or that its members will interact in a manner that generates a way forward.

Definition 2 offered the refinement that *intelligence is the somewhat general capability for and tendency toward complex adaptive information processing in response to or in quest of novelty.* This characterization of intelligence bridges gaps in the simpler definition by emphasizing "tendency toward" and "quest of novelty." These dispositional facets of intelligence are favored by progressive archetypes, which by definition foster good knowledge processing and express values and commitments important to collaborative thought through positive symbolic conduct.

ARGUMENT 3: FROM REGRESSIVE ARCHETYPES

Never mind how progressive archetypes promote organizational intelligence; consider how regressive archetypes erode it. The knowledge processing between individuals would involve errors of communication, spiraling discord, failure to pool information, reluctance to follow through on others' decisions, and so on. The alienation and antagonism produced by negative symbolic conduct would make people uncooperative and factionalized in the short term and perhaps would destroy the group altogether in the long term. Such a configuration could hardly function in an intelligent way.

ARGUMENT 4: FROM ALIGNMENTS WITH THE LITERATURE

The notion of organizational or collective or interactive intelligence is not new. A 1967 book by Harold Wilensky, *Organizational Intelligence* (New York: Free Press), launched a discussion that has continued in various quarters, as several authors have offered their own conceptions of groups, teams, organizations, and communities and how organizational intelligence works. Many of those conceptions fit the model here, because they give key roles to the effective handling of knowledge within organizations through collaborative conversations.

For example, Wilensky defines intelligence in organizations as "the problem of gathering, processing, interpreting, and communicating of the information needed in decision-making processes" (p. 3). Haeckel and Nolan, in a 1993 article in the *Harvard Business Review*, write of the ability to access knowledge and information (connecting); the ability to integrate and share information (sharing); and the ability to extract meaning from data (structuring). Chun Wei Choo, in his 1998 book *Information Management for the Intelligent Organization* (Medford, NJ: Information Today), states that the intelligent organization is skilled at creating, acquiring, organizing, and sharing knowledge and at applying this knowledge to designing its behavior. Note that Choo's categories are close to those used here to characterize the flow of knowledge in a collective: generating, communicating, integrating, and acting upon knowledge. James March, in his

1996 book *The Pursuit of Organizational Intelligence* (Oxford, UK: Blackwell), examines the theme through the lens of decision-making processes. He focuses on a group's capacity to process information, formulate plans and aspirations, interpret environments, generate judgments and strategies, and monitor and learn from experiences. He defines organizational intelligence as the ability to perform well, making good decisions to ensure the survivability of the organization.

Michael McMaster, in his book *The Intelligence Advantage* (Woburn, MA: Butterworth-Heinemann, 1996), argues that business is a cognitive activity. If we understand the model of distributed intelligence that is a corporation, we can design both structure and practices to call forth the maximum emergence consistent with the desired productive results. Adopting an information-processing perspective, McMaster points to a number of characteristics important for organizational intelligence, many of which involve effective communication and coordination among individuals and subunits, for instance:

* Social language and agents that create a natural tendency for relationship and communication as the basis for alignment and shared commitment

* Connections as the source of innovation and adaptiveness

* The number of internal and external connections of each element along with the combinations required for a complete piece of information to be stored, formed, and accessed

* Communication operating freely within a structure, but requiring accumulation of other free communications to achieve meaning or relevance in action

Of course, these authors have their own conceptions of organizational intelligence. No doubt they would disagree with many particulars of the model presented here. After all, the round-table model has its own distinctive face and features, including the notion of round-table interaction and the claim that organizational intelligence

emerges from the predominance of progressive archetypes. Therefore, these sources support not so much the archetype model specifically as theories in the general spirit, theories of organizational
intelligence that emphasize the effective processing of knowledge
among people over time.

YES, BUT, REBUT

Yes, a number of factors support the round-table model. But naturally there are rivals. Here are four fairly straightforward alternatives
that deserve brief hearings and rebuttals. Recognizing their shortcomings helps clarify what the round-table model offers.

ALTERNATIVE I: SMART PEOPLE

Perhaps the simplest contrarian response to the round-table model
asserts, "What really makes a group smart is a lot of smart people."
This has a surface plausibility. Certainly, smart participants increase
the potential for organizational intelligence, by providing more of a
resource for it to draw on. Moreover, it has had vigorous advocates.
Malcolm Gladwell writes in the *New Yorker* about the cult of talent
promoted by the management consulting firm McKinsey & Company, which recommended filling an organization with the best and
the brightest as the key to success. The not-so-stellar example of this
approach was Enron, which drew in new and impressive MBAs constantly, encouraged intrapreneurship and strong competition, and
promoted seemingly strong performers rapidly—so rapidly, Gladwell
argues, that how well a person was really performing had few objective indices.

We know what happened to Enron. Its fast and loose culture
destroyed it. The smart people theory of organizational intelligence
may be simple, but here simplest is also simplest-minded, akin to saying that what makes a computer powerful is a lot of fast transistors.
The computer with the fast transistors is potentially more powerful,
but only if they operate in the right configuration. Likewise, smart
participants do not necessarily make the collective smarter. Many

communities and organizations have plenty of smart participants but obtuse collective behavior. Sometimes it's because the left hand doesn't know what the right hand is doing. Sometimes it's because divided philosophies interfere with working well together on anything important. Sometimes it's because personal competition gets in the way of fruitful collaboration. Sometimes it's because all those smart people think too much alike and have no way to see beyond the valley they're in. The paradox of bright participants and dumb collective behavior motivates the whole theme of organizational intelligence.

ALTERNATIVE 2: SMART LEADERSHIP

A somewhat more plausible variation of the smart-people objection looks not to the general participants but to smart leadership at various levels: "What really makes a group smart is smart leaders."

The puzzle here pivots on what *smart* means. King Arthur said in Chapter 5 that we want not just intelligent leadership but leadership for intelligence. Recalling the archetypes of leadership from that chapter, an answer-centered leader may be smart enough and experienced enough to do most of the important thinking for a group. Can this lead the group to success? Under the right conditions, certainly. Does this help to create an intelligent organization? Certainly not. The same can be said about vision-centered leadership, which frames and energizes the activities of the collective with a broad vision, and leadership by leaving alone, which stands back, watches, and selects.

The inquiry-centered leader advances the thinking of the group with a mosaic of strategies laid out in Chapter 5, but even a leader in this style may not be sufficient. Sometimes a group has long-standing regressive cultural norms that a leader figure new to the group, however progressive in style, may not be able to budge. Instead, the leader's progressive style may be perceived as faddish, and the leader as not long for the role.

Moreover, an inquiry-centered leader is not always necessary. A group may lack a standout leader but function in an intelligent way because progressive interactions are the cultural norm for the group.

So inquiry-centered leadership is a contributing factor but not the whole story by a long way.

ALTERNATIVE 3: SMART STRUCTURE

Another rival to the round-table model is a structural theory of organizational intelligence, which claims that the intelligent functioning of a group depends on its internal organization. A structural theory might say, "Clear chains of command, good division of labor, rich formal and informal lines of communication both horizontally and vertically, no excess layers of hierarchy, creates an organization that functions more intelligently than those that lack such features."

Certainly, appropriate structure is relevant. The right structure can foster progressive archetypes, which of course affirms the round-table model. To underscore the point, Wilensky identifies a number of negative structural features that contribute to "intelligence failure." For a sample:

* Many ranks in hierarchy
* Emphasis on rank in style and symbolism
* A tall pyramid narrowing sharply at the top, providing long promotion ladders for a few
* Great specialization and interdepartmental rivalry
* A large number of organizational units involved
* Specialization on a geographical basis
* Overcentralized intelligence.

Wilensky underscores how such structures interfere with good information processing. In the same spirit, as touched on in the previous chapter, Rosabeth Moss Kanter criticizes the "segmentalism" of many organizations and promotes participative structures that cut across normal boundaries. Elliott Jaques argues as part of his notion of the requisite organization that organizations often have extraneous layers of hierarchy that impede nimble and wise responsiveness. Many others have also pointed out how certain kinds of structures constrain and others promote collective intelligence.

But none of these analysts assert that structure is the lion's or even the leopard's share of organizational intelligence. Structure basically is a matter of an organization's contact architecture—the occasions and roles through which people connect. Even the most enlightened contact architecture is at best enabling. It allows the needed interactions without making them progressive. Culture, leadership, and other factors figure into the mix. An organization with a divisive culture and selfish leadership is not likely to function in an intelligent way, however well structured.

ALTERNATIVE 4: SAME OLD SAME OLD

The round-table model encourages deeper and more refined processing of knowledge within an organization. The round-table model foregrounds progressive interactions, which help collectives and their participants to learn. So someone might say, "Isn't the round-table model just another way of saying 'knowledge management' or 'organizational learning'?"

To sketch in the background, knowledge management has emerged over the last several years as a particular perspective on organizational functioning. Knowledge management foregrounds how knowledge gets created, channeled, and applied within an organization and how that process can be better managed. As noted earlier, there are many different approaches to knowledge management. Some emphasize the technical infrastructure of databases and networks of expertise that can be created to serve an organization better. Others emphasize the importance of tacit knowledge and human contact.

Organizational learning also is a concept with many faces. The general idea is that organizations as collective entities learn in senses that go beyond the learning of the individual members. Organizations can acquire new routines and new structures that make them more adaptive. They can build areas of expertise, embodied partly in people and partly in organizational memory—information resources such as databases, manuals, and other records.

Back to the question, "Isn't the round-table model just another way of saying 'knowledge management' or 'organizational learning'?"

Not remotely. For one thing, the round-table model is a specific theory. Knowledge management and organizational learning are not theories at all but general ideas with many versions. For another, the round-table model has distinctive features not found in any particular version of knowledge management or learning organizations— the idea of archetypes itself, the progressive-regressive contrast, the dominance of regressive archetypes, and so on.

That said, certainly there are important affinities between the round-table model, knowledge management, and learning organizations. The round-table model addresses factors that help to manage knowledge within organizations, and progressive interactions foster learning at both the individual and organizational levels.

THE ASIAN EXECUTIVE'S QUESTION

Singapore rises out of the Pacific with such a splendid cadenza of urban architecture, it's sometimes hard to remember that there's an ordinary hunk of island geology underneath. I've enjoyed visiting Singapore a couple of times, and on one occasion had a chance to speak to a cosmopolitan group, some Singaporeans and some visitors, about an early version of the ideas in this book. I've always remembered an Asian gentleman who stood up after I had explained some ideas about feedback. He politely noted that this was not how things worked in his country.

He was challenging whether these notions about organizational intelligence generalize across cultures. It's a good question!

"I would never expect direct feedback from my subordinates on policy matters, concerns, and such," he continued.

"Yet," I said, "there are issues of knowledge processing involved that have nothing to do with culture. In order for organizations to function well, the flow of knowledge is a logical necessity. Whatever the social customs, not knowing is an impairment."

"There you are right," he acknowledged. "And I do know what's on my subordinates' minds."

"How do you know?" I asked.

"I just know," he said.

This inscrutable utterance was certainly a conversation stopper. I turned to another question, but my thoughts have circled back to the exchange many times, and I have often pondered the role of culture in organizational intelligence. We do not need to drift into speculations about employer telepathy to make respectful sense of the Asian executive's point. For one thing, to "just know" certainly involves reading the nuances of another person's actions and expression beneath the level of direct statement. We do this all the time in social situations. For another, to "just know" in the formal context may benefit a great deal from casual exchanges outside the formal context. Japanese businesspeople (and I do not recall where the gentlemen was from) exchange information much more frankly in informal settings off company time than during large formal gatherings on company time. In whatever way one unpacks the oracular "just know," the Asian executive alerts us all that the account of organizational intelligence outlined here might not stretch well across the diverse cultures of the world.

Moreover, it is important to recognize that organizations have cultures, too, sometimes remarkably distinctive ones. Alpha Aromatics on this side of the street and Beta Bearings on the other side may house internal cultures that contrast far more than do national cultures. In asking about the relevance of the round-table model across cultures, we should bear in mind not just national and ethnic but organizational cultures.

So what's the answer? Does the archetype model hold across cultures in its basic analysis and recommendations? So important a matter deserves a crisp, categorical answer and here it is: Yes with a little bit of no.

One part of the yes looks to the general outline of the theory, the points of the round-table model. At this level, the model certainly holds across cultures. Any community or organizational culture will include archetypes of interaction, some progressive, some regressive. The regressive ones will tend to be more robust because they are simpler and earlier learned, although less nuanced and more egocentric. The overall intelligence of the group will reflect the balance of progressive over regressive archetypes of interaction in the mix.

Another part of the yes looks to the analysis of particular archetypes

in terms of knowledge processing. How well an archetype of interaction processes knowledge is a fairly objective matter, cultural
acceptability aside. To recall familiar examples, communicative feedback simply and straightforwardly delivers more information than do
negative and conciliatory feedback, whatever the local culture may
sanction. Likewise, inquiry-centered leadership promotes patterns of
exchange that favor organizational intelligence more than leadership
in answer-centered, vision-centered, and leaving-alone styles, whatever the local culture may approve.

In sum, if a particular community or organizational culture
embodies biases against archetypes that are progressive from the
standpoint of knowledge processing, it will tend to be a less intelligent community or organization. It may thrive for other reasons—
because of leaders knowledgeable enough to make the right strategic
moves, because of good connections, because of a monopolistic position, because of an expanding demand, or because of guaranteed
sources of support, as with some public services—but not because of
effective pooling of the many minds involved.

When we turn to the symbolic conduct carried by archetypes of
interaction, we come to the little bit of no. The symbolic significance
of different styles of interaction certainly varies across community,
organizational, ethnic, and national cultures. With the Asian executive in mind, recall from Chapter 3 the concept of nemawashi, the
Japanese practice of working things out through small informal
exchanges in advance of the big formal meeting. The importance of
face in Japanese culture attaches a sharply negative symbolic value to
arguments in the formal setting. Westerners are reasonably comfortable with such exchanges. Accordingly, the nemawashi archetype
serves the needs of knowledge processing in Japanese culture in a way
well aligned to the culture's patterns of symbolic conduct. In the
same spirit, frank talk about interpersonal conflicts, budget concerns,
and questionable policies that may be symbolically inappropriate in
the work setting may be acceptable, or at least tolerable, in the lan-
guorous milieu of a bar after hours.

To sum up, as an analytical framework, the round-table model is
culture neutral. Also, the knowledge-processing advantages and dis-
advantages of particular archetypes of interaction are culture neutral.

However, positive versus negative symbolic conduct can differ substantially from culture to culture. Accordingly, organizational intelligence calls for archetypes that are both reasonably effective from the standpoint of knowledge processing and well aligned with what the culture counts as positive symbolic conduct, as with nemawashi.

When there are no good solutions to this dilemma—when, for instance, it is symbolically unacceptable to provide communicative feedback in any setting, the boardroom or the bar, when any answer not from a superordinate is not a good answer—the culture cannot be a smart one. Whatever success it achieves will have to occur by means other than an effective merging of minds.

I have to warn once more that this is not a sweeping argument against hierarchical cultures. A figure in a position of command can certainly practice inquiry-centered leadership, offer communicative feedback, and so on, while clearly and decisively retaining command responsibility. Autocracy, not authority, is the problem. No doubt command hierarchies create conditions under which the pathology of autocracy is more likely, but they do not cause it.

MAKING THE WEATHER

"Okay," says the critic. "The arguments are lined up like lieutenants graduating from West Point. But can they fight the war? Maybe they explain the knowledge weather, but what you want is not just any weather but Arthurian weather, Camelot weather, round-table weather, the right kind of weather. And you can't make the weather."

Often you can.

The round-table model of organizational intelligence aspires to explain, but it also hopes to help. It writes a rough prescription for how to get groups, teams, organizations, and communities to function more intelligently: Focus on hot spots like collective decision making, feedback, and leadership; keep alert for the regressive and progressive archetypes; discourage regressive archetypes and foster progressive archetypes.

One can also skip the particulars and put the general idea of progressive versus regressive interactions to work. I presented some of these ideas to a group of educators a while ago. A couple of days later, one came up to me and told this story.

> I had to have a difficult conversation with someone who works under me. We needed to move something along, and yet I suspected that she was going to resist. Well, she did. We waded through the conversation for a while. And then I remembered the ideas about progressive and regressive interactions.
>
> So I stopped. I quickly explained the idea to my colleague. And then I asked point blank, "Now this conversation we've been having—how do you see it? Is it progressive or regressive?"
>
> My colleague said it was certainly regressive. I confessed that this was my impression, too.
>
> So we stood back from the situation and made a few rules for ourselves, to try to make the conversation more progressive. And you know what? It worked! We proceeded to have a civil exchange and gradually worked our way through some touchy issues.

When the woman related her experience, I was struck by her direct use of the progressive-regressive contrast, and a little surprised that it could be deployed so straightforwardly. But she did it: She and her colleague made their own knowledge weather.

On another occasion, I introduced some of these ideas. Then I invited the participants to forget about the archetypes I had mentioned, identify in their own words the regressive archetypes that troubled them most, and explore how they themselves might act to make things better. At first, they mentioned several patterns of authority that they found noxious, even though many of them themselves held positions of authority. But then someone said, "You know, we're complaining all the time about how things work from the top, but what about patterns of participation?"

Immediately the group shifted gears and listed regressive patterns that didn't come from the top—the person who complains a lot on the side but never contributes to the substantive discussion; the person who won't let an issue go even if it's been settled to almost everyone else's satisfaction; the person who floats along with whatever happens, always doing just enough to get by. It was surprising how easily and intuitively they could draw on their own experience to point out regressive patterns and follow up with practical ideas about making things better.

However, a cantankerous critic might say, "What if my boss or my dean or my team leader or my coach is one of those dragons? They just won't hear anything but their own words, and they breathe fire often as not. Or what if it's a generally nasty setting? Everyone behaves like dragons. Isn't it pretty naïve to think that I can do much to make our knowledge weather better in real dragon situations?"

The round-table model of organizational intelligence can help us understand even dragon situations and acquire some useful moves. As the earlier chapters illustrate, there's almost always some wiggle room for people with progressive mind-sets. However, we have to be realistic. It can be very difficult to change the regressive style of an authority figure through action from below. It can be very difficult to change an entrenched group culture through solo efforts.

This should not surprise or even dismay anyone. A good theory—Newton's laws of motion, for instance—never tells us how we can do anything we please. If it did so, it would be magic, not science. A good theory tells us how we can easily do some things, why others are difficult, and why still others are plain impossible. Please, cantankerous critic, ask for what ways and means there are, not miracles.

So there it is, the round-table model of organizational intelligence, the whole enchilada, all three scoops, jumbo bucket, large-size double cheese. Now it's appropriate to turn back to the particular, continuing to chart out how particular hot spots work and how they can work better. Upcoming in the next three chapters: collaboration, conflict, trust, and development toward a progressive culture.

TOOLBOX

This is a big-picture chapter, and it invites a big-picture toolbox, emphasizing the overall knowledge weather of a community or organization.

* *Look for organizational intelligence*—not just in isolated interactions but in the *large-scale aggregate effects* of many thoughts and actions combined through a multitude of interactions over time.

* *Look at the knowledge flows* to evaluate the overall organizational intelligence of a collective—how well knowledge is generated (or imported); communicated; integrated into decisions, solutions, and plans; and then acted on.

* In the same spirit, *look at the contact architecture*—who interacts with whom in what roles—that sets the stage for progressive and regressive interactions. Keep in mind face-to-face, paper-based, and electronic contacts.

* *Try to see in archetypes*—not just the particular archetypes identified in various chapters of this book, but whatever the strong recurrent patterns are. Pay particular attention to the archetypes around typical hot spots of interaction.

* *Remember* that, apart from alertness to particular archetypes, attention to *the general idea of progressive versus regressive interactions,* with attention to both knowledge processing and symbolic conduct, can itself be a useful tool for detecting and addressing problems.

7

COLLABORATION, NOT COBLABORATION

ONE OF SEVEN

Dinner was a long two hours and a ride home away when the planning meeting began at 5:30 P.M. Felicia, a well-known professor with a formidable reputation for scholarship, listed seven agenda items on the flip chart. So far so good.

At 7:00 P.M., when she closed the meeting precisely on time, Felicia shrugged and checked off only the first item. So far so bad.

What occurred between 5:30 and 7:00 that got us almost nowhere? One person said one thing, another person said another, a third a third. The conversation stayed in the neighborhood of the topic, but it wiggled, it jiggled, it jogged left, it jogged right.

And we also spent part of the time in meeting gridlock. At one point, a gentle argument developed between two of the participants. They volleyed back and forth for 10 minutes while the rest of us listened. Later on, the whole group got seduced by a very secondary matter, discussing it for a quarter of an hour before concluding that it was better considered at a much later date. During all this time Felicia sometimes participated in the conversation, sometimes put a question to the group, sometimes suggested we move on, sometimes called for more conversation on a point, and sometimes expressed uncertainty about what to do next.

We were trying to plan a complex international exchange program. This was the fifth meeting. I was one of about 20 people in the group led by Felicia, all of us with considerable enthusiasm for the enterprise. The planning group met weekly for several weeks on Tuesday evenings, because this was the only time that people could readily schedule. Felicia was very smart and very gracious, not at all autocratic. But she knew nothing about facilitating a group.

We each had areas to think about between meetings. By the second meeting, a colleague and I had a set of recommendations for our area.

"That's good," said Felicia. "Of course, we have a process here. We'll want to take it up in the group sometime soon. Meanwhile, any quick reactions?"

There were a couple, and two weeks later my colleague and I put a tweaked set of recommendations on the table.

"Good to see this again," said Felicia. "Of course, we have a process here. We'll review it all in due course."

A week later, during that notorious one-of-seven gathering, the list of recommendations still waited in its manila folder, and would continue to do so for several Tuesdays to come.

After six or seven weeks, it became obvious to most of us that nothing much was getting done this way. After nine weeks, Felicia saw the light. She hunkered down over coffee somewhere with a couple of buddies and simply made a plan. To her credit, the plan respected much of what had been mentioned during the conversations. There were some reservations, but no one was in the mood to process it much more. If we were not unanimously for the plan, we were unanimously for unanimity!

The plan quickly won the group's approbation. The specific recommendations my colleague and I and others had offered about particular areas also earned rapid approval. The exchange program happened, and it was pretty good, but everyone could have done without a dozen weeks of evening meetings.

Collaboration is one superhot spot of organizational intelligence. Clumsy collaborations are commonplace. Sometimes they take the chaotic form of our hapless effort to plan an exchange program. Sometimes they reflect the dominating influence of one person, without truly tapping the diverse minds in the group. Sometimes they involve people agreeing too readily without any critical distance—as happened at the end of our 12 weeks of meetings, although it worked out all right.

The dark side of collaboration deserves a name of its own. Let's call it *coblaboration*. The aim is to collaborate, but the result is blab that does not really pool the minds around the table, going nowhere in any one of several different ways, or all of them. Collaboration, not coblaboration, is what this chapter seeks. It applies the idea of progressive and regressive interactions to analyze how collaboration often goes wrong, sometimes goes right, and can go right more.

THREE FACES OF COBLABORATION

Collaborations are not easy, especially in larger groups. They often involve largely regressive interactions rather than progressive ones. Fundamental reasons for this were introduced as early as Chapter 1. Problems that require thinking typically are harder to share than problems that require physical work, as in the lawnmower paradox: Pooling physical effort (as in 10 people with 10 mowers mowing a lawn) is usually rather easy; pooling mental effort (as in 10 people designing a power mower) is usually rather hard. The difficulties also relate to the five-brain backlash of Chapter 4: Above about five people, the added value of another head often does not compensate for the added complication introduced by an extra head.

We all know that collaborations often go wrong, but exactly what goes wrong? The round-table model of organizational intelligence recommends identifying progressive and regressive patterns of collaboration, examining which archetypes tend to dominate, and exploring shifts of dominance to favor progressive interactions.

At the most general level, there are some distinctive and destructive patterns.

⌇ *Three faces of coblaboration:* Three pathological archetypes occur over and over again in collaborative conversations: Brownian motion, downspiraling, and groupthink.

BROWNIAN MOTION

Physics provides one of the best ways to describe what happened on that chaotic fifth Tuesday. In 1827, Robert Brown, an English botanist, was examining pollen grains suspended in water through a microscope. He noticed that the grains jiggled about in a random path for no apparent reason. Later, scientists gave an explanation: Molecules of water, always in motion (as with the molecules of any substance at a temperature higher than absolute zero), were colliding with the pollen grains and other small particles at random, nudging them this way and that. Brown was observing the effects of this molecular game of billiards. The phenomenon took on his name—*Brownian motion*—the random motion of particles bouncing around due to molecular impacts.

The talking version of Brownian motion is all too familiar from the one-of-seven meeting and its kin. The conversational focus is like a pollen grain bounced around by the molecules of individual comments. Each comment connects to something—what was said just now or a few minutes ago—but the net effect is drift. This pathology is especially strong with a complex problem and a large group. In the well-known book *How to Make Meetings Work* (New York: Jove, 1976), Michael Doyle and David Straus have another name for it: the *multiheaded animal syndrome,* the many heads around the table talking in different directions instead of thinking together.

Brownian motion is a problem of absence—the absence of organizing forces. It's not that participants are attempting anything contrarian. They're doing what comes naturally—responding to something said before. Ralph speaks against Sarah's recommendation to add two new features to the widget. She presented that five minutes ago. After that, Kevin laid out why focus group testing of the widget should start now. Ralph's comment has nothing to do with Kevin's statement. He just got his turn now. Kevin, for his part, was responding to what someone before Sarah said about the colors the widget might come in. And there are seven other people ready to say something, too.

With several voices in play, responding to something said before is not nearly enough of a rule of coherence to achieve coherence. Some very ordinary absences release the Brownian tendency. But what are the absent forces of organizations? One is lack of time track-ing. Entangled in conversation, people naturally forget the clock. Another is the predilection to organize conversations in terms of top-ics (discuss the widget) rather than outcomes (decide on the features set, decide on the colors, make a plan for focus group testing). Orga-nizing agendas in terms of outcomes gives them much more momentum and helps maintain focus. Still another common absence is the lack of a group memory of the conversation. Shared represen-tations such as notes and diagrams on flip charts, whiteboards, or a projected computer display can help to provide a group memory and stabilize the discourse. (Here's what we've decided so far about fea-ture set, color, and focus group testing. Now what's left to decide?) Although very ordinary, organizers like time tracking, outcome-based agendas, and shared representations are often underused, and it matters a lot.

Downspiraling

In Brownian motion, people jump around too much; in downspiral-ing, they get stuck. The discussion spirals down into a conversational black hole from which it's difficult to escape. This also happened during that Tuesday evening, one time when an argument developed between two participants for several minutes and another time when the whole group deliberated extensively about a matter plainly better considered at a later meeting.

Several different circumstances promote downspiraling. Argu-ments are hard to leave behind even when they have gone beyond the point of productivity—after all, there is always the question of who has the last word—and they often pull other participants in unneces-sarily. Topics that are not particularly timely gain momentum when one person makes a point, another follows that with another com-ment, and other people begin to think of things they would like to say, too. Sometimes a feeling of necessity or perfectionism fuels downspiraling: Let's all debate until we're really sure of the widget features and colors. But, wait—that's a downspiral. Why settle every detail now, since we want focus group testing anyway, and that will generate more data!

GROUPTHINK

Brownian motion has people jumping around too much, and down-spiraling has them stuck in a hole, but groupthink catches them set-tling too easily into comfortable conclusions. Groupthink, a negative archetype of interaction identified by social psychologist Irving Janis, involves people thinking too much alike. Toward the end of planning the international exchange program, we fell into groupthink: Felicia and a couple of friends produced a pretty good plan out of frustration and brought it to the whole group, and the rest of us, also out of frustration, did not want to press some remaining concerns and went along. It worked out all right, but it was far from an ideal process.

In general, Janis warns of groups with excess cohesiveness, commitment, and compliance, leading to various forms of blindness, such as failure to explore or take seriously alternatives and lack of critical perspective. Ralph hears Sarah's suggestions for new widget features; the features sound reasonable on the surface—and maybe Sarah is the boss and doesn't like to be crossed—and it doesn't look like that big a deal, so Ralph says sure, and Kevin across the table hears Ralph's okay and feels the momentum and says sure, and pretty soon they're all one happy family singing the same widget song. Groupthink fails to capitalize on the diversity of experience and perspectives in the group. It misses the complexity of the problem on the table and the opportunity to treat the problem richly, sacrificing them to group cohesiveness.

Many factors can foster groupthink, from the general desire to keep the peace and cement relationships to a boss who dislikes dissension. However, Janis warns that groupthink is not an unmitigated evil: It can be adaptive when cohesiveness is of overriding importance. Also, groups certainly can make bad decisions for reasons other than groupthink.

WHAT FACILITATION DOES AND WHY IT IS NOT ENOUGH

If only the widget committee had better facilitation! If only Felicia had been a good facilitator back in the one of seven meeting! In part, effective collaboration is a matter of avoiding the three pathologies. Like a riverboat pilot watching out for shoals and eddies, a good facilitator steers the conversation around the hazards, toward the intended destination. David Straus, in *How to Make Collaboration Work* (San Francisco: Berrett-Koehler, 2002) defines four key roles for a facilitator—process guide, tool giver, neutral third party, and process educator. This chapter is not meant to be an exposition of the subtle art and craft of facilitation (see Doyle and also Doyle and Straus), but just for the record:

* *Brownian motion.* A facilitator can define the agenda in terms of outcomes rather than topics, press people to stay focused, keep an eye on the clock, and maintain a group memory on flip charts or whiteboards or recruit someone to do it for the group. A facilitator can reframe comments to make the connections to the evolving outcome plain and sustain a center of gravity.

* *Downspiraling.* A facilitator can monitor what issues are worth processing and for how long, and directly suggest that the group move on. A facilitator can moderate and mediate arguments.

* *Groupthink.* A facilitator can avoid pseudotests of agreement such as "Anyone disagree? Okay, let's move on," call for different points of view, ask people to think for a minute about their positions on an issue before sharing perspectives to allow individual points of view to crystallize, and ask subgroups to think about a problem independently and bring their ideas back to the main group.

While touching on what facilitation achieves, it's worth asking who facilitates. Conventional wisdom says that the facilitator should not be the boss. As the power figure of the group, the boss already has an advantaged position, and playing the role of facilitator simply adds to it. While this is good general counsel, in my experience much depends on the style of leadership. Bosses like King Arthur who are first-among-equals inquiry-centered leaders and reasonably alert facilitators can conduct collective conversations quite well, and it's often appropriate for them to do so.

All this is good as far as it goes, but fruitful collaboration calls for more than good facilitation. As usually understood, facilitation addresses the discussion side of collaboration specifically, when people gather to talk things through. Collaboration is a much larger undertaking than just talking things through. Indeed, often people spend too much time talking things through rather than seeking a better balance between talk time and solo work or work in smaller subgroups. The three pathological faces of coblaboration show themselves not just for lack of good facilitation but for deeper reasons that have to do with the structure of the problems addressed and the attitudes of the participants.

The rest of this chapter probes these deeper reasons. With apologies to Clint Eastwood and the famed spaghetti western, it examines the good, the bad, and the ugly of collaboration. It addresses the dominance of regression, analyzing how *good* progressive collaboration often becomes regressive as it falls victim to *bad* ways of sharing problems and the *ugly* spectacle of poor citizens of collaboration. It explores what archetypes of interaction underlie the bad and the ugly and what factors besides good facilitation can push practice from the bad and the ugly toward the good.

THE GOOD: WHAT COLLABORATION MEANS, HOW IT HELPS, AND WHEN IT HELPS

With Brownian motion, downspiraling, and groupthink lurking like trolls beneath every conference table, collaboration in groups of more than three or four people may hardly seem worthwhile—and commonly it isn't. Many worthwhile ways of combining human effort are not truly collaborations, and better not being so.

What Collaboration Means

Combined human effort occurs in other ways besides true collaboration. It's often simply—and often very effectively—a matter of people working on complementary jobs within the same setting. When different lawyers in the same firm take different cases, or when different teachers in a school take different classes, they participate in a common effort, share an infrastructure, and function as colleagues, but this is not collaboration, because they work largely independently. Likewise, the purchasing department and the accounting department play strongly complementary roles to advance the activities of a firm, but they do not collaborate directly that much.

Collaboration also means more than just consulting with one another. If I ask you for some tips about buying a house, and you query me about some point of cognitive science, this does not make us collaborators. There is a valued relationship but no genuine joint venture. I listen to your advice, you hear mine, and then we each act independently.

Collaboration also signifies more than participation in a community of practice, in which people talk shop and share lore, as sometimes happens during coffee breaks, within craft unions, or at certain conventions. A community of practice is a powerful venue for sharing knowledge, but the participants are not typically working on the very same mission.

True collaboration occurs when people strive together toward the same outcome in ways that directly share the work, thinking, and responsibility. It's when the team assembling the annual report devises a common vision for it, splits up the parts, and reads one another's work to ensure uniform style and a strong coherent message. It's when people representing different interest groups develop a new personnel policy conversationally. It's when a faculty committee, over months of meetings, specs out an academic position, advertises for it, interviews candidates, and makes a recommendation. It's when programmers on a project map out a common structure, do their parts, and keep interacting to see that it all works together. This is what collaboration refers to in its root meaning—co-labor, working together, not just side by side. Sustained fruitful collaboration on matters that call for thinking is perhaps the purest expression of organizational intelligence.

How Collaboration Helps

Collaboration is all about *more*. People can often get more done by working together collaboratively than by working apart or in compartmentalized and departmentalized ways. Sometimes *more* means greater efficiency, fewer person-hours for the task, but to settle for "more" meaning only efficiency would be to take a very narrow view of what collaboration can accomplish. Collaborations can easily be less efficient in the sense of total person-hours invested but still eminently worthwhile. Here are several other collaborative "mores":

* *More as sooner.* Finishing the overall job much sooner by dividing the job into parts that people can do in parallel and then combining the parts, as when different people write parts of a complex report or computer software system after figuring out the overall structure. Total person-hours might be lower or higher, but in any case, the job gets done fast.

* *More as greater quality.* Producing a greater-quality outcome by taking advantage of diversity for creativity and greater critical perspective, as in brainstorming an innovative idea for research and development and watching out for its traps and pitfalls.

* *More as making possible.* Doing something that cannot be done by a single person acting over a longer period, either because it involves parallel roles (as with a string quartet or a sports team) or because it involves complementary kinds of expertise not readily found in one person (designing a product, advertising campaigns, or military missions).

* *More as a committed, unified group.* Producing an outcome with general commitment to carry on together because of the shared process, as in stakeholders collectively talking through a decision. The feeling of common decision and common cause may be much more important to future success than the efficiency of the deliberation.

* *More as learning.* Generating considerable individual and collective learning that becomes a resource for the further endeavors of the community or organization.

No matter what the collaborative "more," collaboration is a round-table idea, very much King Arthur's cup of tea.

WHEN COLLABORATION HELPS

Sometimes collaborations go very well indeed. Remember from Chapter 1 how the Hawaiian group therapeutic practice of ho'oponopono can facilitate thinking through difficult interpersonal issues, as with the shouting episode that disturbed Mr. Kealoha's family and would have left behind it hihia, a relationship of negative entanglement, were it not attended to. Also, there was the drama of the U.S.S. *Palau,* the Navy ship that suddenly lost electrical power as it approached San Diego harbor, calling for extraordinarily flexible coordination across the command hierarchy to avoid disaster. These are not isolated episodes. Most of us have experienced rich collaborations at one time or another.

However, Harvard teamwork scholar Richard Hackman warns that collaboration often is not a good choice for the task at hand. Much depends on background conditions that favor a collaborative approach. Here are some of the important background conditions mentioned by Hackman and others:

* *The mission lends itself to collaborative conversations.* Hackman notes that teams generally do not handle nuanced creative tasks such as writing a novel very well. We'll return to this theme later in connection with archetypes of problem sharing.

* *The mission is fairly well defined.* Or, it becomes well defined through initial and continuing efforts. Otherwise, the group wallows around too much.

* *There is good support for the practical requirements of collaboration.* Tractable calendars, handy venues for meeting, and effective communications technologies are made available. Partly this is a matter of a good contact architecture, so that people can conveniently maintain the conversations needed to get things done.

* *There is a good mix of members.* Members have most of the necessary skills and readiness to learn more and to learn to work together.

* *The setting honors and rewards collective performance.* Many settings lack incentives for sustained collaboration. The Deal (my committed effort in specified directions for salary, status, etc.—Chapter 5) tends to be defined in terms of individual achievement. Besides tinkering with incentive systems, vision-centered and inquiry-centered leadership can help.

* *There is a culture of trust among participants and a feeling of psychological safety.* For more about both, see the next chapter.

Absence may make the heart grow fonder, but it makes collaborations founder. Without most of these background conditions, collaborations will sink in a sea of chaos, inconvenience, and ineptitude. But the presence of all of them does not ensure success. Down inside the details of collaborative interaction are a number of ways for it to go wrong, even when the conditions are right.

THE BAD: THE PITFALLS OF PROBLEM SHARING

King Arthur and the Knights of the Round Table are all abubble about launching a new product line of high-end armor, the Knightingale Line.

GALAHAD: Now your standard pauldron is simply a bore. No style at all. Grail seekers certainly will not secure the grace of God in so common a knightly dress.

GUINEVERE (*Invited to sit in and contribute her fashion sense*): No sensitive effort to mix or match. It's rather, well, shabby.

LANCELOT (*Lancing what he privately takes to be a lot of nonsense*): I curse the cuisse and grieve upon the greave.

ARTHUR (*Calculatedly oblivious to Lancelot's jab*): So, decided! We'll roll out the Knightingale Line, the very latest in style and technical effectiveness, a configuration no noble can resist. Now, what is this new look going to look like? How will we market it? How will we price it? Let us talk it all through.

Uh-oh. Arthur is strolling into Felicia land, the dominion of one of seven. Yes, Arthur wants organizational intelligence. He longs to draw on the fashion sense and practical savvy of his knights and Guinevere toward the new rollout. But how well will they manage this without Brownian motion, downspiraling, or groupthink? The results depend on sharing the problems in an effective way. One doesn't want to put the pauldron where the vambrace belongs.

Problem sharing lies at the very heart of collaboration. A collaboration typically involves a long-term mission with a variety of specific problems to address. The international exchange program mentioned earlier included problems of program goals, financing, selection of host institutions, and process for selection of scholars, among others. The rollout of the Knightingale Line includes problems of product design, pricing, advertising, marketing, production, and so on. Effective collaboration means sharing the problems in some good fashion—coming together, defining the problems, deciding who works on what and which problems to deal with as a group, going off to do work, coming back together again in various combinations, and thereby moving the mission forward.

So how can we share problems? Simple logic helps to sort out the fundamental archetypes of problem sharing. There are not very many basic ways a group can contribute ideas and take joint responsibility for a problem. The group can talk the problem through together, or divide or delegate it in some way but with everyone retaining a voice at critical stages, as follows:

Talk through.   Get to the results through a highly interactive conversation. (This taps the richness and diversity of people's experience and perspectives and maintains full participation.)

Entrust.   Collectively generate general ideas and considerations. Then entrust one person or a small group to go off and produce a plan or draft for consideration by the whole group. (The particular problem doesn't divide up easily or is too small to bother to divide up, so it's better for one person or a small group to work it out.)

Divide up.   Divide up the task jigsaw style and perhaps offer advice about the parts. Then people go off individually or in smaller groups, do their parts, and gather again to evaluate results and put the pieces back together. Dividing up amounts to entrusting different parts of the problem to different groups. (It's more efficient, takes advantage of individual expertise, and keeps everyone involved in everything as sources of ideas and feedback.)

Initial take.   One person or a small group brings in or generates on the spot an initial take—a first draft, outline, or sketch of a concept that's relatively specific—to get the conversation started. In much the same spirit, one can also speak of a "trial balloon," "putting a stake in the ground," or offering a "sacrificial plan." (The initial take makes the conversation concrete. If large parts of the initial take survive criticism, all the better.)

Everyone has encountered these four archetypes of problem sharing at one time or another. The question is not so much what they are, but which fits when.

Like other archetypes in earlier chapters, these have their trade-offs around knowledge processing and symbolic conduct. Talking through is always tempting. It's the simplest thing to do (a processing advantage up to a point) and fully participative (an advantage of symbolic conduct up to a point). However, the larger the group, the less efficiently conversation can pool diverse insights, because of limited floor time per person. The tipping point comes when the conversation starts to mire seriously in Brownian motion, downspiraling, and groupthink. In large groups facing complicated issues, the three inevitably threaten trouble, and total reliance on talking through is asking for just that. Talking through tends to be both regressive and dominant, the dinosaur of collaboration.

Good problem sharing is a *which-hunt.* It calls for savvy selection. When our group of 20 tried to plan the exchange program, there wasn't much of a which-hunt. We mostly used the first archetype, trying to talk almost everything through, and the discussions got us entangled in a briar patch of issues and viewpoints. Problem sharing could be a briar patch for the Knightingale Line too. Arthur seems about to engage the Knights of the Round Table in talking it all through. Don't bother to check with your local armor shop soon.

To see the dilemmas of which-hunting, let's keep the Knightingale Line in the wings and look at a very simple example: constructing a shopping list versus composing a poem. Many of the items on a shopping list come to mind readily. Also, they are not much entangled with one another. More formally, they are loosely coupled, simply sitting on the same list without interacting much. To be sure, there may be minor interdependencies. You might need chocolate sauce for the ice cream, and the pickles might be located close to the cereals in the store, so you'll want to grab them at the same time. But such couplings as these are not very complicated.

Composing a poem is a very different undertaking. Each line probably calls for considerably more effort than adding *ice cream* or *pickles* to a shopping list. Just as important, the lines of a poem are tightly coupled with one another. How one line plays depends a great deal on the art and artifice of the lines that come before and after.

Imagine a committee composing a shopping list for a birthday party and composing a poem for the birthday boy. The committee handles the first task with speed and grace. Some people think of items that others do not. In five minutes, the shopping list is done, and they address the poem—which soon becomes a cumbersome camel of a poem (a camel, in the classic quip, being a horse designed by a committee). The participants flop around in different directions, struggling to produce lines of good wit and fit, and collectively they really cannot.

General good sense about which-hunts for problem sharing comes down to this: Talking through functions best when it's easy to suggest ideas and aggregate or prioritize them. The less this is so, the less well talking through will work, and the better other archetypes will serve. Efforts to use a purely conversational process for problems that do not fit generate Brownian motion and downspiraling, and sometimes groupthink as people become fed up and lunge for closure.

THE RULES OF WHICH

If the shoe fits . . . but when does the shoe fit? With the foregoing perspective in mind, one can analyze which archetypes fit what sorts of problems.

☞ Matchmaking between problem-sharing archetypes and the problem:

* *Talking through* suits problems that call for quick ideas easily integrated or prioritized.

* *Entrusting* fits best when a group can easily produce initial ideas and advice, but the final form is highly integrated.

* *Dividing up* fits best when the problem factors readily into large parts that can fairly easily be put together later.

* *Initial take* best fits something that's fairly easy to produce, so that the contributor will not feel overcommitted and others will not see the initial take as preemptive.

Let's look at the four archetypes one at a time.

TALKING THROUGH

This method of problem sharing suits problems that call for quick ideas easily integrated or prioritized—as in a shopping list, a meeting agenda, somewhat independent components of a program, steps of a simple plan, or a pro-con evaluation.

ARTHUR: Let's begin by sketching some visions for the Knightingale look itself. Now, let us remember that we are not of a mind to settle anything. This is no more than initial input for the design team. Ideas are the game, and they can be tame or wild. Then we'll do some simple prioritizing.

Arthur has the right approach. Ideas, options, priorities, and pros and cons are easily conceived and readily organized. Simply talking can capture diverse ideas for the Knightingale Line from around the table and screen them intuitively toward some high-promise options. In the same spirit, a team of academics might sketch elements of a curriculum; a team of lawyers might outline the basic approach to a case; a club might list and choose among options for a seasonal outing; a sports team might develop two or three new strategies to try; a marketing team might brainstorm and prioritize several markets to investigate.

ENTRUSTING

This approach to problem sharing fits best when a group can easily produce initial ideas and advice, but the final form is highly integrated, as with a mission statement, a program description, a formally stated policy, a legal statement, or a detailed sketch or diagram.

> ARTHUR: Excellent. We have a fine collection of ideas for the Knightingale basic look. But what will the basic look truly look like? We have to move forward to the stage of sketches, then prototypes. Did I say "we"? Guinevere and Lancelot, far better that you take these ideas and craft some sketches over the next week. Guinevere, you can examine the matter from a stylistic standpoint, and Lancelot from a technical. What say you?

Guinevere is pleased to do just that, and also Lancelot, despite his misgivings about the entire undertaking. After all, it's quality time with Guinevere (you may recall there's something going on there), and even at the king's request—how can he lose?

Again Arthur has the right idea, at least about the design process, if not about pairing Guinevere and Lancelot. The parts of a suit of armor are tightly coupled functionally, and also aesthetically according to the Knightingale vision. It would prove horrendously wasteful to work out particular designs in the whole group. In the same spirit, faculty members, after a general discussion of program characteristics, might ask for a volunteer to draft several pages of catalog copy for the group to look over. An engineering group might ask a couple of members to construct the design for a prototype.

DIVIDING UP

This manner of problem sharing fits best when the problem factors readily into large parts that can fairly easily be put together later, as with different topics to be investigated and reported on or loosely coupled components of a design or plan.

> ARTHUR: Now, the market for Knightingale. There we have another puzzle. Consider our diversity as a kingdom. There's the north market, the east market, the south market, and the west market, each with their particular preferences and economies. What adjustments do we need to make? How can we avoid the twin threats of overdiversification and one-size-fits-all? Let's divide up the market research and we'll gather again in a few days to appraise the results. Now, who will stand for the north?

The market research for Knightingale demands considerable time and could not readily be done around the table anyway, because the information doesn't sit in the room. The north, south, east, and west regions are readily separable. Any overall patterns can be extracted from the four reports.

In the same spirit, a group producing an annual report might assign different authors to different sections. Developers of a complex software system might give different components to different individuals, with clear specifications up front about how the components will talk to one another. An advertising team might arrive at a general vision for a new campaign and split up to think about different media—television, radio, magazines, Internet—then come together again to vet ideas and keep it all coordinated.

INITIAL TAKE

This style of problem sharing best fits something that's fairly easy to produce, so that the contributor will not feel overcommitted and others will not see the initial take as preemptive—for instance, a draft agenda for a meeting, a draft slogan or title, or a quick sketch.

ARTHUR: We haven't spent a word on the pricing. Let us not treat the matter now in any case, since so much else is undefined. But Galahad, you have always taken some care with appearances and purchased many a fine assembly of armor. For the next meeting, perhaps you can bring in some preliminary notions to get us started, without investing much time.

Arthur's caution not to spend much time is crucial. If Galahad constructed an intricate pricing plan without any initial counsel from the group, the group might avoid challenging his ideas to keep the peace (groupthink) or arouse Galahad's defensiveness when they aired their concerns. The phrase *initial take* and others like *trial balloon, stake in the ground,* and *sacrificial plan* express a similar spirit. It's understood that an initial take may not survive the hour, but nonetheless does a service by launching the conversation in a concrete way. Of course, initial takes can be more extensive and elaborate when prior discussions establish a strong context, and when the members of the group are comfortable with one another and flexible about rethinking things.

THE BALANCING ACT OF PROBLEM SHARING

King Arthur, first among equals at the Round Table and steersman for its journeys, not only has to bear in mind the general fit between archetypes and problems; he also has to recognize how other factors influence the choice, nudging one way or another:

☞ The balancing act of problem sharing:

1. The larger the group, the less sensible talking through becomes and the more attractive entrusting and dividing up become.

2. The more effective the facilitation, the better a larger group can share a problem by talking it through.

3. The more symbolic significance complete participation has—"I had a chance to make my case," "I was there, I voted for it"—the more important talking through becomes, so long as knowledge processing is adequate, even if not ideally efficient.

Regarding point 1, a large group is not an efficient setting for talking a problem through, because only one person can talk at a time, which does not tap the diversity of judgment and experience in the group very well. In contrast, a larger group provides more brain-power for entrusting or dividing up a problem jigsaw fashion, if that suits the problem.

Regarding point 2, good facilitation mitigates the Brownian motion and other ills of group size. Groups of two or three do not generally need a facilitator. With five or more, as the five-brain back-lash sets in, a facilitator becomes more and more worthwhile. A skilled facilitator can capitalize on the diverse perspectives in a rela-tively large group and keep the process orderly.

Regarding point 3, knowledge processing is not the only consid-eration. Often groups talk a problem through for reasons of symbolic conduct, because all the participants want a share of the conversation. Important decisions in which everyone has a stake are a good exam-ple. Discussions around a new personnel policy involving many kinds of stakeholders and strong feelings might score low on efficiency of knowledge processing. However, if the group can see the discussions through to an accord that most stakeholders feel good about, this would be worth far more.

THE UGLY: THE CHALLENGE
OF COLLABORATIVE CITIZENSHIP

Simply potholes of technique—we could view the challenges of collaboration as no more than that and quite enough to worry about. But something more than technique figures in regressive pat-terns of collaboration, something a little bit ugly. Say the knights are seated at King Arthur's Round Table, thinking about the Knightin-gale Line, but not taking any responsibility for keeping the table round. Each says whatever comes to mind. Galahad busies himself preparing his comment while not listening to Lancelot's recom-mendation. Guinevere, speaking after Galahad, ignores his remarks and asserts three reasons why Lancelot's plan should certainly be accepted. And so on.

All too often, people are not *good citizens of collaboration*. They fail to monitor and guide their behavior in ways that advance the collective effort. Being a good citizen of collaboration involves spirit and commitment at least as much as technique. Artful facilitation can help, but no gathering of minds can thrive if it's only the facilitator who cares about a well-coordinated collaboration. For a round table, the responsibility needs to be spread around.

Trials and traps of collaborative citizenship can be understood in terms of archetypes. Let's acknowledge some familiar archetypes of collaborative citizenship, then profile particularly good citizenship.

Impulsive.   Often people participate in interchanges impulsively, regardless of the current topic, the time available, and so on. They speak too haphazardly, too often, and too long. Between contacts, they develop tangents. (If I have something on my mind that might be a contribution or simply interesting, why not say it!)

Aggressive.   Some people sometimes participate aggressively, pushing positions, elaborating arguments, taking strong stances, and repeating points. (If I see the way forward, why not campaign for it!)

Passive.   Some people show a passive pattern, not saying much, and between contacts doing no more than they're asked to, if even that. (Perhaps I don't know that much about this, am not that interested in it, feel I can't risk a stance, and just want to get past it.)

Responsible.   Responsible citizens of collaboration attend to their responsibilities between points of contact and during interchanges sustain a balanced productive discourse. (The fruitfulness of the collaboration depends critically on keeping the table round!)

The now-familiar criteria of knowledge processing and symbolic conduct warn that the first three of these archetypes tend to be regressive. They undermine effective knowledge processing while displaying various forms of egocentricity. Yet it's easy to understand why they often dominate. All three reflect the tremendous momentum of the *natural* thing to do. It's natural to say what's on your mind. When passionate about something, it's natural to take an assertive stance. When your interests and talents do not encourage a particular collaboration, or when you're in a threatening climate, it's natural to fall into a passive pattern and wait the matter out, rather like waiting out a rainstorm. We get pulled into these patterns spontaneously by our own characters and commitments and the surrounding circumstances. In the case of coblaboration that opened this chapter, impulsiveness ruled, aggravated by occasional episodes of aggressiveness on the part of one or another participant and unfettered by good facilitation.

That said, we should not condemn the first three archetypes to the dustbin of irredeemably disastrous practices. As with negative and conciliatory feedback and other regressive-in-trend archetypes, sometimes the three do positive service. Impulsive interchanges can work well when only two or three people are involved, and the matter at hand is not forbiddingly complex.

Some situations demand an aggressive approach, as when a team member recognizes a serious ethical dilemma others do not yet see.

The 1986 space shuttle Challenger disaster is a classic example. Engineers at Morton Thiokol, maker of the solid-fuel boosters, persistently brought forward serious concerns about the booster segment O-rings. There were tense discussions prior to a decision to launch the Challenger despite the cold weather. Unfortunately, NASA pressure led Morton Thiokol's management to override the engineers' reservations, and the Challenger exploded shortly after launch.

Even passivity can make a contribution, freeing floor time for others when the passive participant in fact has nothing much to contribute.

THE ART OF CITIZENSHIP

Yes, the regressive archetypes have their progressive moments. That acknowledged, in general collaboration benefits from responsible citizenship, with its high commitment to the common enterprise and high process awareness. So what is it like?

Progressive interactions offer an answer at a general level. *Responsible collaboration* means striving to sustain progressive interactions. *Responsible citizenship* means managing one's conversations to advance good knowledge processing within the group and to broadcast positive, cohesive, affirming messages through one's symbolic conduct rather than negative and divisive ones—but not at the cost of simply being agreeable and falling into groupthink.

More concretely, several sources directly address the responsibilities of citizenship within a collaborative context. Doyle and Straus admonish participants in a group initiative to:

* Monitor the facilitator and help and advise as needed.

* Participate freely. Because the facilitator has undertaken the principle burden of tracking the interchange, you do not have to fixate on it.

* Pay attention to the *memory* of the conversation—notes on the whiteboard, your own accumulating notes, and so on.

* Listen, listen, listen.

* Don't be negative.

* Don't be defensive.

* Don't always sit next to the same people all the time, to establish different kinds of connections and feelings of closeness.

My colleague Daniel Wilson speaks of cultures of conversation and proposes lists of *generative* and *degenerative* moves that shape these cultures (Table 7.1). The generative moves are progressive, showing good knowledge processing and symbolic conduct, the degenerative moves just the opposite. Keeping your moves generative in an interactive setting is part of your citizenship responsibility.

Further counsel comes from Jon Katzenbach and Douglas Smith's *The Wisdom of Teams* (Boston: Harvard Business School Press, 1993). The authors emphasize points similar to those in Table 7.1. They also underscore how important it is for team members to articulate and clarify the mission of a collaboration and the particular

TABLE 7.1 Moves That Shape Cultures of Conversation	
Generative Moves	Degenerative Moves
Clarifying. Asking clarifying questions, rephrasing, etc.	*Dismissing.* Ignoring ideas, waiving them aside with a word.
Probing. Eliciting implicit assumptions, criteria, underlying goals.	*Asserting.* "This is the only way."
Testing. Offering and testing ideas publicly.	*Defensiveness.* Becoming entrenched, not really hearing concerns.
Openness. Welcoming feedback, taking it seriously, discussing it.	*Negative critique.* Only negative feedback, as in the negative archetype of feedback.
Constructing. Comparing, connecting, integrating ideas.	*Isolating.* Disconnected discourse; no effort to connect ideas, acknowledge other's views.

goals that arise at particular stages, and mark progress relative to these goals. Authentic participation in a collaboration means not taking the mission, goals, and progress for granted but participating in the construction, reconstruction, and monitoring of them. It's natural for particular goals and even the mission itself to evolve as the work generates new information and cultivates greater insight. To ignore this and maintain a view written in stone from the beginning is a failure of citizenship, not a virtue.

Katzenbach and Smith also see a commitment to learning as a critical asset. It's a rare team that at the outset has all the knowledge and skills needed to carry a complex initiative forward. Learning, not just doing, is part of the game. Areas of learning may include technical knowledge about the mission, broad perspectives on its place in the larger scheme of things, process skills, patterns of working comfortably with one another, and more. To treat learning as a peripheral part of the process is again to fail in one's collaborative citizenship.

Mark Haskins, Jeanne Liedtka, and John Rosenblum describe an especially strong version of collaborative citizenship that they call *relational collaboration.* They report on an extended investigation of professional service organizations, where they often found a remarkable commitment to collaboration not just team by team or group by group but as a general ethic and mindset. The authors identify several key characteristics of this collaborative attitude, among them the sense of a calling, a pervasive caring attitude, conscientious steward-ship, and an abundance of creative energy.

No question about it: The art of citizenship is something of an acrobatic undertaking, calling for courage, commitment, and skill. However, this need not mean memorizing the Ten Commandments of Collaborative Citizenship and badgering oneself to toe the line. Spirit is most important of all. Given the spirit, useful moves and strategies are easily enough remembered or picked up along the way, and the occasional backslide is readily repaired.

HERE THERE BE DRAGONS

Collaboration isn't always a trial. One of history's most notable doc-uments was paradoxically both the product of smooth collaboration and in large part the construction of one individual. On June 11, 1776, the Second Continental Congress of what was to become the United States of America adjourned for three weeks. The delegates anticipated that the Congress would vote to declare independence from England on reconvening. Although the Congress declared a recess, a few of its members had homework to do. Five, including John Adams, Benjamin Franklin, and Thomas Jefferson, were charged with drafting a document that would announce the secession and articulate the arguments behind this act of defiance. The com-mittee of five in short order passed along the task of producing a draft to one person, Thomas Jefferson.

Jefferson proceeded to write a draft. He then checked it with Adams and Franklin and received feedback that led to some minor adjustments. Then the entire committee approved the revised ver-sion, which went to the Continental Congress when it reconvened on July 1, 1776. The day after, the Congress approved the Lee Res-olution, advanced by Richard Henry Lee of Virginia before the recess, which formally made the break with England. Then the Congress turned to tinkering with the draft declaration. This con-versation proceeded for a couple of days with various deletions and emendations, although the document remained principally Jefferson's. On July 4, 1776, in the late afternoon, the Congress finished its editorial work and formally adopted the Declaration of Independence.

This particular collaborative process was remarkably smooth. Sir Jefferson and his fellow Knights of American Independence slew the dragons that often plague collaboration. The reasons for their success are plain. The process involved entrusting—from the Congress to the group of five and then from the group to Jefferson—and entrusting is one of the easiest collaborative procedures when the delegates do their work well. Moreover, Jefferson proceeded in a nondefensive way. He first checked with two close colleagues, Adams and Franklin, then brought the adjusted document to the whole group, which in turn presented it to the entire Congress for further editorial attention.

Jefferson and his colleagues were fortunate with one another's practical sense of collaboration. Neither Jefferson nor any of us could always be so lucky. The smart problem sharing and responsible citizenship necessary for smooth and productive collaborations often trip over power struggles, rivalries, chaotic conversations, and the like. While the three pathologies of Brownian motion, groupthink, and downspiraling can be troublesome, they respond readily enough to group awareness and artful facilitation. The true dragons lie beyond. Four particularly deserve examination: *galloping democracy, lurking autocracy, feuds,* and *spoilers.*

GALLOPING DEMOCRACY

Perhaps the subtlest dragon of collaboration is too democratic a mind-set. People fall in love with talking everything through. Let's hear from all, and all once again! Calling for closure counts as bad manners, lest anyone feel disenfranchised. It's democracy at a gallop. Imagine that the attendees of the Second Continental Congress had all wanted to be in on the sentence-by-sentence crafting of the Declaration of Independence. Or imagine that the five entrusted with the task had insisted on sitting down together to write—five hands holding one quill.

Galloping democracy is a pathology of collaborative citizenship. Although wonderfully positive symbolic conduct, it's too much of a good thing. What makes it a dragon to deal with is the subversive tone of trying to do so. Efforts to cage the dragon can seem like oppressive moves that threaten the democratic spirit. Good timing helps. Too soon, and people feel the heavy touch of oppression; after enough participants have become fed up with the way galloping democracy gets nowhere fast, some practical suggestions for moving things along are likely to be better received.

LURKING AUTOCRACY

If galloping democracy is a good thing gone too far, lurking autocracy is its evil twin, democracy going nowhere. The lurking autocrat is the leader figure who presses for preconceived solutions while maintaining the pretense of collaborative process. Chapter 5's look at leadership anticipated this dragon: the authoritarian variant of answer-centered leadership. Here it appears with a further twist, authoritarianism in a democratic mask.

Just as the problem is similar to some in Chapter 5, so are potential solutions. Other people involved in the pseudocollaboration can at least try to function in inquiry-centered rather than answer-centered ways, striving to open up the conversation.

FEUDS

Sustained antagonism between members of a group can poison a collaboration. The enmity might reflect prior rivalries, jostling for status or power, or simply two personalities that rasp eternally against one another. The likely consequence is flare-ups over ideas and issues that do not seem to warrant it. The flare-ups are indirect expressions of the real conflict. Not only do such salvos darken the atmosphere of collaboration with their very negative symbolic conduct; they may also draw others into a pattern of escalation. What would have become of the Declaration of Independence if Jefferson and Adams had had a feud?

When such feuds have appeared in groups where I have had some responsibility, I have always felt tempted to try to cure them, but I cannot report much success. The mutual wounds are too hard to soothe. In the short term, a policy of containment rather than cure seems to work better. If people cannot be collegial, at least one can encourage them to be civil. If they would never want to pair off with one another for some group task, at least they can contribute along separate tracks. If their skirmishes are too public, at least they can be asked in the name of the group to keep the lid on.

That's in the short term. In the long term, deep-seated antagonisms take their toll. It seems unwise to keep people in sharp conflict within the same collaboration, unless circumstances make this imperative. If historical antagonisms persist in the communications office, perhaps it needs to be split into two different functions, or someone has to go elsewhere. If the steering committee meetings often get derailed by debates between old-timer Oswald and young-blood Yolanda, perhaps Oswald or Yolanda or both should find other worthwhile roles. There are always battles within any organization, but there is no reason why ardent antagonists have to work side by side in the uncomfortable intimacy of a collaborative relationship.

SPOILERS

Sometimes collaborations include participants who are agents of chaos. They are not just impulsive or aggressive occasionally, as we all are, they are forever disruptive—pushing points of view with too much persistence, adopting stances that seem overcritical, sending the conversations spinning off in unhelpful directions. It's easy to wish that they simply were not there.

Be careful what you wish for. Such wishes are sometimes hasty. A little chaos can be good for a group—annoying, but generative. Socrates was not much loved by Athenian society, because he constantly adopted unpopular critical stances toward all manner of matters. He styled himself as the gadfly (according to Plato's account in *Apology*), whose sting kept people alert to problems that they might otherwise slumber through. Basically, Socrates was accusing the Athenians of groupthink. Of course, Socrates paid a price for his irritating role, convicted of impiety and corrupting the youth of Athens and sentenced to drink the poison hemlock. But he had a point: Collaborations can be too feel-good for their own good sometimes.

But what if the spoiler is just a spoiler? What might ·be done when the disruption outweighs any positive benefits? It's almost always regressive—bad symbolic conduct and poor collaborative citizenship—to redress an agent of chaos directly in a public setting. What often works better is to establish clear general rules of conduct at the outset, so that disruptive behaviors constitute a clear and plain violation of them. Then the agent of chaos either will get the point without any further action or can be asked to take a nap with some grace on the grounds of the rules just made.

I remember a recent meeting where the leader anticipated a firestorm in a group that settled most matters by near consensus. The leader uncharacteristically began by warning the group how things might escalate and announcing that he would use Robert's Rules of Order, which he generally did not do except in a perfunctory way. Although Robert's Rules of Order are hardly the sine qua non of fluent conversation, in this case they infused the proceedings with a remarkable civility, moderated what were likely to be the loudest and longest voices, and allowed the facilitator on one or two occasions to ask people simply to hold their peace.

We can rarely hope for as smooth a process as Thomas Jefferson and his colleagues managed around the Declaration of Independence. However, the good news here is familiar by now: Dragon situations are not intractable. They leave room for some strategies that sometimes help a good deal. Besides that, it's important to remember that communities and organizations get work done by means other than collaboration. Compartmentalization of functions works quite well for many situations, a way forward not to be forgotten when collaboration does not suit the task or, just as often, does not suit the people who have to do the task.

TOOLBOX

* *Strive to be a developmental leader,* whether as boss, facilitator, or simply participant, transforming coblaboration into collaboration.

* *Try to see in archetypes,* as always.

* *Attend to the three pathologies* of Brownian motion, downspiraling, and groupthink. Watch out for the factors that foster them (for instance, in the case of Brownian motion, lack of time sense, conversations organized around topics rather than outcomes, and no group memory).

* *Use good group facilitation* to help with these pathologies, without expecting it to solve all the problems of collaboration.

* *Attend to the background conditions* for a worthwhile collaboration: Does the mission lend itself to sharing? Is there good practical support in terms of frequent face-to-face or electronic opportunities to communicate, reward systems, and so on? If not, consider approaches in which people complement one another without close collaboration.

* *Make smart choices among the four archetypes for problem sharing:* talking through, entrusting, dividing up, and initial take. Remember that talking through often is not the best way, although people gravitate to it.

* *Foster responsible collaborative citizenship.* Remember that the rival archetypes of impulsive, assertive, and passive citizenship come more naturally but do not serve the collaboration as well, except in special circumstances. Attention to facilitation, generative rather than degenerative cultures of conversation, group learning, and related matters can help.

* *Watch out for the four dragons of collaboration*—galloping democracy, lurking autocracy, feuds, and spoilers.

ठ

CREATIVE CONFLICT, TRAGIC TRUST

A TRAGEDY OF TRUST

Never mind King Arthur, ponder King Lear. With no round table in sight, William Shakespeare's *King Lear* is a tale of conflict and a tragedy of trust.

The aged Lear, grown tired of managing his kingdom, proposes to divide it up among his three daughters, Goneril, Regan, and Cordelia, the youngest and most beloved of all. But first, Lear calls for professions of love. Goneril offers a well-buttered statement, and Regan outdoes her sister with absurd declarations that place Lear pretty much at the center of the universe. But when Lear turns to Cordelia and asks for her words, he doesn't hear what he wants. Sure in her balanced commitment and piqued by her sisters' extravagance, Cordelia says, "Nothing, my lord." Warned by Lear that "Nothing will come of nothing" and pressed to speak again, she states, "I love your Majesty according to my duty—no more, no less," which, although it avoids the sisters' flamboyance, might seem a little cool under the circumstances.

Lear is not pleased. He trusts the effusive Goneril and Regan, but not the reticent Cordelia. He gives half his kingdom to Goneril and her husband, the other half to Regan and her spouse, wanting only that they support 100 knights at arms for his retinue. He proposes to live with his two loving daughters in turn, and he banishes Cordelia, who is fortunate in that the king of France, one of her suitors, recognizes her merit and makes her his queen.

Oh Lear, you might as well have trusted the tide not to turn. Goneril and Regan do not live up to the deal. They show no interest in supporting Lear's retinue and treat him with disdain. Then things get complicated and bloody in the way that Shakespeare and his audiences so cherished. Cordelia and the king of France find out about the ill treatment of Lear. Cordelia leads an army to restore justice, but loses to the combined forces of Goneril and Regan. Goneril's husband, the Duke of Albany, recognizes Goneril's perfidy and, himself a good man, turns against her. The score at the end: Goneril dead by her own hand, Regan dead because Goneril poisoned her out of spite, Cordelia dead because she was hanged in prison at the sisters' orders, and Lear dead of grief at the fate of his one true daughter.

Trust is a positive concept, but *King Lear* is a tragedy of trust. In Shakespeare's tale, trust plays the role of a destructive force. The king trusts both too little and too much. He demonizes Cordelia for what he perceives as a lapse of fealty. After that, Cordelia can do no good. And he angelizes Goneril and Regan, placing full faith in their flowery espousals and expecting a serene senescence in their loving hands.

CALM AS A CLAM

Trust is a positive concept. In business, government, and our personal lives, we want plenty of trust, but, as Lear learned, not too much. Conflict is a negative concept. In business, government, and our personal lives, we want plenty of calm. However, just as there can be too much trust, there can be too little conflict.

I said never mind King Arthur, but consider King Arthur again. It's visitor's day at the Round Table. There you are, sitting in the corner, just as citizens in many countries can observe their senates or parliaments at work, watching what makes Arthur's table round. You notice that on this day matters seem stupendously calm—calm as a clam, clams being beings who seem to manage a perpetual state of meditation that would put any yogi to shame. Arthur proposes such-and-such; everyone says sure-you-bet. Galahad proposes so-and-so; everyone, even Arthur, says yes-yes. Pretty soon, you're thinking this is altogether too calm. The items on the Round Table are very boring indeed, or else everyone's suffering a hangover from Woodstock at Camelot, or it's simply a serious case of galloping groupthink. Clams are calm but not very creative. More initial dissension would hold more generative potential.

There's nothing very startling about this:

🔊 *Creative conflict:* From plants and animals to human relationships and on to organizations, communities, and nations, the world abounds with examples of creative conflict.

We probably hold negative views of conflict in part because we remember vivid episodes of destructiveness but not how conflict often figures productively. At the biological level, conflict drives much of evolution, which creates truly remarkable creatures—like us, for instance, and those clams. Come to think of it, they must be quietly competing with mussels or oysters or whatnot. They're not as calm as they look.

At the level of nations, conflict often means war, but even wars, despite their many costs, can be generative in certain specific ways, such as fueling technological advances or spreading legal, civil, and cultural practices of civilization, as the Roman empire certainly did, for all its faults. Also, conflict among nations sometimes involves ingenious processes of social maneuvering, such as Gandhi's use of peaceful resistance to pry India away from British rule.

In the business world, competition within free markets helps to provide products and services at reasonable prices and to fuel innovation. Economist Joseph Schumpeter wrote of *creative destruction*, arguing that the displacement of old ways by new ideas and practices is both the natural order of things and fundamentally productive. In this Darwinian view, adaptation and extinction, as organizations repurpose themselves in the face of fresh challenges or go bankrupt, are both part of the rhythm of progress. All this applies within businesses and other organizations as well as across them: People and groups champion ideas and projects; some win out and some fall away, a process that certainly can be creative if the competition occurs on a reasonably fair playing field.

The nineteenth-century German philosopher Hegel even enshrined conflict in his panoramic view of history, recognizing a process of thesis and antithesis, the conflicting positions, followed by synthesis, which puts thesis and antithesis together in a more enlightened construction that captures important features of both. Hegel's view is a vote for the necessity of conflict: Without the struggle between thesis and antithesis, there's no synthesis. Things stay stuck on the original thesis.

To sum up, trust can be negative, and conflict can be positive. Moreover, as we shall see, conflict and trust are intertwined in both creative and destructive contexts. Creative conflict involves high trust—trust in the others involved or the system in play—whereas destructive conflict involves low trust. Conflict, trust, and the interplay between them are hot spots in collective life and essential themes in fostering organizational intelligence.

THREE WAYS OF SETTLING CONFLICT

Conflict happens when people press for different answers about something that calls for resolution. The different answers might concern almost anything—who gets King Lear's kingdom, who controls Jerusalem, what product line to develop, what contractor provides most European carriers with the next generation of airplanes, what kinds of nuclear testing to permit, who takes out the trash. What's crucial is that the context calls for resolution. Someone will control Jerusalem, so who or what combination does so is an issue. Some contractor will provide the next generation of airplanes, so which one?

To all this, the traditional lament is, "Why can't we all just get along?" Because, of course, there are too many reasons to disagree and press for resolution. Turning to communities and organizations, Lee Bolman and Terrence Deal, in their well-known book *Reframing Organizations* (San Francisco: Jossey-Bass, 1991), point out how resources are always limited, high-status positions are scarce, and some roles are more desirable than others. Questions about who gets what budget, who gets what office space, who gets to manage others, and who gets the more desirable roles always will arise. In families it's not much different. There, too, resources are limited, and more- and less-agreeable jobs need attention. Even between nations, the same principles apply. Such inevitable conflicts aside, people's personal styles, perceived offenses, and multitudinous other factors generate further aggravation.

If conflict is inevitable, the round-table model of organizational intelligence encourages us to examine which archetypes it manifests. Conflict is host to amazing and dismaying diversity. People may persist in a conflict, yield simply to get away from it, or avoid conflict in the first place. The plan for today may be the final resolution of the problem at hand, a path of investigation to generate information, or a resolution for a trial period. But none of this dissects the process by which conflicts get resolved. Modes of resolving conflict are especially important. Although mixes and melds certainly occur, the following three modes stand in high contrast to one another:

Consensus resolution.   Often people or groups resolve conflicts by consensus or near consensus, figuring out what option to go with; or what to try first, then next; or a compromise, deal, and so on. (Consensus or near consensus keeps collaborative relationships intact; we can continue to move forward together.)

Civil resolution.   Often people or groups resolve conflicts through appeal to a governance structure of some sort—the boss, a vote, a jury. This civil mechanism decides which side wins or what balance or combination. (A civil resolution ideally provides different sides with a fair hearing, and at least makes the decision so that things can move forward.)

Power resolution.   Sometimes people or groups resolve conflicts through power—through wielding political or administrative authority in their own behalf, or physical conflict, or other means of direct conflict (for instance, financial maneuvering); or one party has the power to depart the conflict and does so (for instance, quitting a position, shifting roles, or moving to another place). (Sometimes civil mechanisms do not exist or are unacceptable, and matters reduce to who has the power to win or leave.)

Why do these three archetypes arise over and over again? Because they reflect a fundamental three-way logic: To reach a resolution, either we have to agree, or some group or other person decides, or the matter comes down to who has the power to do what.

It may seem odd to group under *power resolution* such diverse tactics as administrative fiat, physical force, and leaving the field, but they share something important: A person or group pursuing any of these need not convince anyone—not the other side or a judge or voters. It's simply a matter of getting away with what you have the power to get away with, including just plain getting away from the battlefield.

Likewise, it may seem odd to group under *civil resolution* both an authority-oriented mechanism such as the boss's decision and a democratic mechanism such as voting. But again, they share an important property. Authority figures and voting both are civil structures that provide an orderly way of resolving conflicts and moving forward (among other functions; they often have other responsibilities, too, such as formulating policies). To resolve the conflict, the parties at odds must convince the deciding agent. Of course, if one of the conflicting parties *is* the boss, the boss wins through administrative or political power—a power resolution. For a true civil resolution, the authority figure should be neutral, deciding on behalf of the individuals involved and the interests of the organization.

It's natural to wonder how the thriving art and craft of conflict resolution fits into this scheme. By and large it falls within *consensus resolution*. Typical conflict resolution techniques try to achieve a better mutual understanding and a mutually agreeable resolution among the conflicting parties. The combatants may attempt conflict resolution strategies themselves, but more likely, they will need the help of a neutral mediator. The presence of a mediator may make the process seem like civil resolution. However, the mediator is not a judge who makes the decision, but a facilitator who supports the conflicting parties in arriving at a mutual decision.

REGRESSIVE AND PROGRESSIVE CONFLICT

We have three fundamental archetypes for settling conflicts. Which archetype gets the round-table prize for most progressive interaction, best knowledge processing, best symbolic conduct, and most superior servant of organizational intelligence?

The clear loser in this competition is power resolution. Characteristically, power resolutions do not involve good knowledge processing between those at odds. The sides may not be communicating much at all. If they are, each side is likely to withhold information, misrepresent itself, and view with suspicion the others' statements. Each side is likely to blame the other without recognizing its own contribution to the conflict. Even if both sides make an effort to be open, each will tend to stereotype the other and hear what the other says as self-serving. Thus, knowledge processing between sides is poor. Knowledge processing within each side often suffers, too. The tendency to stereotype the enemy and the pressures of the struggle can easily lead to poor individual and collective thinking.

As to symbolic conduct, the choice by one or both sides to attempt a power resolution projects profoundly negative messages, driving the groups apart. To put this another way, attempts at power resolutions immediately create acute distrust, a theme to which we'll shortly return.

However, one carnivorous characteristic of regressive interactions does not entirely hold. Contrary to the dinosaur paradox of Chapter 2, power resolutions do not always tend to dominate the more progressive consensus and civil resolutions. The reason seems clear enough: Power resolutions are so often so negative in short-term and long-term consequences that people reach for consensus and civil resolutions instead. However, battles around the world at any level, from gangs to nations, testify to the continued popularity of power resolutions.

Comparing consensus and civil resolutions, it's tempting to say that consensus is most progressive, because, the argument would go, consensus involves the best knowledge processing and broadcasts the most affirmative symbolic conduct. However, the trade-offs between consensus and civil resolution are too tricky to declare consensus the round-table winner.

One problem is that both consensus and civil resolution have big pitfalls, what we've called pathologies. Reaching consensus involves a collaborative process that is subject to the ills diagnosed in the previous chapter. The discussion process can prove too easy (groupthink) or too hard (Brownian motion and downspiraling) to serve well. Consensus resolution can yield a false consensus, with everyone superficially on board but some people sabotaging the effort as it moves forward from there.

Civil resolution also has its pathologies. If it's a matter of a vote, those who vote can be unduly swayed by emotional arguments and other misplaced appeals, a problem the founding fathers of the U.S. government recognized in the Greek version of democracy (see Chapter 1). If it's a matter of executive decision, a supposedly neutral authority may be corrupt, another theme revisited later.

But never mind pathologies. Even in ideal form, consensus resolution isn't decisively more progressive than civil resolution. As to knowledge processing, people caught up in a debate certainly can strive in a collaborative spirit to work toward a reasonable resolution, but it may take a painfully long time. Third parties in a civil process— a boss or a voting group—can sometimes bring distance and detachment that might improve the quality and speed of the knowledge processing. The presence of a civil mechanism can even be freeing for the contenders, allowing each to concentrate on making the best possible case. As to symbolic conduct, certainly there is powerful symbolism in striving to reach consensus, but there is also powerful symbolism in the operation of a good civil mechanism. The reflective boss, the wise judge, a vote on a well-discussed issue all stand for a commitment to working things out in orderly ways that avoid the third option—power resolution.

Finally, it's important to acknowledge that some issues do not lend themselves to consensus or even near consensus between the parties in conflict. A civil resolution is the best that one can hope for.

If two people are vying for the same directorship, or two salespeople for the same account, or two political parties for one presidency, consensus resolutions make little sense.

All this helps to map the archetypes of conflict resolution and some of their trade-offs, but it leaves masked the forces that push toward one or another archetype of resolution. Many of these forces concern the other theme of this chapter—trust.

HOW TRUST WORKS

Richard Farson's *Management of the Absurd* (New York: Simon & Schuster, 1996) takes delight in propositions that ruffle the sleek fur of common belief. One of them counters the notion that organizations are robust. Instead, Farson suggests that "Individuals are almost indestructible, but organizations are very fragile." Farson argues that human relations are fragile and organizations are built out of them. When human relations go deeply wrong, we are hurt and upset, but we survive, move on, and do something else with someone else. However, the group, team, organization, or community may suffer and even collapse. Committees may fall into bickering and fail in their missions. Executive groups may falter because of divergent visions and rivalries at the top. Mergers may fail as enmity and rivalry between the merging organizations snowball due to differences in corporate culture.

Trust is one of the building blocks of cohesiveness in teams, communities of practice, networks, and communities and organizations of all sort—but a fragile one. So, how can we understand trust? Where does trust come from when it comes, and why does it go when it goes? How can we not be King Lear, who trusted the wrong people for the wrong reasons? Although trust occupies the world of interpersonal feelings and sensibilities, the concept has a remarkably clean and orderly logic along the following lines.

One of the most notable features of trust is its *practicality*. Trust suggests peace of mind, but peace of mind translates into pace of action. The world is a vexed mix of opportunities and dangers. Even living rooms have their subtle threats. Do you trust that chair to support your weight, the fireplace to keep the fire within its hearth? When we trust, we can plan and act without fretting too much about the trusted dimensions of the situation. Otherwise, we have to keep checking. Thus, besides helping us to feel better about our circumstances, trust is supremely practical.

The language of trust often has a sweeping quality. We say, "Elizabeth is completely trustworthy" or "You can certainly trust in George." However, such attributions are not as broad as they seem. We make such statements in contexts that implicitly delimit the kind of trust. Elizabeth can be trusted to get her work done on time, but not to save you from drowning in a pond. George can be trusted to take care of your children for a day or two while you're away, but not to manage your stock portfolio well.

When we do trust George or Elizabeth in some role, our trust involves two complementary judgments. One of them is *capability.* We trust in the capability of an inanimate object, another human being, a group or organization, or even an animal, to come through in various ways. We trust the chair to hold us up, a colleague to finish work on time, the post office to deliver the mail, and Lassie to come home. The other judgment we make concerns *commitment.* Although chairs cannot display commitment, individuals, organizations, and some animals can. We trust the colleague to finish on time not just because of capability but because of the colleague's commitment, and the post office to deliver the mail because of its institutional commitment, and even Lassie to come home because of her commitment.

We arrive at this dual judgment of capability and commitment in many different ways—intuition, contextual cues, systematic evidence from past experience. A mix of long-term experience and our immediate sense of things allows us to judge how much we can trust the capability and commitment of a thing, person, or institution. Sometimes we trust because of experience with the specific person or situation, but we also often place trust in *roles,* without knowing anything about the specific case. We trust a teller in a bank to be honest, a physician to be knowledgeable, a bus driver to drive a bus reasonably well, a seeing eye dog to watch out for its master. Simply being in such a role is a kind of evidence. We know that behind the roles lie selective processes that favor these attributes and weed out those who do not live up to them. The fact that roles are not always lived up to means we need to maintain a certain measure of alertness, but roles provide at least a starting place for trust.

Of course, sometimes our judgments of capability are mistaken. When the chair collapses beneath us, we feel disappointed (to say the least), but not betrayed—or at least not betrayed by the chair, although perhaps by the chair-maker. When a colleague lacks the capability to follow through on a task, again we feel disappointed but not betrayed. The colleague has done his or her best, but did not prove up to the task. When our judgments of commitment are mistaken, then we do feel betrayed—as when, for example, our colleague goes to the race track instead of finishing the job, or a delivery service commonly loses packages. Both could have done better had they invested more effort. Thus, a sense of disappointment is the red flag of our frustrated judgments of capability, and a sense of betrayal the red flag when our judgments of commitment prove misplaced.

All this reveals a remarkable systematization in what might at first seem like a fluffy feel-good intuition. To sum up:

↝ The logic of trust:

* *The practicality of trust.* Because we trust certain people, institutions, and things, we can move forward without worrying about them.

* *What we trust.* Even though we speak loosely of trusting this or that person, institution, or thing, what we really trust is highly contextual—that person, institution, or thing in specific roles.

* *Two sides of trust.* When we trust people or institutions, we rely on judgments of both capability and commitment—the capability to come through and the commitment to do so.

* *When we trust.* We trust when we infer (from intuition, evidence, context, etc.) that the required capability and commitment are there.

* *When trust is violated.* We feel disappointed when the capability turns out not to be there and betrayed when the commitment turns out not to be there.

TRUST IN THE LAND OF LEAR

The ideal story of trust in our lives would go something like this: We make judgments of trust grounded in experience. Although we sometimes misread the signs, on the whole we proceed in reasonable ways, undertake reasonable risks, and live reasonably happily ever after.

Of course, it's not like that in the real world of the shop floor, the sales office, the faculty meeting, the U.N. task force, or the executive suite. We actually live in the Land of Lear, where misjudgments about trust are common. We trust other people and groups too little, demonizing those whom we feel have somehow betrayed us. And we trust too much, angelizing others, which of course sets us up for demonizing them later when they almost inevitably betray that excessive trust. This is the tragedy of trust.

In other words, trust often falls into a risky pathology. It's *categorical* trust, not sufficiently nuanced and sensitive to circumstance. The consequences may be minor, but sometimes they are profound.

Why does trust become categorical? Not only trust but many judgments that we make slip and slide toward the categorical. Several psychological factors nudge judgments in that direction. Here are some of them.

* *Unreasonable expectations.* People often expect others to be paragons of capability and commitment. Unreasonably, they want angels. Autocrats want angels of obedience, bureaucrats want angels of procedure, democrats want angels of wholehearted thoughtful participation, fanatics want angels of commitment, and so on. Then, when those expectations are violated, they do an attitudinal back flip, feeling profoundly disappointed and betrayed, demonizing instead of angelizing—also not reasonable. I remember feeling betrayed a number of years ago when an associate unexpectedly left a project with relatively little notice. The consequences were readily managed, however. After time had given me more distance on events, I concluded that my expectations had been unreasonably idealistic. Although he

was committed to the project, an exceptional opportunity came his way, one it would have been foolish to pass up.

✳ *Unexpected expectations.*   It's easy for people working together to have different ideas about what's expected of one another. You think you can deal with my question next week, whereas I imagine you understand how urgent it is. You take it for granted that we'll push ahead on several important fronts evenly, whereas I take it for granted that we are both prepping for Tuesday's critical meeting. You assume you should apply a new policy flexibly, whereas I'm afraid of legal ramifications and feel it's obvious that we need to be strict. When I discover that my question isn't answered, we aren't ready for Tuesday's meeting, or policy breaches have occurred, I'm likely to trust your commitment or ability less. We'd both be better off if we had the habit of clarifying expectations!

✳ *The fundamental attribution error.*   This concept from Stanford social psychologist Lee Ross concerns how people explain their own actions versus others' actions. We tend to explain others' actions by character or personality but our own actions by situational factors. Why was Paul late for work on Tuesday? I might mention character: "Paul's a late kind of guy, unreliable that way." But if I were Paul himself, I might say quite honestly, "I spilled coffee at breakfast and had to clean it up, and then on top of that traffic on I-95 was terrible." Why did Paul finish the annual report early? I might mention character again: "Paul really comes through when it counts." But if I were Paul himself, I might confess, "I thought it was important but I also had a slack weekend, so I worked on it." All these judgments could have some truth in them. However, it's hardly reasonable to see others' actions as largely determined by character and one's own actions as largely determined by situations. The sweeping nature of character attributions can lead to categorical trust or distrust, with its angelizing or demonizing.

✳ *Overgeneralization.* It's easy to imagine that the person who is often late will not come through when it counts. But perhaps the person will. We casually generalize from trusting or distrusting a person in one respect to another, a risky step. We can all think of people we would trust in one way but not in another. Sound judgments of trust are not sweepingly categorical—you can trust him with anything—but specific and nuanced—you can trust him with this sort of thing but not that sort of thing.

✳ *Selective processing of information.* There are those who can do no wrong in the eyes of the emperor, and others who, it seems, can do no right—at least for some emperors, whether they are presidents, division chiefs, or coaches. Bosses of this sort suffer from the syndrome of categorical trust, and so do we all to some extent. Like all mental models, judgments of trust, once formed, generate selective processing of information that tends to confirm them. Once a person has concluded that another is trustworthy or untrustworthy, the mixed and messy evidence of everyday relationships is likely to strengthen the judgment already arrived at. The rich get richer and the poor get poorer; once an angel, always an angel; once a demon, always a demon. It may take a virtual avalanche of contrary evidence to change the judgment.

The collective moral of these several points is:

☞ Don't trust your trust! Cultivate reflective trust.

Our judgments of trust tend to be too categorical. A better archetype than categorical trust is *reflective trust*—a thoughtful appraisal of who realistically can be trusted for what, along with getting expectations out on the table when they might be unclear. Reflective trust entails a more measured and nuanced appraisal of how much you can trust who with what. Reflective trust involves deeper knowledge processing and also leads to more positive symbolic conduct, through not broadcasting unreasonably positive and negative expectations.

Reflective trust brings us to another psychological twist:

> *The Pygmalion principle:* While we do well not to trust too little and not to trust too much, it seems better to trust a little too much than a little too little.

The reason comes from symbolic conduct: Trust is inspiring; distrust is deflating. When Alicia trusts Benedict to untangle a conflict in his area of responsibility, monitor some legal ramifications of a project, or conduct an analysis with professional rigor, Benedict is likely to know it. Maybe Alicia tells him directly, but often as not he picks it up from her manner—her confidence and lack of hovering. Even if Benedict does not feel all that committed, he will likely try to rise to the occasion. However, if Alicia doesn't trust Benedict, he's likely to detect this through her manner, feel less committed, and, in turn, not trust Alicia as a work partner or boss.

The natural metaphor for the inspirational power of trust is the Greek myth of Pygmalion, recast by George Bernard Shaw into a modern play of the same name, which was later adapted into the well-known musical *My Fair Lady,* in which a cockney flower girl is transformed into an elegant society lady by a misanthropic scholar of dialects, who, of course, falls in love with her along the way. Psychology has picked up this metaphor to speak of the *Pygmalion effect,* in which people's belief in the positive attributes of others often strengthens those very attributes. Of course, there is also a reverse Pygmalion effect, in which people's belief in others' negative attributes brings them out.

The Pygmalion effect would predict an outcome for *King Lear* different from the one Shakespeare wrote. The trust vested by Lear in his older daughters should inspire them to honorable behavior, while the trust withdrawn from Cordelia should undermine her commitment. Neither occurs in *Lear,* nor need it in real life. The Pygmalion effect is perfectly real but not perfectly reliable. This is why it's smart to trust a little too much, which does not risk a great deal, but not to trust a lot too much.

BETTER CONFLICT THROUGH TRUST

Maybe love and marriage really do go together like a horse and carriage. But whatever the case with love and marriage, conflict and trust certainly do go together, a conceptual marriage smoother than many real ones. People are warned never to expect to change their partners' characters for the better, but trust can do exactly that—convert conflict from destructive to creative, or, in the words of this book, from regressive to progressive.

How? Here are the three archetypes of conflict resolution identified earlier, matched up with three areas of trust:

Archetype		Area of Trust
Consensus resolution	↔	Trust in the common vision (a cause, mission, collaborative relationship, etc.)
Civil resolution	↔	Trust in the civil mechanism (bosses, voting, courts, etc.)
Power resolution	↔	Trust only yourself and yours (close family, in-group, ethnic subgroup, etc.)

Note that the arrows go both ways. Not only does trusting the common vision encourage (although not guarantee) consensus resolutions but effective consensus resolutions also build trust in the common vision. Not only does trusting the civil mechanism encourage civil resolutions, but effective civil resolutions build trust in the civil mechanism. And, less laudably, not only does trusting just yourself and yours encourage power resolutions of conflicts with outsiders, but power resolutions encourage trusting just yourself and yours.

TRUST IN THE COMMON VISION

When you trust in the common vision, you believe that there is a joint sense of what's important. Your goals and the goals of others in the group are the same or, at the least, complementary. Moreover, you believe that the people have considerable commitment to this common vision with its shared or complementary goals and can pursue it with some success—commitment and capability, the two earmarks of trust.

It's a commonplace in the corporate world that a well-articulated and sustained common vision can help to advance an organization. James Brian Quinn writes in *Intelligent Enterprise* (New York: Free Press, 1992) of the impact of *frontier visions* that reach toward the future with a spirit of innovation. One example is the classic DuPont slogan, "Better things for better living through chemistry." Another is Intel's commitment to operating as a revolutionary force in society, often reiterated by Gordon Moore and Robert Noyce, two of Intel's founders. Quinn emphasizes that slogans are only an entryway into more elaborated values and philosophies that sustain engagement.

When there's trust in a common vision, many conflicts are not fundamentally adversarial. Yes, Molly says tomatoes and Mabel says potatoes. They argue about whether tomatoes or potatoes should prevail. However, when their debate concerns matters of means within the overarching ends and general approach defined by the common vision, their shared commitment provides a basis for working through the conflict: Will tomatoes or potatoes serve the common vision better? A consensus may well emerge. Certainly it's worth trying.

This does not mean that groups with a common vision need only consensus resolutions. Even with a common vision, people will have their individual interests, and of course some conflicts will reflect these. Molly and Mabel may find that even extended and mediated discussion does not break their tomato-potato deadlock. It may be that some kind of civil mechanism will be needed—voting, the head chef's decision, or whatever else. However, their differing perspectives on how to serve the common vision at least enrich the discourse in the group, contributing to creative conflict and helping to avoid the trap of groupthink.

Research on creative versus destructive conflict supports this picture. Morton Deutsch, the noted social psychologist, developed an important distinction between two kinds of interdependence: promotive and contrient. *Promotive interdependence* applies to situations in which people are interdependent in synergistic ways. They share goals, or their goals are complementary, so one person's pursuit of goals helps to advance another's. A common vision helps to create promotive interdependence by establishing broad shared goals. *Contrient interdependence* refers to situations of inherent conflict: One person's pursuit of goals inherently gets in the way of another's.

Dean Tjosvold, in an analysis building on Deutsch's concepts, connects these notions of interdependence to creative versus destructive conflict. When conflict occurs within promotive interdependence, it tends to be productive. Because people's goals are the same or synergistically linked, their arguments concern means; their divergence enriches the mix of possibilities toward pursuing the goals, and consensus, or near consensus, or at least amicable resolutions are likely. Tjosvold argues that experience with positive conflict in such contexts even helps to resolve psychological conflicts internal to individuals. In contrast, in contexts of contrient interdependence, the circumstances are fundamentally adversarial. Although the conflict may generate multiple perspectives helpful to the larger community, the conflict itself will lead to winners and losers, or to the half-win, half-lose of compromises. Tjosvold reviews considerable evidence for the creative consequences of promotive interdependence and the destructive consequences of contrient interdependence, reporting that such findings have been found across cultures, not just within Western cultures.

At this juncture, the practical person might comment, "I get it. But what do I do? The common vision is either there or not, and if it's not, so much for consensus resolutions. I'm calling my lawyer."

Fold your cell phone up and put it back in your pocket. To say that the common vision is either there or not oversimplifies things. Common visions are built by people to meet needs. A dispute among communities and corporations about water rights might lead to a comprehensive vision for conservation and sharing, to everyone's long-term benefit by avoiding the notorious *tragedy of the commons,* in which overuse of a resource harms all. Manufacturers promoting competing formats for media such as CDs or videotapes often do well to construct a common vision of the market and its needs and a common standard to serve it, else the confusion about what works in whose machines and uncertainty about what standard will win in the end stand in the way of strong market development. Thoughtful discussion helps; visionary leadership helps (see Chapter 5); shared experiences over time help. To favor progressive conflict and boost the chances of consensus, one can strive to build and fine-tune such visions.

Even when people share a common vision, they may need to be reminded of it in times of conflict. Mabel may find herself more at odds with Molly than their shared commitments warrant. While they hover over precisely how the molehill should be built, the mountain they share looms behind them unseen.

One enemy of a common vision is the language of blame. Say Mabel and Molly disagree sharply on how some changes in staff responsibility should have been handled. Mabel blames Molly for insensitivity to people's concerns. Molly blames Mabel for ignoring the need to get on expeditiously with an urgent matter. In their book *Difficult Conversations* (New York: Penguin, 1999), Douglas Stone, Bruce Patton, and Sheila Heen contrast two archetypes: the *blame system* of conducting disputes and the *contribution system*. The language of contribution asks Mabel and Molly both to speak about how their actions contributed to the situation. It doesn't deny that one or the other might be more responsible, but it does suggest that in complex organizational settings events rarely depend on a single individual's behavior. The language of blame is a regressive archetype, the language of contribution a progressive one.

Another enemy of building a common vision is categorical trust, the sort exemplified by Lear's tragedy of trust, the kind that says you're either with us or against us, on the bus or off the bus. Besides cultivating a common vision, it's also important to foster reasonable expectations. Of course people are not going to agree 100 percent, not even on the details of the vision. Of course people's goals are not going to be perfectly aligned. With reflective rather than the purist categorical trust, substantial alignment is enough.

Even situations that appear fundamentally adversarial can sometimes be reframed to foreground a common vision. This is exactly the strategy of negotiation based on interests advanced by Fischer and Ury (see Chapter 2). Recall that an archetype of negotiation from positions typically dominates negotiations. Each side takes a position; either the sides reach stalemate, one side gives in, or the two sides compromise. In contrast, negotiation from interests asks each side to articulate interests—areas of need and concern—toward identifying common and complementary interests. Often, although certainly not always, the result is a joint problem that both sides can work on creatively—in other words, a common vision both can trust and pursue. This common vision makes consensus solutions rather than adversarial solutions much more likely.

Finally, the mutually reinforcing relationship between trust in the common vision and consensus resolutions deserves emphasis. Every successful consensus resolution, even a small one, increases one's sense of common vision. It's worth working case by case for consensus resolutions, to build an abiding trust in their prospects.

TRUST IN THE CIVIL MECHANISM

Legal canons in the United States ask that judges avoid not only impropriety but also the *appearance* of impropriety. You'd think avoiding the real thing would be good enough, but it's not.

Why not? It's a matter of symbolic conduct. Trust in the system is crucial, and even the suggestion of bias will undermine that trust. When you trust the civil mechanism—whether it's a judge, the boss, a vote, or whatever else—you believe that the civil process of resolving conflicts proceeds without bias. Your side and the other side get a fair shake. The process reflects the merits of the issues and the needs of the group, not those of special interests. You also believe that the process advances in a reasonably efficient way toward a reasonable resolution. Here again the two earmarks of trustworthiness appear—both the commitment of the civil mechanism to doing a good job and its capability of doing so.

Civil mechanisms face a special challenge in sustaining your trust. Your standard cannot be, "Always decides in favor of me, the torch of truth, the leader of light, the womb of wisdom!" When the director approves someone else's plan, you can't automatically conclude that the director is biased. When your favored candidate loses the vote, you can't automatically conclude that the vote was fixed. In general, when the civil mechanism decides against you, you may feel that it made a mistake in that instance, but you still can hope to feel that it made a reasonable mistake, while nonetheless paying fair and thoughtful attention to the matter at hand.

Francis Fukuyama's book *Trust* (London: Hamish Hamilton, 1995) underscores the importance of trust to productive societies. Fukuyama draws a distinction between high-trust and low-trust societies. In high-trust societies, people pretty much trust one another as well as the social institutions—schools, businesses, and government agencies. Both peccadilloes and mortal sins occur from time to time, but by and large the customs and practices of those cultures maintain people's trust, and, when they do not, corrections follow. Fukuyama praises their customs with the apt phrase, the art of association.

In low-trust societies, people can trust only those close to them and cannot trust the social institutions. The legal system and other governmental institutions may be corrupt or grievously inefficient, or, for a double somersault into the swamp, both. Low-trust societies make life much harder. Recall that a basic function of trust is simplifying life. We can move forward without worrying about those matters when we have a basis for trust, concentrating instead on other matters. Trust is liberating. Reciprocally, epidemic lack of trust is profoundly impairing, a burden both to human well-being and practical productivity.

What does it take to build trust in the civil mechanism? Often, getting started means putting into place a civil mechanism where none yet operates, so there's no civil mechanism to trust. Getting one going may mean establishing policies for handling certain kinds of conflicts; articulating rules, laws, or policies; defining which boss deals with what disputes in a command hierarchy; and the like.

Typically, civil mechanisms explicitly forbid power resolutions. If your neighbor has borrowed your lawn mower and not returned it, you cannot simply break into the neighbor's garage and take it back. Leave your crowbar in the basement and call the police. Even optional civil mechanisms often help, as in voluntary mediation of conflicts or a deliberate choice to involve the judgment of a group in the hope of breaking a stalemate that impairs moving forward.

Of course, simply putting a civil mechanism in place does not materialize the desired trust through some kind of social sorcery. Perhaps an organization establishes a director for a certain area, convenes a review panel to appraise particular lines of work, or creates a standing committee to rule on a range of disputes. From the first, the director or panel or committee should be free of obvious signs of bias. You don't want a director who is known to play favorites. You don't want a panel or committee that is obviously loaded toward one or another narrow viewpoint. Over time, the civil mechanism must establish a track record for fairness, reasonableness, and efficiency. All three are not just practical accomplishments but symbolic conduct, testifying through action to the trustworthiness of the system.

Perhaps the hardest situation to deal with is a sick civil mechanism, one either stained by corruption or tattered by inefficiency and obtuseness. This is a true dragon case, and one revisited at the end of the chapter.

TRUST ONLY IN YOURSELF AND YOURS

When you trust only yourself and yours—those very close, such as family, immediate in-group, gang members, ethnic subgroup, and so on—you have confidence in your commitment to your mutual interests and your mutual ability to advance those interests and not much confidence in any outsider's inclination or ability to help.

Trusting only in yourself and yours is profoundly adversarial. It leads to power resolutions of all sizes, from firecrackers to Armageddon. Over and over, society has responded to this insupportable risk through a basic strategy of trust: Establish civil mechanisms, make them trustworthy, and require people to abide by them. Even groups that have little trust in outsiders or larger civil mechanisms normally have both some civil mechanisms and patterns of individual trust within the group. Otherwise, they cannot survive for long as groups.

Business practices move toward trusting only in oneself when they flout civil structures designed to keep order in the world of transactions. Appropriately, many examples concern antitrust cases— for instance, a 1946 conspiracy among major tobacco companies, who were purchasing tobacco not needed for production in order to make it unavailable to smaller companies; the 1984 breakup of AT&T for monopolizing carrier services and equipment provision; and the case against Microsoft for systematically undermining Netscape's presence in the Internet browser market by giving away the Internet Explorer browser preinstalled in the Windows operating system.

None of this argues against aggressive competition but rather warns of the chaotic world that pure power resolutions lead to, unless civil mechanisms step in to squelch them.

A Green Thumb for Trust

To sum up, trust is the fiber of progressive rather than regressive conflict. Trustworthy civil mechanisms and, where possible, trust in a common vision leading to consensus resolutions help to convert conflict into resolutions that are productive and even creative.

℞ Some simple rules of thumb for cultivating trust toward progressive conflict:

Building Trust in a Common Vision

* When there does not seem to be a strong common vision, try to construct one.
* In times of conflict, foster the language of contribution rather than that of blame.
* In times of conflict, remind one another of the common vision, lest it get lost in the brushfire.
* Try to reframe seemingly adversarial situations in terms of a common vision, as in negotiating from interests rather than positions.
* Strive for a history of thoughtful consensus resolutions (not groupthink), because this reinforces the sense of common vision and fosters further consensus resolutions.

Building Trust in a Civil Mechanism

* When conflicts not readily resolved by consensus occur frequently and do obvious harm, establish civil mechanisms to deal with them. Different mechanisms (boss, vote, judge, jury, etc.) are appropriate to different contexts.
* Create mechanisms without obvious initial bias and strive for a good track record, both of which carry enormous symbolic significance.

* Use the civil mechanisms to forbid power resolutions that result in serious harm to life, limb, property, or abrogation of rights.

IN GENERAL

* Recognize that trust is fragile, whether it's trust in the common vision, in civil mechanism, or in anything else. Avoid actions that break trust yourself, and create disincentives for actions that break trust.

* Remember that trust concerns not only the commitment but the capability of what's trusted. Strive for consensus and civil processes that are not only fair but thoughtful and efficient.

* Try to foster reflective trust rather than categorical trust, which is so brittle that it easily falls into old King Lear's sad tragedy of trust.

HERE THERE BE SUPERDRAGONS

Developmental leaders face no greater challenge than dealing with tangles of conflict and trust. Dragons thrive in those dark forests. Some of those dragons are merely bad, and some of them are really bad.

To acknowledge some merely bad dragons, there's groupthink, Brownian motion, and downspiraling, three pathologies of collaboration from the previous chapter. Consensus resolution of conflicts, certainly a collaborative process, easily falls into these hazards, and people then lose trust in the process. But groups can minimize these pathologies—for instance, by using some of the tactics discussed in the last chapter. Related problems are inefficiency and poor thinking in civil mechanisms. Committees can dither, lawyers can use various tactics to delay judgments, and individuals can procrastinate on difficult decisions. It can be challenging to streamline and fine-tune civil processes. However, at least efforts toward reform are more likely to meet with inertia than with active resistance.

Continuing with some merely bad dragons, there's silent conflict: Morton and Merton can't seem to coordinate their separate areas of responsibility for a particular mission, but it's really all about the younger Morton's promotion over Merton two years before. Such circumstances call for looking beneath the surface to find and soothe the sources of the malaise—not easy, but approachable—unless you have *superdragons*.

Yes, there are the merely bad dragons, but then there are the really bad dragons, the superdragons, the ones that are truly rough and risky to deal with. I nominate three: *broken trust, corruption,* and *animosity*. For all three, sometimes you can help, but sometimes there's not much you can do.

BROKEN TRUST

Trust is like Humpty Dumpty, much easier to break than to put back together again. Once a serious breach of trust occurs, repairing it can be a matter of years or never. This happens at all scales, from partners in marriage to partner nations. Some of the world's most enduring conflicts feed on a long history of distrust, with individual memories of moments when the other side broke what little trust there was going back decades, and social memories going back centuries.

The easy-to-break, hard-to-repair character of trust underscores the dangers of categorical trust mentioned earlier. Categorical trust is inherently brittle, because by angelizing the other it sets itself up for trouble. Categorical trust makes Humpty Dumpty particularly brittle.

So important and troublesome a superdragon certainly deserves taming. One way forward is the Osgood proposal, fashioned in the 1950s as a tool of diplomacy but applicable to broken trust of all sorts. The Osgood proposal recommends three steps toward rebuilding trust.

1. Party A announces some conciliatory action and carries that action forward reliably. In an international conflict, this might mean declaring and maintaining a cease-fire for a limited period regardless of Party B's actions. In an office conflict, Party A might declare, "I've been griping endlessly

about Party B's approach to this. I'm not sure that's really productive, and I'm just going to hang it up for a while."

2. Party A then invites Party B to join the effort at reconciliation in some fashion. In the international conflict, Party B might mirror the cease fire. In the office conflict, Party B might make more room for comparing and contrasting different plans rather than just pushing one.

3. Only when several conciliatory attempts fail does Party A desist. Even then, Party A tries simply to match or mirror the other party's negative actions without escalating retaliation or rhetoric.

The Osgood proposal is not magic, but it embodies an essential insight: Trust cannot be rebuilt without one party taking a chance. This is both the strength and the weakness of the proposal—the weakness because often neither party feels politically or emotionally able to make conciliatory gestures and sustain them through two or three cycles of rebuff.

CORRUPTION

A colleague once told me about a deep dilemma at a major corporation where he had worked. You would probably know its name, but let's call it Mordred Enterprises, named after Mordred, the betrayer of King Arthur, and also because its initials neatly spell ME. The top executives of ME were all about "me." They comprised an old-boy network full of favoritism. The next tier of management and on down generally proceeded in a more balanced way, as best they could within the sometimes odd decrees from the top tier. The old boys were not awful people, nor were they doing anything wildly illegal. Nonetheless, when conflicts arose about courses of action for the company, the kinds of civil resolution they provided were often corrupt—shaped by their "me" rather than by the true interests of the company.

In general, corruption of civil process is a deeply regressive archetype of interaction, one that leads to deliberately biased knowledge processing with negative symbolic conduct that can easily destroy the solidarity of the organization or community. Basically, it's a form of parasitism. The people involved are enjoying benefits of their positions that are not truly theirs to enjoy, at the cost of the general well-being of the collective and its members.

So what to do? At least in mild cases of corruption, it's tempting to adopt a therapeutic perspective. If only we could foster enlightenment, help the participants to see the mischief they do, recognize the error of their ways, put the past behind them, turn over a new leaf.

Yes, but how many therapists does it take to change a light bulb? The classic answer: Only one, but the light bulb really has to want to change. The fundamental problem with corruption is that the people don't want to change. Why should they? They have a good thing going.

Rather than a therapeutic approach, a surgical approach has more promise—do a little cutting and pasting, rearrange the structure of the situation. This usually means firing someone, moving someone, convicting someone, reconstituting certain groups, redefining certain processes, making visible practices that haven't been visible before so they can't be misused, that sort of thing.

What makes corruption a superdragon is the inherent difficulty of such tactics. Remember, this light bulb does *not* want to change. Whereas problems of efficiency or thoughtfulness can be, and sometimes are, solved from within, problems of corruption almost never are. Resolving them requires a power base higher up in the organization— or outside the organization, as in the case of legal interventions. Often, invoking such a power base involves whistle blowing from someone below who is not party to the corruption, a risky action that frequently backfires. And often there simply is no relevant powerbase to turn to. Remember again Mordred Enterprises. The members of the top echelon were not doing anything particularly illegal, but they were making decisions that were not in the best interests of the company. Many members of management a level down were acutely aware of the problem, but who do you turn to?

ANIMOSITY

Having made much of *King Lear*, perhaps we should make something of *Othello*. Lear's daughters Goneril and Regan show callousness toward Lear, but Iago, villain of *Othello,* shows *animosity* toward the Moor.

Animosity is worse than callousness. Animosity goes beyond putting one's own interests first, never mind who gets in the way. Animosity entails the active desire to harm another person or group. Animosity often arises from a history of repeatedly broken trust.

The entrenched ethnic and historical conflicts of today's world— Israel and Palestine, Northern Ireland, Cyprus, and so on—all involve a bubbling animosity. It's not just that people on each side want a fair shake from now on. Many of them feel that they have been injured by the other side for a long time and want to hurt the other side back. Likewise, in Shakespeare's play, Iago resents Othello and wants to hurt him, to bring him down, and so he does.

Animosity is a wildly regressive archetype of interaction. In its most extreme form, animosity becomes especially frightening: People and groups are eager to harm others even at the cost of certain harm to themselves. The fanatics who crashed airplanes into the two World Trade Center towers and the Pentagon in September 2001 are a dramatic example.

Animosity within communities and organizations rarely takes such virulent form. Still, it inevitably arises. Individuals or groups just don't like one another—often because of perceived offenses or sometimes simply because of stylistic differences or rivalry—and they dislike one another badly enough to want to do each other harm, so they undertake actions that generate subtle or obvious conflict. They start rumors about the other party, they speak against the other party's plans for no other reason than to thwart them, they sabotage the other's initiatives by gaining control of key resources, and so on. Such internecine warfare not only does needless harm in itself but tends to poison the atmosphere of the group.

So what to do? As with mild cases of corruption, it's tempting to adopt a therapeutic approach, to try to lead the warring parties toward an enlightened tolerance, if not amity. But, again, this light bulb does *not* want to change. The parties at odds do not simply want a fair peace—as they see it, there is no peace that is fair to both sides. They don't want to get past it all; they want to get at one another.

Again, a surgical approach has more short-term promise, whatever may be accomplished in the long term. A surgical approach restructures the situation to prevent the harm without expecting to quell the animosity. This can mean requiring civil conduct in public settings, making the actions either party might take to harm the other unacceptable, perhaps subject to punishment. Often it simply means keeping the combatants apart to limit their opportunities. They work on different things, meet with different people, and so on.

Such tactics help with this dragon, but a couple of factors make it a superdragon. First of all, these tactics do not so much resolve the conflict as contain it. It's still there, ready to breathe flame again in the right circumstances. Second, one can easily miss the presence of this dragon. The conflict of the moment is not the real conflict, or it's only the tip of the iceberg. Yes, Isaac protests that Joseph's plan will prove far too costly, but Isaac is basically out to get Joseph, and that's what it's really about. Yes, West Eastland sides with North Southland on the issue of the trade embargoes on South Northland, but West Eastland has no real interest one way or another, only a long-standing enmity with South Northland. The enemy of my enemy is my friend.

An Ounce of Prevention

Once full-grown, the superdragons of broken trust, corruption, and animosity are vigorous survivors—much better that they hardly get started at all. It's naive to imagine that the round-table model of organizational intelligence or any other framework can establish settings that are trust-secure, corruption-proof, and animosity-free. Intrinsic characteristics of human nature spawn these dragons. However, one certainly can create settings that discourage them and stunt their growth when they do occur.

 Two basic principles toward discouraging and limiting broken trust, corruption, and animosity are: (1) Make it practically difficult and risky, and (2) make it countercultural.

This may be old news, but at least it's good news, and worth a couple of paragraphs. The law, including lawlike policies within organizations, is one classic approach to making broken trust, corruption, and animosity practically difficult and risky. Contracts, for instance, articulate each party's intentions and obligations and allow for legal enforcement. While the fundamental relationship between the parties ideally reaches much further than the document and involves interpersonal trust, the document functions as a back-up system to ensure clarity of expectations and discourage blatant violations.

Naturally, this works only when the law itself can be trusted to function fairly and effectively. Besides laws and policies, physical devices, such as locks and TV monitors, as well as technical practices, such as systematic bookkeeping and auditing, have enormous importance. Standard procedures of open discussion, shared rather than secret information, and the like also contribute. Such devices and practices make corrupt and harmful acts more difficult to execute, at least without exposure.

As to the countercultural aspect, making breaches of trust, corruption, and animosity countercultural, not considered good behavior, frowned upon, is a powerful force—but it's not a force that can be taken for granted. In many settings, all three are expected and even acceptable. In Fukuyama's low-trust societies, breaches of trust are commonplace. In some settings, corruption is taken for granted, a way of life that even has its own rough rules. Not to participate is naïve. In some cultures, animosity thrives. You are expected to have strong, polarized views, to hate your rivals, to take personal revenge for supposed wrongs. There is an intolerance of tolerance itself.

In the business world, Enron again presents a tempting example of culture gone awry. Enron executives sought to pack the company with bright young aggressive executives and promoted them rapidly according to their success in closing deals, without a lot of attention to how sound the deals were in the long term and with a high tolerance for practices that skirted legal boundaries. Inevitably, such policies would create a culture that was high in competition and selfishness, with people who were neither particularly trusting nor trustworthy.

This brings us back to the theme of trust in a common vision.

One of the simplest ways to immunize a culture against broken trust, corruption, and animosity is to build a common vision. A common vision makes all three look small, because they undermine it.

Of course, a common vision *within* a select group sometimes takes the form of a common enemy *outside* the group. Adolph Hitler knew this all too well. Superdragons indeed.

TOOLBOX

* *Too much trust* and *too little conflict* are both threats to organizational intelligence. Watch out for naïve trust and feel-good peace. Strive for reflective trust and creative conflict.

* *Keep an eye out for the archetypes*—the tragedy of categorical trust, with its angelizing and demonizing, and the resolution of conflicts through consensus, civil mechanisms, and power.

* *Don't trust your trust.* Beware of angelizing and demonizing. Discourage it in others, and cultivate reflective trust.

* *Remember the Pygmalion principle*—trust a little (but not a lot) too much.

* *Consensus resolution* and *trust in a common vision* are partners. Build each through the other.

* *Civil resolution* and *trust in the civil mechanism* are partners. Build each through the other.

* *Cultivate consensus and civil resolutions of conflict.* Handled well, either one can make conflicts progressive rather than regressive.

* *Suit the approach to the circumstances.* Attractive as consensus sounds, it's not always feasible or preferable. Many conflicts lend themselves more to a civil resolution.

* *Avoid power resolutions* of conflict, with their very negative knowledge processing and symbolic conduct.

* *Beware the superdragons* of broken trust, corruption, and animosity. Work to make them practically difficult and countercultural.

* *Repair broken trust* through systematic conciliatory action, as in the Osgood proposal.

9

CLIMBING TOWARD CAMELOT

PRESTO CHANGE-O

Try this experiment. Pick up any issue of the popular business magazine *Fast Company*. Turn to a random page. If the page happens to be all ads, keep turning for a page with an article. Now take stock of what you find.

Here is my report for eight random pages from a particular issue of *Fast Company:*

* Unlearning in order to be creative
* Making work fun
* Clarifying what you think and rethinking
* Managing fear
* Dealing with resistance
* Innovative ways of dominating a market
* How not to play it safe
* Transformational leadership

But never mind my report. Continue with your own inventory of the issues you picked. Examine the articles. Examine the text boxes.

You will notice something quite intriguing: *Fast Company* is made of advice.

I tried the same experiment with a popular health magazine. Same result: It was made of advice.

Presto change-o. Today, in a world increasingly intricate and sometimes dismayingly problematic, we have an open love affair with change. We applaud and often join the crusades for superior leadership, greater health, better government, improved education, thriving economies, and more humane and effective communities and organizations of various sorts. We are not credulous like Voltaire's satiric figure Candide, who took the current state of world affairs to be the best it could be and kept making excuses for it. We are critical. We see the problems and devise solutions. We view today merely as a foyer to a brighter future—if only we can figure out how to step forward.

There is no lack of advice in this book, either, although it's not as thick and fast as that of *Fast Company*. The round-table model analyzes how progressive interactions build organizational intelligence and encourages people to step in that direction by giving communicative feedback, exercising inquiry-centered leadership, avoiding coblaboration, and cultivating trust in a common vision and civil processes. A brighter future awaits groups, teams, organizations, and communities, a future with round-table interactions that foster collectives smarter in both the cognitive and humanistic senses.

Most of the advice in *Fast Company* sounds pretty reasonable, and I hope that the counsel in this book sounds reasonable, too. Certainly, the analysis tries to reflect cognitive and social fundamentals of the human condition; however, it's all nothing but talk until you do something about it. There are some huge wart-ugly dragons under the bridge between talk and action. The dragons collectively amount to what we might call:

☞ *The idea-action gap:* A name for the wide and persistent gulf between good principles and practical action displayed by individuals and organizations.

Scholars of organizational life Jeffrey Pfeffer and Robert Sutton have another name for this: the *knowing-doing gap,* which doubles as the title of their book (Boston: Harvard Business School Press, 2000).

The calamitous reality is that people get lots of advice and act on hardly any of it—even good advice, even advice to yourself that you really truly believe in, say advice to quit smoking or lose weight. People receive the advice like a priest's blessing, they say presto change-o, but nothing much happens. The everyday wisdom of folk psychology gives plentiful testimony to the omnipresence of the idea-action gap. It's the New Year's Resolution effect. And "There's many a slip twixt the cup and the lip." And "Talk is cheap." And "The road to hell is paved with good intentions."

As with individuals, so with organizations: Guidelines for building stronger teams, arriving at common visions, or restructuring governance see far more talk than action. Chapter 6 introduced four knowledge processes fundamental to organizations—generating knowledge, communicating knowledge, integrating knowledge, and acting on knowledge. In some respects, acting on knowledge is the toughest of them all. We can do research and spread the results around and formulate plans, but until we actually step out to make changes, everyone can maintain the roles and rhythms they're used to. Speaking of hot spots in individual and community life, change is the hot spot of hot spots.

In their book *Clued Up* (London: Pearson Education, 2002) business authors Alan Robertson and Graham Abbey compare the idea-action gap to a hostile environment, such as a jungle, filled not only with evident obstructions but "unseen and unobvious threats, wild things, predators, noise and movements that we don't recognize." Are they dramatizing? A bit, they confess, but they want to emphasize that many of the features behind idea-action gaps are not obvious, especially not at first—features such as novelty and complexity, others' incomprehension, changing circumstances and the way they sometimes leave us behind, and people's wariness or outright resistance. A central point in *Clued Up* is that you have to look for the clues in order to bridge the gap.

Of course, the gap is not always so great. Advice can sometimes prove wonderfully useful. It serves best when we're relatively new to something, but not so new that the advice won't make sense, when we don't bring a lot of baggage and can readily benefit from guidelines. Advice sputters out in our minds like a wet fuse when it asks us to redirect deeply ingrained beliefs or patterns of behavior, as in losing weight, quitting smoking, adopting more democratic stances when we have autocratic habits, practicing appropriate authority and leadership when we tend to be too democratic, listening when we so much love to talk, trusting at least a little when we lean toward distrust, and so on. In other words, the idea-action gap is most troublesome when we want to change well-established archetypes. Unfortunately, changing well-established archetypes is exactly what cultivating organizational intelligence demands. This crusade brings us into direct confrontation with the dragons under the bridge.

How can the bridge from idea to action be crossed to foster progressive rather than regressive interactions and build more intelligent organizations and communities? How can we make round the tables where we sit, and promote round tables in other settings? Paradoxically, all this chapter can do about such heady questions is offer more talk—but the right kind of talk can help to make a difference.

POETRY IN MOTION

Presto change-o! Open Sesame! Abracadabra! Shazam! These are the incantations that transform reality—but only for stage magicians and fantasy novelists. What are the truly potent words? What can one say to oneself or others that makes a difference in what we do, especially a difference toward more progressive patterns of interaction in groups, teams, organizations, and communities? The right kinds of talk are very important in bridging the idea-action gap. It's worth distinguishing two manners of speech that often get mixed up: *explanation theories* and *action theories.*

Explanation theories are theories that explain things—the orbits of the planets, the meaning of *King Lear*, the social functions of trust, the self-adjusting character of free markets, or the tribal roots of hierarchy in organizations. They are the cordon bleu of the academic life. Their deployment and defense are the main dishes of erudite journals and technical conferences.

However, explanation theories serve up ideas in a highly abstract form, rather detached from practice. Newton's laws of motion explain a lot, but write no clear recipe for placing a human being on the moon or even racing a bobsled. The law of supply and demand

and the notion of free markets explain a lot, but write no specific formulas for antitrust legislation or import and export taxes. The principles are relevant but need subtle reasoning and rich experience to translate into specific practical forms.

Action theories are theories that tell us directly how to accomplish things. These are what fill the pages of *Fast Company.* These are theories about getting results. Sometimes they take the form of edicts, sometimes folk tales, sometimes parables, sometimes jokes, sometimes slogans, sometimes steps, sometimes checklists. From the Ten Commandments to Ten Tips for Buying a Home, we are counseled to cope with the complexity and uncertainty of life's missions through such action theories. Advising ourselves and others about what path to follow is not our only tactic, but it is one of the most universal, conspicuous, and diverse forms of education.

Explanation theories and action theories are both immensely useful, but in different rhythms. Practices such as planning a project, running a meeting, conducting a negotiation, or giving feedback are best informed by streamlined action theories in the foreground, with explanation theories in the background.

Which brings us back to the idea-action gap. One fundamental reason why ideas fall short of action is that they do not offer very good action theories. Everyday experience logs plenty of evidence of this. Often, the advice we get is an explanation theory disguised as an action theory. It pretends to guide action in the moment, but it's really a very abstract principle at great remove from practical action, like Newton's laws and the bobsled. When people have time to stand back and think things out, it can be powerful, but it's almost useless in the moment, on the ground.

Another way ideas can fall short of action is to call for too much of it—less of a map than a maze, too many steps, too many concepts, hard to remember, hard to use. The advice is not lean, pointed, and energizing enough to focus our efforts well.

One can sum this up metaphorically as follows:

☛ *Action poetry:* The language of real change needs not just explanation theories, or even action theories, but good action poetry—action theories that are built for action— simple, memorable, and evocative.

Action poetry has a back-pocket quality. Like combs and keys, an action theory well expressed is not cumbersome but compact, not complicated but straightforward. It is handy and ready at hand. It helps us to act simply and effectively. Sometimes the language is expressive, even metaphorical, sometimes simply spare and to the point, but either way evocative. It functions with the compressed and compelling efficiency of poetry.

Let's bring back an earlier example, Fisher and Ury's notion of negotiating from interests rather than negotiating from positions (Chapter 2). The fully decked out strategy involves many ribbons and bows and a rich rationale, but the fundamental idea can be said in five words: Negotiate from interests, not positions. The words emphasize a simple contrast that in itself can take you some distance. Another example from earlier is communicative feedback (Chapter 3), which leads with clarification, continues by identifying and honoring positive features, and only then turns to concerns and suggestions—simple, lean, and direct.

A look at various organizational change initiatives warns that good action poetry is often in short supply. Many models, theories, and frameworks designed to illuminate organizational life do just that—if one has hours to stand back and think things out; if one can seize time to engage members in extended development of ideas, perspectives and practices; and if people can learn to pause, reflect, and select their actions thoughtfully in the midst of the rush. But these are hard standards to meet. The words and concepts do not call up mental snapshots that make the ideas memorable and actionable in real time and in stressful situations. They lack that back-pocket handiness.

I've tried to write this book with such challenges in mind. The story is not simple, but there are a number of conceptual and verbal hooks that should help. Top-level ideas like knowledge processing and symbolic conduct or progressive versus regressive archetypes can be used directly in a commonsense way, as Chapter 6 discusses toward the end. You can quickly and intuitively assess whether a conversation, meeting, or exchange of e-mails seems progressive, whether it appears to be processing knowledge well, whether the symbolic conduct is positive or negative, and what archetypes seem to be in play.

The accounts of group decision making, negotiation, feedback, leadership, collaboration, trust, and conflict recall familiar situations and emphasize important categorical contrasts. Remember, for instance, the leadership archetypes of answer-centered leadership, inquiry-centered leadership, vision-centered leadership, and leadership by leaving alone. Or remember the conflict resolution archetypes of consensus resolution, civil resolution, and power resolution. It shouldn't be too hard to recall what these mean and why they are important. The contrasts underscore the threat and damage done by regressive archetypes and the gains inherent in progressive archetypes. They recommend relatively simple structural transformations of practical action in the progressive direction.

All of which might do the job all by itself, if only pretty good action poetry were enough. However, the reality of the idea–action gap demands more than pretty good action poetry. It requires agents of transformation who are ready and willing to act in progressive ways. Moreover, sustained impact calls for microcultures of progressive interaction. The next two sections bring these points to life.

THE ONE-EYED WOMAN

A colleague of mine—we could call her Guinevere in the Arthurian tradition, but let's make it Gwen for short—is a clever participant in the endless parades of meetings that march through both our lives. I'm always grateful when our parades intersect, because I know that this particular gathering has a much lower probability of meetingitis.

Gwen has a knack for moving things along gracefully. Even when not leading a meeting, she asks questions and makes suggestions that untangle the typical Gordian knots. She helps us to avoid Chapter 7's coblaboration, groupthink, and downspiraling, the triple threat of the conversational collective. She helps to bridge the idea–action gap and create a culture of progressive interactions.

Moreover, Gwen acts with awareness. It's not that she has read this book, but she has the knack. Recalling Robertson and Abbey's jungle metaphor for the idea–action gap, she's jungle-wise, clued up. Like a good sentry, she sees the threat creeping forward through the

bushes and blocks it. She sees in archetypes—the archetypes of interaction on which so much depends—although she probably wouldn't
call them that.

"In the country of the blind, the one-eyed man is king." This
principle certainly applies to life within communities and organizations. The reality is that most people are archetype-blind. Naturally,
people recognize the problems and opportunities of collective life in
a rough way, but they don't usually see analytically, in terms of specific patterns and alternatives. They do not detect the archetypes that
channel our interactions in sometimes more and sometimes less productive ways. When Alice tells Baker everything that's wrong with
his position and nothing that's right about it, neither Alice nor Baker
identifies the negative approach as an entrenched counterproductive
pattern of feedback. When Carol and Dwight begin to downspiral
into an epic discussion of a trivial point, most people simply bring
their own viewpoints to the fray.

Not Gwen. While keeping one eye on the substance of the conversation, she saves the other eye for the archetypes of interaction.
Where archetypes are concerned, she is the one-eyed woman in the
country of the blind.

One-eyed people like Gwen can be called *developmental leaders*.
They are, if not the kings and queens, at least the knights of fostering
more progressive interactions. Whether the boss of a group or simply
a participant, a developmental leader acts in ways that help the group
develop more progressive practices, and the beginning of this is seeing in archetypes.

Seeing in archetypes sounds like a splendid idea, but what does it
mean practically? The thought balloon of a developmental leader at a
critical moment might read like this:

SITUATION 1. Here we go again. We're trying to talk through
this complicated issue and there are too many of us and it's
going to take forever. It would be a lot better to divide the
problem up in a different way. (See Chapter 7.)

SITUATION 2. I notice he's not listening. His leadership is all
about his answers. How can we get more of the big questions on
the table and give them some serious attention? (See Chapter 5.)

SITUATION 3. Whoops. The conversation is getting a little nasty here. This is almost a fight. This time, I think we're beyond hope of a consensus. So what's a civil means of resolving it? Whose job is it really to decide? (See Chapter 8.)

Seeing in archetypes is cognitively quite a trick. It happens on the fly. Gwen participates in the substance of a meeting with one eye open for trouble. Seeing in archetypes is less a matter of inspection and dissection—who has time in the middle of interactions?—and more a matter of noticing what's going on. It involves a receptive alertness rather than stand-back analysis. It involves tracking loosely the knowledge processing and symbolic conduct of meetings, one-on-one conversations, instructional sessions, and other kinds of interactions. Seeing in archetypes is a little like driving while maintaining a conversation: Mostly you sustain the conversation, but you notice events important to steering—a ball rolls out on the street ahead of the car, or a light turns yellow ahead of you—and you make adjustments.

Beyond what one-eyed seeing involves, what does practical action entail? An ideal developmental leader tries to adopt progressive archetypes regardless of what others are doing. When giving feedback, the person offers communicative rather than negative or conciliatory feedback. When collaborating with others to start a project, the person brings to the table not fully developed ideas but trial balloons or sacrificial plans held loosely to avoid the dangers of early entrenchment. And so on, as described in previous chapters and summed up in their toolboxes.

Besides acting progressively, the developmental leader makes the archetypes visible to others. For instance, imagine a developmental leader who is not even a boss or facilitator but simply a participant in Situations 1, 2, and 3 described previously. The person concerned about talking through a complicated issue (Situation 1) might put an alternative plan on the table:

You know, we're ten minutes into this conversation and I'm seeing how complicated it is. It's a real conversational tangle. Often that's not the kind of thing we can talk through effectively from beginning to end. I wonder if it would make

sense to collect first impressions from everyone and then have
a small group try to untangle it for the next meeting.

The person concerned about the answer-centered leadership
(Situation 2) might gently try to win time for some of the difficult
issues:

> That direction certainly makes a lot of sense. Still, we all
> know that this is an important decision so let's be sure before
> we make it. A couple of puzzles that might really be serious
> have come up in passing. I wonder if we could commit our-
> selves to spending, say, half an hour taking a hard look at
> them, with everyone around the table pitching in. I've heard
> at least these puzzles. . . .

Of course, this might not divert the freight train, but maybe it would.
   The person concerned about the escalating argument (Situation
3) might reframe the situation:

> I know we usually try for consensus. And maybe we can still
> get there. But we seem to be pretty entrenched on opposite
> sides. Can we stand back for a minute and ask, in a pinch,
> how do matters like this get settled? Whose decision is it?
> And what does that imply for whether to talk about it more
> right now and how?

The true harvest of all this comes not from the particular occasion but the long-term effects. A developmental leader seeds the conversational soil, and others start noticing archetypes, too. A more
intelligent culture of conversation grows and thrives.
   To summarize:

☞ Marks of the developmental leader are:

* *Seeing in archetypes.*   The developmental leader tries to see
  for himself or herself on the fly what's going on.
* *Acting visibly.*   The developmental leader acts progressively
  and fairly conspicuously.

Thereby, developmental leaders function as exemplars, facilitators, and mentors within a group, helping to move it toward a progressive culture.

Of course, most developmental leaders have never read this book. They do not think in this vocabulary of progressive versus regressive interactions or knowledge processing and symbolic conduct. They're "naturals," like Gwen. In their own ways and in their own terms they have learned to see in archetypes and to act visibly in favor of progressive archetypes. There have always been occasional developmental leaders. The ideas in these pages can help us cultivate more of them.

None of this means that we should expect one-eyed people to be paragons. That one eye is probably not open all the time. I recall a particularly dedicated participant in a setting where colleagues and I worked—Liam, let's call him. Liam had the responsibility for managing an office with several other employees. He took a number of progressive practices to heart, but suffered from entrenched habits and showed a lot of backsliding. However, he built a strong spirit of confidence among his colleagues. When he slipped off the track, subordinates or not, they told him so in graceful ways, and he accepted the feedback with respect. Soon he and his office mates were working with new energy and trust. Even if the one-eyed person has that eye for archetypes open only part of the time, a lot can happen.

POCKET CHANGE

Imagine a group with a one-eyed person, one of those developmental leaders. The person stimulates a better pattern of interaction in the group, but still, that's just one eye on the archetypes. Now take a snapshot a couple of months later, when most individuals in the group have caught on to the art and craft of progressive interactions. This group no longer depends on a single person. People regulate themselves and one another naturally through mutual habit and commitment. When a facilitator is needed for a complicated conversation, almost anyone can facilitate pretty well. When matters of feedback, collaboration, or conflict come up, people deploy progressive archetypes through a kind of common will: "Let's use a ladder of feedback on this!" "Let's see if we can divide this problem up rather than talking it through." We have a microculture of progressive practice, a pocket of progressive change.

What do such pockets of change look like, what do they feel like, and how do they function? A measure of insight comes from a concept prominent in organizational theory today—communities of practice (COPs), an idea developed by Jean Lave and Etienne Wenger. A community of practice is a group of people who share a practice with one another and cooperatively support one another's mastery.

For example, Julian Orr, an anthropologist at Xerox's Palo Alto Research Center, undertook a classic study of Xerox machine technical representatives—basically, machine repairers. He found something surprising: Repair by the book did not play the critical role. Too many problems fell outside what had been coded and cataloged. The tech reps learned the most from one another. They shared lore over breakfast, lunch, and coffee. Sometimes one would go with another to untangle a tricky problem. In this way, sophisticated twists and turns of the craft of Xerox machine repair spread throughout the group. John Seely Brown and John Duguid emphasize how the tech reps communicated by storytelling, exchanging their war stories as Arthur's knights might have shared craft and lore through their tales of deeds done.

COPs provide a way of addressing one of the most frustrating dimension of professionalization, the extended development of expertise over time. They thereby offer an approach to one important aspect of knowledge management, the management of the knowledge resources of organizations. As with the Xerox tech reps, formal training programs are generally notorious for not accomplishing nearly as much as one would like. The just-in-time character of informal exchanges in a social network, the war stories told around the water cooler, and the tricks of the trade lubricated by a glass of beer often do the job better. For that very reason, the World Bank, Motorola, Johnson & Johnson, and many other organizations have initiated and supported widescale electronic COPs or other kinds of social networks with many of the same characteristics—and with significant success.

Communities of practice such as the Xerox tech reps tend to be somewhat progressive automatically. After all, a COP reflects a commitment to share lore through collegial relationships, and, in such a context, many of the typical troublesome archetypes of negative feedback—authority-based leadership, and so on—fall away.

Furthermore, the idea of COPs illuminates the pockets of progressive practice that developmental leaders create. Such microcultures *are* COPs, with a particular focus. The people involved do not necessary share a specialized professional activity, such as Xerox machine repair. They may have different roles within a larger organization—say, someone from finances, someone from sales, and someone from production—or even across different organizations. The practice they share is not their professional specialization but progressive practice, the art and craft of sustaining progressive interactions. The tips that they can give one another and the ways they can coordinate smoothly reflect this practice held in common. One might call such groups *communities of progressive practice.*

Here's an example of cultivating such communities. As mentioned in Chapter 3, a few years ago, some colleagues and I had the opportunity to work at length with the administration of a large university. We dealt not with deans and other academicians, but with hard-core administrators—financial officers, purchasing agents, lawyers, and buildings and grounds managers. The broad aim was to foster a more positive and effective culture of understanding and collaboration.

The administrators in this setting had considerable commitment, good heartedness, and enlightened leadership, but they also showed considerable rivalry, bureaucracy, and negative criticism of one another's ideas. Our principal strategy for building better community culture was to engage people in action projects. Action projects were short- to medium-term missions undertaken by individuals and small groups in the service of the institution. Some people sought to streamline various office processes, others to develop a scheme to sustain better contact with university alumnae, others to manage buildings and grounds resources better, others to improve human relations within their offices, others to make meetings more efficient, and many mixed goals such as these.

To lubricate the process, we introduced a number of progressive practices through workshops and minicourses. Because of the negative tendency in people's reactions to one another's ideas, communicative feedback proved particularly popular. We also provided a general group problem-solving scheme that discouraged Band-Aid solutions and promoted excavating and understanding the roots of problems.

Any such initiative is bound to have its ups and downs, but the general results were quite satisfying. Many of the action projects produced direct results that benefited the institution. Moreover, participants reported developing skills and attitudes with a progressive character, not only because these had been directly introduced through workshops and minicourses but also because the action projects provided concrete settings for trying them out and improving them.

Besides the positive trend, we observed something else very interesting: The changes were "pockety." They varied considerably from office to office and small group to small group. Much depended on the extent to which a power figure in the group embraced the enterprise and become a developmental leader. In principle, any of the small groups might have been influenced from without by other participants, or from above, because the top administrators supported the initiative strongly. In practice, each group was a little world unto itself, a table round or not so round, a pocket of change or not so much change. To generalize, it's reasonable to propose:

 ℞ *The law of local impact:* The influence of developmental leaders tends to be local, cultivating progressive practices most in groups directly involved with them.

The logic of this should be clear. People are likely to learn the most from a developmental leader by participating directly in a common enterprise. To be sure, a developmental leader in a central position can advocate progressive practices or even arrange for workshops, but this doesn't have as powerful an effect as working together.

HOW CHANGE TAKES FLIGHT

Pocket change is great for the pocket. But many organizations and communities are huge, encompassing dozens and hundreds of pockets—teams, offices, departments, sectors, boroughs, and so on—in complex relationships. Okay, your friendly neighborhood developmental leader helps to create a progressive culture in a pocket, and that's one idea–action gap bridged, but how can that add up to organizational intelligence writ large? The law of local impact not only expresses a potential but lays down a limit. A round table's worth is only that of a table, and one swallow does not a summer make.

Instead of swallows and summers, let's consider robins, titmice, and stealing milk. There is a story about learning among birds that illuminates how change within small groups can escalate to a whole collective. One teller of this story is Arie de Geus, in his book *The Living Company* (Boston: Harvard Business School Press, 1977), drawing from the work of the biologist Alan Wilson.

When milk deliveries began in England in the late 1800s, two species of garden birds found this much to their liking, robins and titmice. Strange as this sounds in today's thoroughly packaged world, the milk bottles didn't have caps. Robins and titmice alike learned to skim the cream, drinking from the bottles that were waiting for their human owners to wake up and take them in.

In the 1930s, the milk delivery system finally saw some innovation. Aluminum caps now sealed the milk bottles. Whatever this straightforward advance might have contributed to preventing spills and keeping the milk clean, it did not entirely defeat the forces of avian nature. Occasionally, robins and titmice would learn to peck through the caps and help themselves to the cream anyway. Moreover, in the long run, the titmice outdid the robins. In a few years, any titmouse you might nod to on the street knew the milk-bottle scam. The robin plunderers remained few.

Alan Wilson, a professor of biology at the University of California at Berkeley, analyzed how the titmice outscored the robins as part of examining how innovation spreads within some species and not others. Individuals within the species have to be able to discover the trick in the first place. Wilson found that both robins and titmice had their Edisons. Occasionally, and about equally often, an individual robin or titmouse would figure out the capped milk bottle. However, to connect this to organizational themes, robin society has a poor contact architecture and titmouse society a good one for spreading practices. Robins are territorial. They stake out their private realms and defend the boundaries. Titmice, in contrast, form small foraging flocks with changes in membership every now and then. This meant that when a robin Edison made a milk-bottle breakthrough, other robins usually did not learn about it. When a titmouse Edison made the same breakthrough, other titmice in the flock would see, learn, and do, and others would learn from them as flock membership rotated, until an entire population of bottle-top pirates emerged.

Aesop did not allow his fables to leave a lot to the imagination, instead spelling out the moral at the end, and so shall I. A few enclaves of progressive practice do not make an intelligent collective. However, if some people who are part of each pocket catch the spirit, become developmental leaders, and carry progressive styles to other groups in which they participate, it's the same as with titmice and milk bottles. Soon a community will emerge with mostly round tables, a community in which most interactions have a progressive character most of the time, a community that, because of superior knowledge processing and symbolic conduct at all levels, is more intelligent.

In other words:

☞ *The law of global impact:* Transformation toward a culture of progressive practice depends on a contact architecture that mixes people enough to foster propagation of progressive practices from group to group ("flock to flock") along with a critical mass of developmental leaders to seed the process.

Vision and policy from the top as well as formal training can help to foster the progressive transformation. They may be essential to getting it started. But they do not do the actual work of transformation. This is done by the developmental leaders, if people mix enough and there is a critical mass of such leaders. Such a transformation is a systems-level phenomenon, one not so easily understood or appreciated, as Peter Senge argues in *The Fifth Discipline* (New

York: Doubleday/Currency, 1990). It's all too easy to imagine that a weekend training program for key people together with a little follow-up could put progressive practices in place. However, the good effects hoped for will depend on systemic properties such as how widely those who have received the training are sprinkled throughout the organization, whether they have caught enough of the spirit and craft to begin to function as developmental leaders, whether their roles help them to establish pocket communities of progressive practice, whether the organizational culture is receptive enough to allow this to happen in a number of pockets, and whether the contact architecture of the organization mixes people well enough for progressive practices to spread. All this needs to be thought about systemically.

And there's a further catch: It's not reasonable to expect progressive practices to spread as easily as stealing milk. People quickly learn from the human flock matters of direct individual benefit—ways of skimming the cream—such as where the best fishing holes are, or the best antique shops, or the best singles bars. But learning progressive practices from one another is more challenging. It's learning something of *indirect* individual benefit, by way of collective benefit, something inherently both less motivating and less visible.

Therefore, it's sufficient for the Edison titmouse merely to steal the cream in front of other titmice, but not sufficient for the developmental leader merely to act progressively. Stealing the cream, or parking your SUV next to the best fishing hole, is sufficient visibility for that sort of thing, but simply acting progressively is not enough to cause other human beings in complex social contexts to catch on. The developmental leader needs to act not just progressively but with high visibility, not so much proselytizing as alerting, exposing, and explaining—raising consciousness casually in the natural flow of working together.

THE DRAGON UNLEARNING

Unlearning is a particularly nasty dragon guarding the passage from idea to action. Changes in attitude and practice generally arrive with some difficulty when they arrive at all, no matter whether they concern organizational intelligence or something else. It's often easier to learn how to handle situations for the first time than to relearn how to handle them in a new way. The first time, we travel light. The second time, we carry the baggage from the first time, and that cumbersome baggage can make us miss the train.

Most people already have been around the block a few times and have gained the very real benefits of experience. But they've also accumulated all that baggage. Most organizations settle into patterns that lie not in the head of any one participant but in organizational structures and routines. This is one factor that makes organizational mergers tricky. Each organization has its distinctive style of leadership, paths of advancement, and ways of managing problems, and all its members have learned them. Now somebody has to unlearn. It's also a factor that makes change within an organization tricky: Somebody has to unlearn. Accordingly, the problem of unlearning deserves a close look.

The dragon Unlearning seems to have three heads, as though one set of jaws were not enough. The three correspond to fundamental archetypes of interaction, ways in which past learnings interfere with current learning opportunities in collective settings.

Frame defenses. Often, a person's current frame of reference—established beliefs and attitudes—generates resistance to an innovation (It won't work, or it won't work here, or I already do that, or it's a fad, or it's a good thing in principle but won't take hold, or it's a threat to how I've set things up, or I'm tired of all these initiatives that never really accomplish anything.)

Habit defenses. Often, when people accept an innovation in principle, entrenched habits reassert themselves, particularly in moments of urgency or threat—just when the new practice may be most needed. (Established habits are so automatic that they readily reappear, especially when stress leads people to fixate on the matter at hand.)

System defenses. Regardless of individual belief and readiness to act, often the social system around a person resists an innovation. (There's no time for it; it threatens others' interests; the setting gets polarized into "missionaries" and "unbelievers"; there are too many change initiatives at once; there's no incentive structure.)

As with many previous archetypes, these three should seem familiar, because they reflect common experience. Indeed, in many circumstances, this three-headed dragon is one we want to have around. The archetypes keep emerging because a certain conservatism regarding change is valuable. Innovations often are not viable. The status quo reflects the legacy of prior learning at the individual and system levels, a legacy that needs some protection. Accordingly, archetypes of frame, habit, and system defense resemble some others examined in earlier chapters, such as answer-centered leadership or conciliatory feedback: They often make positive contributions. However, like guests at the party who seem to have more energy than the hosts, they overstay their welcome.

Why not let our constant guest King Arthur illustrate the dragon Unlearning. The king, recognizing the power and humanity of the round-table style, decides to carry the word to the North Country. Sensing the need for simple words and practical guidance (what we would call *good action poetry*), Arthur articulates his round-table philosophy with care and pragmatism and calls the round-table style *grailing* to suggest a committed quest. Then Arthur and his entourage sally forth to bring grailing to the North Country.

Arthur plans a two-pass process, one to introduce grailing, and the second, a couple of months later, to check on progress. The first pass seems to go well, with much applause at Arthur's workshops, but the second pass holds some surprises. When Arthur returns to Castle Framenlock two months after the introduction of grailing, there is little grailing to be found. Chatting up the knights of Framenlock with the help of numerous flagons of ale, Arthur and his team discover reactions like these:

KNIGHT 1: I essayed grailing once or twice, but it pains me to report that the method did not appear to work.

KNIGHT 2: God's truth is that I already do grailing and have for some time, or what surely amounts to more or less the same thing.

KNIGHT 3: I acknowledge the attractiveness of the philosophy. But it will never take hold here in this noxious backwater, so why in all common sense should I bother?

KNIGHT 4: With due respect, Camelot simply cannot direct our local lord and his knights in what to do about such small matters.

KNIGHT 5: It is a gracious practice, to be sure, but I cannot let my subordinate knights lapse into soft womanish ways.

In other words, at Castle Framenlock, Arthur discovers frame defenses in abundance, with established beliefs, attitudes, and interests producing resistance to and dismissal of grailing. Indeed, anyone who has tried to manage change processes will recognize such phrases as "I tried it and it didn't work," "We already do that," or "It won't work here." As noted earlier, such defenses can be legitimate, because many change initiatives are not well conceived. But they can also be mere excuses.

The grailing team proceeds to Castle Habitrance, Arthur grumbling all the way and anticipating the worst. However, at first Arthur finds reason to feel encouraged. The knights of Habitrance have considerable praise for the virtues of grailing: It offers an enlightened vision, a way forward, a modern look, an energizing style.

Arthur and his team spend some time at Castle Habitrance observing how the local lord and his knights interact in advancing the affairs of the small realm. Gradually they discover an unsettling reality. Although the knights of Habitrance talk the talk, they do not so often walk the walk. Sometimes they use a few elements of grailing, but without getting to the heart of it, and they do not even seem to recognize their tokenism.

Sometimes they catch themselves slacking:

KNIGHT 1: God's wounds! It is true that I find myself weak in my grailing. I shall try harder!

However, they usually fall into error again, especially when difficult matters need attention.

> KNIGHT 2: I knew not what else to do. We had to advance in the matter somehow.
>
> KNIGHT 3: By the cross, my previous self simply took over as though I had no will.

In other words, at Castle Habitrance, Arthur encounters habit defenses. Arthur comes to realize that it's one thing for knights to accept grailing in principle, but another for grailing to penetrate the daily and hourly texture of their lives. Indeed, anyone who has managed processes of change will recognize problems of missed opportunities, backsliding, and especially backsliding in more stressful situations.

Disappointed again, the group moves on to Castle Systemuck. Arthur, this time paying more attention to what people do than to what they say, is gratified to discover that grailing plays an occasional genuine role at Castle Systemuck. Informal meetings among friends and colleagues, the way one knight manages his small staff and another deals with local affairs, show flashes of the philosophy. However, in larger settings and among the real power figures at Castle Systemuck, no such signs appear.

The usual mix of ale and chat reveals the Castle Systemuck story. The knights get the idea of grailing pretty well, and even seem to have enough self-awareness to override old habits. But grailing does not fit so well within the dominant Systemuck culture.

> KNIGHT 1: My heart is strong for grailing. However, the bishop is quite conservative. He has little tolerance for such novel practices, and it is my duty and indeed need to maintain good standing in our community.
>
> KNIGHT 2: For myself and my friends, fine. But the merchants are canny folk, and they will take full advantage of me if I emphasize grailing in my dealings with them.
>
> KNIGHT 3: Now if we were all of the same mind about this, if we were to a soul committed to grailing, all would be well. But

with only a few of us secure in this new enlightenment—well, it is difficult to grail when the noble person next to me has no such disposition!

These could be excuses, Arthur tells himself. But after investigating Castle Systemuck further, he concludes that they are only partly so. The culture and procedures of Castle Systemuck create system defenses. Indeed, anyone who has managed processes of change will recognize how systemic factors often conspire to resist change. Organizational scholar Edgar Schein has devised an apt name for this: the *organizational immune system.*

All in all, Arthur returns from his second journey deeply disappointed. He could bring the word about grailing, he could introduce the local knights to some of the key practices, but frame defenses at Castle Framenlock, habit defenses at Castle Habitrance, and system defenses at Castle Systemuck defeated his best efforts to spread the word.

The challenge of getting grailing to take hold is no myth. Call it a parable instead. When therapists encourage family members to adopt smoother ways of relating to one another, when managers in corporations try to initiate better practices, when innovative educational programs guide teachers toward deeper pedagogies, when political and social leaders try to introduce unfamiliar civil structures to a society full of strife, the dragon Unlearning stirs. Frame defenses, habit defenses, or system defenses—and not uncommonly all three—guard the patterns of the past against frameworks for the future.

THE THREE ARTS OF UNLEARNING

With a three-headed dragon to dodge, a serious innovation might seem to have little hope of crossing the bridge from idea to action. However, there is a countervailing force. Hope rests in a character we have met before, the one-eyed person in the country of the blind, the developmental leader, the person who sees in archetypes, recognizes the forces at work, and has some prospect of dealing with them. Indeed, for each of the three defenses one can recognize countermoves toward frame breaking, habit breaking, and system breaking.

Frame breaking, habit breaking, and system breaking are all complicated worlds in themselves. A thorough look at them would fill another few chapters. However, it's possible to visit these worlds briefly and develop some sense of what developmental leaders can do, whether they are managers, political leaders, facilitators, or simply savvy and dedicated members of the group. Here, then, is a brief guide.

Frame Breaking

Frame defenses try to sustain frames of reference reflecting established beliefs and attitudes. Therefore, frame breaking involves throwing these stubborn mental models into question and ultimately shifting them. Developmental leaders of progressive change can undertake several moves in this direction.

Having a Good Reason. One of the simplest strategies of frame breaking is giving people a really good reason to try. There must be something attractive about the innovation at hand. It must promise gains over the status quo—greater savings, efficiency, productivity, influence, or leader status or contributions to health, stability, or some other state of affairs that the key people really want. Participants, and especially decision makers, do not need to embrace the innovation wholeheartedly from the outset, but they at least need to recognize its potential and engage it with an experimental spirit.

Quite reasonably, the innovation must be sold, whether it be knowledge management, communities of practice, virtual meeting spaces, or something else. While this may seem evident, enthusiasts of a particular innovation often behave as though its merits are so obvious that it will sell itself. Instead, the case usually needs to be made.

Raising Consciousness. Often, people are not resistant to a change agenda in principle. Nonetheless, they fail to recognize how established frames of reference will assert themselves as the process unfolds. It helps simply to alert people that doubts and questions are likely to arise.

For example, one company was developing new methods of collaboration using digital media. Experience showed that these online conversations disturbed many people's expectations about what was public and what was private, how articulate their initial thoughts needed to be, and related matters. Accordingly, the company established warnings about what would feel strange or worrisome at first. Knowing what to expect, participants faced the problems with more resolve and worked through them.

BRACKETING OLD FRAMES OF REFERENCE.   Asking a person to reject familiar ideas right away for the sake of a new vision is asking a lot. Innovators may find more success in simply asking people to suspend judgment, bracket the old frame of reference, try the new practice, and see what happens.

For instance, teachers often accept innovative pedagogies more readily if they are not presented with elaborate arguments about which way is better, the old or the new. Instead, they get the basic rationale with encouragement simply to try out the new practice in an experimental spirit and analyze its strengths and weaknesses. The practical experience makes a better case than a priori argument and sometimes brings genuine weaknesses in the innovation to the surface, leading to its refinement.

EXPECTATION FOR ACTION.   The transition from idea to action benefits from clear expectations for action. Otherwise, people can talk endlessly about what might be done while doing very little of it. Jeffrey Pfeffer and Robert Sutton, in *The Knowing-Doing Gap* (Boston: Harvard Business School Press, 2000), identify substituting talk for action as a common defense mechanism.

Probably the best way to move toward action is to make concrete action a part of the process from early on, in the spirit of action research as articulated by, for instance, Kurt Lewin, or action learning as developed by Reg Revans. The idea of action projects, discussed in the preceding "Pocket Change" section, is one way to approach this. As just mentioned in the previous subsection, it's often advantageous to move to action almost immediately, deliberately deferring reflection until experience provides more data.

LOW-RISK REALISM.   Medical innovations do not begin with the wide-scale application of speculative treatments. Likewise, the smart innovator creates circumstances in which people can experiment with new ways without feeling too exposed or threatened if things don't go well.

Arranging for people to work in groups is one way to help, because the group participation distributes and dilutes the sense of risk. Establishing modest initial expectations and emphasizing an experimental and tolerant spirit is another. Several organizational theorists emphasize the importance of *practice fields,* selected safe settings in which new practices can be tried with low risk. A practice field might take such forms as a small-scale low-stakes initiative, a group of collaborators with few issues of authority and rivalry, or an occasional off-site meeting with more open standards of communication—or anything else that makes experimentation less risky than in the midst of business as usual.

COMPETING COMMITMENTS.   Often, people articulate new intentions emphatically and still find themselves not following through. This seems particularly puzzling, an idea-action gap without an evident explanation. Robert Kegan and Lisa Lahey, in an examination of what they call *languages of transformation,* point out that the culprit often is another commitment. They write of shifting from "the language of new year's resolutions to the language of competing commitments." When well-articulated intentions do not lead to concrete action, the reason is likely to be an implicit competing commitment—a concern, value, relationship, or other matter not recognized in the formulation of the original intention. For instance, you find yourself not following through very well on plans to conduct a group in a more open way. Why? Perhaps, on reflection, you realize that you fear you will be perceived as arrogant; or you fear losing control of the group, which includes some aggressive individuals; or you yourself have strong convictions about many issues, and you are reluctant to limit your power of advocacy through more evenhanded conversations. Kegan and Lahey suggest that, once we expose implicit competing commitments, we can examine them as assumptions that have been holding us unseen. We can mindfully decide whether and when to hold them. There may be something to those competing assumptions, but we can let go of an assumption experimentally, in fairly safe circumstances—practice fields—to give the new practice a chance and discover what happens.

EXPOSING TALK-WALK DISCREPANCIES. When people do not follow through on a practice, a more difficult path involves leading people to recognize fundamental disparities between their talk and their walk. Organizational theorists Chris Argyris and Donald Schön draw a contrast between single-loop learning and double-loop learning. *Single-loop learning,* which is what we do most of the time, involves fine-tuning established patterns but not breaking out of their implicit frames of reference. *Double-loop learning* requires a confrontation with underlying assumptions that challenge the old frames.

Argyris and Schön's approach to this has a therapeutic character. These authors report that many people offer *espoused theories* that are at odds with their *theory in practice.* For example, the head of the office may espouse a democratic leadership style while in fact behaving autocratically, or espouse delegation while in fact maintaining close control. Argyris and Schön interpret such situations not as problems of hypocrisy but as problems of blindness. People do not so readily see their own behavior or gauge how well it aligns with their espoused theories. In such circumstances, a facilitator can support double-loop learning, helping people to examine their own behavior in ways that expose inconsistencies and lead toward a reconciliation that discards old assumptions.

I venture the opinion that this is by far the most difficult kind of frame breaking, although it may sometimes be the only path that works. The right kind of developmental leader is especially critical, because that person must function in a therapeutic role and have the status and perspective to do so. This usually means someone outside the organization or community in question, not entangled in its power structure, but with sufficient respect and support to act effectively.

HABIT BREAKING

Habit defenses involve the persistence of established habits even when they conflict with new attitudes. Especially in times of stress, old habits of leading with negative criticism can override a new commitment to communicative feedback, or old habits of autonomous decision making can abort an agenda of consulting with others more widely. Therefore, habit breaking requires addressing the psychological factors that give established habits their momentum. The savvy developmental leader attends to these.

RAISING CONSCIOUSNESS. This point is the essentially the same as for frame breaking. People are more likely to cope effectively with habit defenses if they are forewarned that established habits are likely to resurface.

WHENS, WHERES, AND HOWS. When people accept a concept and intend to act, it's still not uncommon that nothing much happens. Psychologist Peter Gollwitzer illuminates this problem. Sometimes people develop detailed visions of where and when to carry forward an idea and exactly what they will do on those occasions. These visions are called *implementation intentions.* Gollwitzer's studies show that implementation intentions make a substantial difference in follow-through with practical action. In two investigations, one concerning completing an essay and the other adopting an exercise program, the rate of follow-through rose from about one-third to 75% in one case and 91% in the other. An important reason seems to be that relatively specific plans better combat the momentum of old habits.

PLANTING REMINDERS. Old habits are sustained in large part by old circumstances—the same meeting rooms, the same people around the table, and so on. Sometimes one can move to a new setting to combat this influence. When one cannot, another approach is to create new reminders in the old environment, either direct messages or cues implicit in salient rearrangements.

Planting reminders is a familiar trick of self-management. To ensure that you take a file home from work, you leave it beside your coat. To pay that bill by the end of the month, you leave it on the dining room table. To remember to call so-and-so, you stick a note on your telephone. The same strategy can work in interactive settings. At a meeting, you might put cue cards around a table that offer a quick guide to communicative feedback. You might ask the facilitator to sit at the head of the table, rather than the boss. You might use a timer to remind the group in half an hour to stand back and take stock of the process.

ACTIVE INHIBITION. It's naïve to suppose that simply and sincerely committing oneself to a new strategy will carry the day against old habits. A sentinel-like alertness holds more promise. Watch out for the old habits asserting themselves and actively inhibit them, pushing them aside in favor of the innovation. This is much more likely to succeed than relying on good intentions to magically reprogram deeply ingrained behaviors.

STRESS MANAGEMENT. It's no news that organizational life spawns stress in such forms as interpersonal conflict, urgent deadlines, competition for resources and personal advancement, and the sheer complexity of juggling multiple agendas on multiple fronts. Unfortunately, stress often undermines newly adopted practices, causing people to backslide to more established behaviors.

Chapter 4 mentioned a classic version of this effect, a 1908 laboratory finding called the *Yerkes-Dodson law.* The discoverers mapped an inverted-U-shaped relationship between arousal and performance: Performance first went up with increased arousal, but then deteriorated as arousal continued to climb. Subsequent research has shown that the relationship between performance and arousal factors such as stress is complex. Some people thrive more on stress than others, and some activities benefit more than others from a certain amount of stress. However, as a broad generalization, the effect of great stress is to narrow attention and fixate it on the main task at hand. This reduces the attention available to sustain new practices, which are, of course, more attention-demanding than well-established practices. When the stress is up, new practices crumble. Accordingly, stress management strategies such as time outs and relaxation techniques can help to keep them in place.

FRAMING BACKSLIDING AS NORMAL. The preceding paragraphs emphasize how forces of habit work against change, and thereby warn that progress will be erratic, with many rounds of two steps forward and one step back. While much can be done to ensure that the steps forward outnumber the steps back, such circumstances also call for managing participants' perceptions. The steps backward stand out more than the steps forward. Statements such as these are not unusual: "Just the other day he behaved as though we'd never started." "You think you've got it, and then you find you haven't." "Its not working. Look how we always slip back."

While some backsliding is inevitable, negative perceptions are not. The adroit developmental leader frames backsliding as a normal part of forward motion. "Something is happening, or there'd be nothing to backslide from. Backsliding tells us where the rough spots are and helps us anticipate them and work harder toward dealing with them."

SYSTEM BREAKING

System defenses involve factors outside the self—cultural attitudes, bureaucratic routines, others' entrenched habits, schedules, postures of power figures, even physical layouts. Sometimes the system resists passively, the established order creating inertia. Sometimes the system resists actively, certain individuals or groups standing against an innovation and even sabotaging it. In either case, the challenge of system breaking is to anticipate how system defenses might operate and take steps to reduce their influence.

The following thoughts draw from personal experience and various sources. An article by Andrew Molinsky on paradoxical impediments to organizational change was particularly helpful.

RAISING CONSCIOUSNESS.   As with frame breaking and habit breaking, alerting everyone to the likely system defenses in the situation can help.

CREATING A LOW-RISK CULTURE.   Risk was mentioned under "Frame Breaking," because even in the friendliest context, people are wary about exposing themselves. Beyond this natural reticence, risk is often a systemic problem. In some organizational cultures, risk runs high. There is little tolerance for failure. Supervisors come down hard on experiments that don't work. Paradoxically, there are often demands to develop new programs quickly and implement them widely, pumping up the stakes. People feel pressure to make things look like they are working, even when they are not.

Writing on risk in organizations, Sim Sitkin warns that high risk suppresses innovation. New initiatives thrive on small-scale pilot testing, low stakes, and plenty of room to make errors that don't sink the boat and from which one can learn. Small-scale failures are seen as a normal part of the process, presenting valuable learning opportunities.

A developmental leader nudges the collective in this direction, or, if that is difficult, at least builds or finds smaller-scale contexts within the larger collective that are fairly safe—often called *practice fields,* as mentioned earlier.

MAKING TIME.   Innovations require time to explore and refine, and this resource is in short supply in most organizational settings. One way to beat the time problem is to introduce innovations in ways that mesh with what has to happen anyway—for instance, melding innovations into meetings, feedback sessions, and the like.

A complementary strategy is to create deliberately protected time for an introductory period. In one initiative in an administrative setting, the leadership set aside an official time each week when all interested administrators were relieved of other duties to meet and discuss new practices.

A third tactic is to avoid too many innovations with the same people at the same time. It's commonplace for multiple innovations, often from different power groups in an organization, to impinge on the same people, who then have to divide their time and effort, leading to rampant tokenism and little real progress.

COPING WITH CHANGE FATIGUE.   In many organizational settings, anything new is the same old same old. People have become jaded with Total Quality Management, reengineering, quality circles, and the other "next great revolutions" that constantly move through the collective landscape like weather fronts, changing the atmosphere for a day or two but not really altering the climate.

To be taken seriously, yet another initiative has to make serious commitments—finding time as described before and planning for the long term, creating sustained expectations. The great asset of developmental leaders here is that they are inherently in it for the long term, because they raise consciousness simply by the way they interact with others. Programs can support, but no program can substitute for, the contribution of individuals acting progressively and making progressive practices more visible.

AVOIDING MISSIONARIES AND UNBELIEVERS. Aggressive change initiatives often create ardent missionaries and a counterforce of steadfast unbelievers. Richard Elmore, writing about problems of large-scale innovation in education, points to this as one of the principal barriers. It is tempting to identify a core group of those who are "really committed and really doing it" and to exclude others from partial or tentative participation, but this exacerbates polarization by creating clear in-groups and out-groups.

It's important to keep the boundaries between participation and nonparticipation flexible, permeable, and blurred—for instance, by keeping people with erratic attendance on invitation lists and by accepting a certain amount of tokenism or half-hearted participation. Developmental leaders know that even in the best innovations there will be a few ardent participants, many middle-of-the-roaders, some reluctant participants, and some antagonists. This bell-shaped curve graphing participation is natural. The trick is to avoid polarizing pressure that turns it into a bimodal curve, with two humps like those of a camel—the missionaries and the unbelievers. Because the missionaries are usually in the minority, such heightened rivalry is likely to destroy the innovation in the medium to long term.

COPING WITH STIRRING THE SWAMP. Many innovations bring to the surface controversies and enmities that have been buried safely in the routine of organizational life. The autocratic habits of one person or the carelessness of another may become topics of conversation. Particularly if the swamp involves highly placed people, stirring the swamp can create a backlash that quashes the innovation. In one large corporation I know of, a long-planned retreat to explore basic management issues was simply cancelled because a top executive had promoted someone with whom he was having an amorous relationship to a high position. He and his cronies recognized that this was likely to become an embarrassing topic of conversation at the retreat, and they decided that the timing was bad.

Developmental leaders have to be aware that such factors are part of the political reality. An innovation that does not stir the swamp a little probably is not accomplishing much. However, this does not mean that anyone has to feel deeply threatened. Helpful tactics include, for example, bracketing certain issues as out of bounds for a while, seeing that certain conversations happen privately, and tagging conversations that seem to be escalating as ones to defer and honestly come back to, but in a safer setting.

THE ROAD TO CAMELOT

The road to hell is paved with good intentions, but the road to Camelot is paved with good *smart* intentions. The moral of the several ideas in this chapter is that change in groups, teams, communities, and organizations toward greater intelligence requires not only good will but considerable savvy about the rather finicky conditions of change, and savvy put into action. Remember, of the four knowledge processes—generating, communicating, integrating, and acting on—the fourth is often the toughest of all.

Let's trace the road to Camelot, admittedly not a turnpike, perhaps more of a winding path up a boulder-strewn slope. The idea-action gap is a central challenge of change not only for organizational intelligence but for any innovation. It's much easier to talk a good game than to play it. Helpful ideas are abundant, whereas the practices enacting those ideas are rare.

One source of the idea-action gap is the idea and its language. Often the idea is too abstract or complex to inform action readily.

Good action theories, rather than explanation theories, expressed in good action poetry are powerful tools of change. Clear, direct, compact, and evocative, they have a back-pocket quality.

In the end, it's not ideas but people with ideas that make things happen. Like the one-eyed woman mentioned earlier, they are developmental leaders. A developmental leader might occupy a power position, but often such people are simply participants with the right kind of savvy.

A developmental leader sees in archetypes. Amidst the clutter of collective life, the developmental leader notices the patterns that play out over and over again. A developmental leader acts progressively but also visibly, framing actions to make the archetypes salient. In these ways, a developmental leader seeds the growth of organizational intelligence across the group.

The law of local impact says that developmental leaders influence primarily those with whom they interact directly. Even a single developmental leader can do much to build a community of progressive practice in a small group. Yes, there are groups dominated by doggedly regressive individuals in which making a step forward is about as likely as seeing a unicorn out the window, but most settings have great potential.

The law of global impact concerns how to get beyond the limits of the law of local impact. It's not so easy to foster a large-scale community of progressive practice. More than anything else, such development calls for learning by doing. Progressive practices spread to the extent that further developmental leaders arise and their participation in various groups generates yet more—as in the parable of the robins and the titmice. Visionary leadership from the top, policies, workshops, and similar means can promote this, but ultimately it depends on an expanding circle of developmental leaders.

Even with a few developmental leaders seeding a microculture, all this will not happen smoothly. Defense mechanisms are a natural and indeed appropriate part of community and organizational life. Frame defenses, habit defenses, and system defenses are likely. The savvy developmental leader has seen them before and can help to get around this three-headed dragon with strategies for frame breaking, habit breaking, and system breaking.

These reflections do not write a simple recipe for utopia. The road to Camelot has many twists and turns. However, the quest for this particular Camelot is important and worthwhile for all of us who live out our lives in communities and organizations—which is, well, just about all of us.

Moreover, there is some comfort in always remembering the law of local impact. Even in a discouraging setting, it's generally possible to act locally to good effect in at least some of the groups in which one participates—and who knows what castles may get built in time?

TOOLBOX

* *Keep an eye on the idea-action gap.* Good ideas commonly fall short of practical action for all sorts of reasons.

* *Beware of explanation theories* as guides to action. They're too far removed from practical action. Instead, reach for *action theories* backed by explanation theories and expressed through good *action poetry*—simple, direct, memorable, with a back-pocket quality.

* *Developmental leaders* are the key to changing toward organizational intelligence. They see in archetypes and act visibly in a progressive way, thereby creating progressive communities of practice around them. Be one.

* *The law of local impact* says that the impact of developmental leaders is largely local, a matter of those with whom they work directly. Training can foster developmental leadership, but don't expect individuals to have a wide impact.

* *The law of global impact* says that progressive practices spread when there is a critical mass of developmental leaders and a contact architecture that mixes people enough. Policies and programs can promote this, but it's the people who do it.

* Communities and organizations have natural and often useful defenses against change—the *frame defenses,* which work against new ideas that challenge old frames of reference; *habit defenses,* in which old habits reassert themselves despite new intentions; and *system defenses,* which resist individual will with various systemic pressures, such as lack of time, entrenched bureaucracy, and cultural norms.

* Expect frame, habit, and system defenses and counter them with strategies of *frame breaking, habit breaking,* and *system breaking.*

Epilog: Rounding the World

The scroll of miseries recited by people under their breaths in the halls of corporations, governments, clubs, teams, and even those most intimate of organizations, their families, seems to have no end: acidic feedback, chaotic collaborations, autocratic leadership, collapses of trust, escalating conflicts. Add your own favorite trauma to the list! Perhaps most alarming is not so much the occasional catastrophe but the generally awkward, inefficient, herky-jerky, muddle-through-one-more-time character of so much of it.

Will things ever change? Yes, if we understand them; yes, if we act to make them better; yes, if we get beyond rounding a table here and there and round the world.

Magellan had it easy. The expedition of the Portuguese explorer Magellan rounded the world in the early 1500s. Admittedly, Magellan himself never made it, falling victim to the resistance of indigenous people on the island of Mactan in the Philippines. Fewer than 20 of the initial 265 men, and only one of five ships, returned, three full years after setting forth. Still, Magellan had it easy.

It's one thing to round a world that's already physically round in order to show that it's round—Magellan's crusade—but quite another matter to round a world that's not at all socially round in order to make it that way—Arthur's crusade. In the first years of our calendar's second millennium, it's all too plain that the world is not, on the whole, a round-table kind of place, even though the world has round tables in it here and there. A skeptic might say that rounding the world is hopeless.

So, one more time, lightly, let's hear the basic story. We began with the lawnmower paradox: Pooling physical effort is usually rather easy; pooling mental effort is usually rather hard. We formulated the fundamental what–why–how question: What is organizational intelligence, why is it so hard to come by, and how can we get more of it?

So, *what is organizational intelligence?* To answer that question, I've offered the round-table model. The model says that organizations are made of conversations. The intelligence of a collective comes from individual contributions combined by people's interactions. Human interactions can be *progressive* or *regressive* or shades in between. Progressive interactions combine lines of thought and experience within the group effectively to advance agendas, and they foster the cohesion of the group. They are process smart and people smart. Specifically, they show good knowledge processing and positive symbolic conduct. Because progressive interactions yield better solutions, decisions, and plans along with group integrity over time, they make the organization or community a better collective thinker over time— that is, more intelligent.

Regressive interactions do not combine thought and experience within the group effectively. They involve poor collective knowledge processing and negative symbolic conduct. Because this generally, although not always, yields inferior solutions, decisions, and plans, as well as instability in the group, it makes the collective less intelligent.

Interactions between people fall into *archetypes of interaction,* recurrent styles of interactive behavior. Some of these archetypes are generally progressive, some regressive. One finds these archetypes around the typical hot spots of collective life we've taken up—group decision making, feedback, leadership, collaboration, trust, conflict, and change. There are other hot spots worth thinking about, too— for instance, operational efficiency, organizational politics, or selecting and promoting people. Ponder these and other hot spots with the general concepts of the round-table model in mind, and you'll begin to see archetypes that play out over and over again, with characteristic patterns of knowledge processing and symbolic conduct.

The archetypes, positive or negative, sometimes reflect people's explicit philosophies and strategies. However, often they do not. They emerge from tacit assumptions, impulses of the moment, simplest paths forward, and the ways in which patterns of interaction escalate between people, without any specific intention on the part of anyone. Thus, major archetypes tend to be recreated over and over again in different settings.

The contact architecture of a community or organization determines who has contact with whom in what formal or informal roles. It supports four broad kinds of knowledge processing: generating knowledge through sifting experience, conducting research, and so on; communicating knowledge face to face, electronically, and by other means; integrating knowledge into solutions, plans, and decisions; and acting on that knowledge. The contact architecture allows all this to occur, but does not determine whether the interactions are progressive or regressive.

The overall intelligence of a community or organization reflects the balance of progressive over regressive archetypes of interaction within a well-developed contact architecture. Organizational intelligence is emergent, like the weather. As we begin to understand the knowledge weather of collectives better, we can take more responsibility for making the weather we want.

So why is organizational intelligence so hard to come by? Several reasons emerge from the basic story and its elaborations in the preceding chapters.

First of all, regressive archetypes tend to drive out progressive archetypes even though progressive archetypes are usually more adaptive—the dinosaur paradox. Recall from Chapter 4 and other places that regressive archetypes tend to be cognitively and emotionally simpler, so progressive practices require more skill and alertness. In times of stress, when cognitive load is high, behavior tends to regress toward simpler earlier-learned behaviors. And it's hard to be progressive when the other guy is being regressive: Both progressive and regressive practices stimulate their own kind, but regressive practices tend to provoke regressive practices more than progressive practices provoke progressive practices.

Moreover, progressive interactions are not always more adaptive. This has been acknowledged from the beginning. For instance, regressive interactions are often advantageous in emergencies (no time for the extra processing of progressive interactions), when one person knows far more than others about the matter at hand (the extra processing can be a waste of time), or when smooth group coordination is far more important than tapping most of the minds in the group (as in some military or sports situations).

In addition, regressive archetypes often serve the interests of power figures, regardless of the overall effectiveness of the group. Organizational intelligence, although generally advantageous for the group, is not so advantageous for power figures who want to use the group for their own interests, directing or draining its resources.

Finally, the process of change is hard. It's the idea–action gap. It's that fourth knowledge process, acting on knowledge, which often challenges established beliefs, habits, and systemic features of the setting, arousing the organizational immune system. With all these factors in mind, we should be pleased to see as many round, or at least elliptical, tables as we do.

And yet, I'm optimistic about the long-term prospects for widespread organizational intelligence. For one reason, the round-table model speaks to the question, *how can we get more of it?* We can cultivate developmental leaders. We can try to build a critical mass of developmental leaders in an organization, along with a contact architecture that mixes people around enough to spread progressive practices. We can cope systematically with the resistance of established beliefs, habits, and systemic factors.

Another reason I'm optimistic despite the ragged track record is that a jerky process of development is not actually a compelling reason to be pessimistic. It's natural to see such a pattern for practices with basically positive but mixed virtues.

Consider democracy, for instance. Remember from Chapter 1 that the Athenian politico Kleisthenes concocted democracy as a way of recovering power from a rival clan. Democracy, in its various versions, displays a jerky history of advances and setbacks that continues today. Democracy is a mixed-virtues practice, inefficient in many ways and subject to uninformed and emotionally swayed voters from time to time. Socrates grumbled about it, and so have many other gadflies of their cultures, including Winston Churchill, who quipped, "It has been said that Democracy is the worst form of Government except all those others that have been tried from time to time." Nonetheless, democracy in various versions is plainly albeit erratically gaining ground. As Churchill said, it's the worst "except all those others."

In the same spirit, we should not be too dismayed by the erratic manifestations of organizational intelligence, and it does seem to me that various practices of organizational intelligence are gaining ground.

However, there is yet a third and perhaps more important reason to sustain some optimism. Arguably, the adaptive advantages of organizational intelligence are increasing in today's world. The driving factor is not social insight but technological development. At one level, digital computation and electronic communications provide us with ways of interacting that can sustain better the web of dialogs underlying progressive interactions, as, for instance, in technologies for telepresence or for knowledge management. But this is only the frosting on the microchip. The broader factor is that technologies of communication and transportation continue to shrink the world, while technologies of agriculture and the production of materials continue to crowd the world.

With more of us more readily and inevitably in touch, organizational intelligence becomes more valuable. People can trade and collaborate as never before, so it becomes especially advantageous to do so well. Globalization gains momentum from this fact and makes it even more of a fact. Even resistance to the problematic aspects of the trend toward globalization involves groups getting and keeping in touch and collaborating. They need organizational intelligence, too.

Moreover, in this more crowded and in-touch world, power resolutions of conflict become increasingly more disruptive and disastrous, whereas civil and consensus resolutions prove more productive and promote sustained affiliations. Note that none of this implies an advance toward some conflict-free utopia. As discussed in Chapter 8, organizational intelligence is not about the absence of conflict. Divergent ideas and interests are inherent in the human condition and part of intelligent functioning. Rather, organizational intelligence includes smart conflict that is less destructive and involves amalgams of dispute and collaboration within civil structures.

To put all this in biological terms, the adaptive pressures favoring organizational intelligence are increasing, so we can expect to see more progressive practices over time, much as when circumstances make a biological trait more adaptive, its frequency in the population increases generation by generation. But we don't have to wait for generations. Social practices are not so much genes as *memes*—zoologist Richard Dawkins's term for ideas that evolve among the cognitive networks of society. They spread more like that trick of stealing milk among titmice. One can even hope that eventually practices of organizational intelligence will reach a point at which enough individuals and groups know and do such things that it becomes very awkward not to know and do them, and pretty soon most everyone will.

This does not mean that we should all spin in our office chairs waiting for the millennium. We finished one millennium recently, the new millennium does not seem to be overflowing with human enlightenment so far, and 3000 is a dauntingly long way off. So no spinning of chairs, please. King Arthur may have been a fictional figure, but his table could be real. Let's pull up to the tables of the world and make them round.

Notes

CHAPTER I

PUTTING OUR HEADS TOGETHER

Social loafing: Max Ringelmann, a French agricultural engineer, experimented with various numbers of students pulling on a rope. He reported in the late 1880s that individual effort lessened as group size increased. The term *social loafing* for such effects was introduced in B. Latané, K. Williams, and S. Harkins (1979), "Many Hands Make Light the Work: The Causes and Consequences of Social Loafing," *Journal of Personality and Social Psychology,* 37:822–832.

David N. Perkins (1995), *Outsmarting IQ: The Emerging Science of Learnable Intelligence* (New York: Free Press).

POWER TO THE PEOPLE

This summary of Athenian democracy is drawn largely from an excellent Web site, The Birth of Democracy, that is part of the Perseus Digital Library, editor-in-chief Gregory Crane, Tufts University, www.perseus.tufts.edu/~hartzler/agora/site/demo/index.html.

COOLING DOWN CONFLICT

The conversation conducted by Mr. Kealoha: This is adapted from E. Victoria Shook (1985), *Ho'oponopono: Contemporary Uses of a*

Hawaiian Problem-Solving Process. (Honolulu, HI: University of Hawaii Press), pp. 13–20.

Account of hoʻoponopono: From Shook, ibid.

Quote about Hawaiian culture: As quoted in Shook, p. 4, from Mary Kawena, Pukui, E. W. Haertig, and Catherine A. Lee (1972), *N na I Ke Kumu,* vol. 1 (Honolulu, HI: Hui H nai), p. 72.

Team Intelligence

Hutchins's work: Edwin Hutchins (1995), *Cognition in the Wild* (Cambridge, MA: MIT Press). The story of the *Palau* is drawn from pages 1–6.

Quote from Hutchins: *Cognition in the Wild,* pp. 5–6.

From Camelot to Reality

Was there an historical King Arthur, and who was he? See *Encyclopedia Britannica Online,* www.Britannica.com.

Lack of organizational intelligence in nations and governments: Barbara Tuchman (1984), *The March of Folly* (New York: Alfred A. Knopf).

The story of abandoning a product too late: Chris Argyris and Donald Schön (1978), *Organizational Learning: A Theory of Action Perspective* (Reading, MA: Addison-Wesley).

CHAPTER 2

Ernesto's Truth

Conversations and change: John Ford and Laurie Ford (1995), "The Role of Conversations in Producing Intentional Change in Organizations," *Academy of Management Review,* 20(3):541–571.

U.S.S. *Palau:* Edwin Hutchins (1995), *Cognition in the Wild* (Cambridge, MA: MIT Press), pp. 1–6.

Process Smart and Deciding Smart

Ford Motor Company and simultaneous design: James Brian Quinn (1992), *Intelligent Enterprise: A Knowledge and Service Based Paradigm for Industry* (New York: Free Press), pp. 206–208; quote from p. 206.

People Smart and the Language of Actions

There is a monograph in Spanish on symbolic conduct: David Perkins (2001), *Conducta Simbólica en las organizaciones.* (Caracas, Venezuela: Fundaexcelencia).

Organizational culture and tacit belief systems: Edgar Schein (1997), *Organizational Culture and Leadership* (San Francisco: Jossey-Bass).

Two Archetypes of Negotiation

On negotiation: Roger Fisher and William Ury (1981), *Getting to Yes: Negotiating Agreement without Giving In* (New York: Penguin, 1981).

The Sinai example: From Fisher and Ury, pp. 42–43.

Contact Architecture

Segmentalism and integrative action: Rosabeth Moss Kanter (1983), *The Change Masters* (New York: Simon & Schuster).

CHAPTER 3

Four Brands of Better Feedback

One minute managing: Kenneth Blanchard and Spencer Johnson (1982), *The One Minute Manager* (New York: Berkeley Books).

Limits of the one-minute reprimand from a behaviorist standpoint: Karen Pryor, personal communication. A contemporary and practical view of behaviorism can be found in Karen Pryor (1995), *On Behavior* (Waltham, MA: Sunshine Books). An excellent practical guide is Karen Pryor (1999), *Don't Shoot the Dog: The New Art of Teaching and Training,* rev. ed. (New York: Bantam Books).

The after-action review: Lloyd Baird, Phil Holland, and Sandra Deacon (1999), "Learning from Action: Imbedding More Learning into the Performance Fast Enough to Make a Difference," *Organizational Dynamics,* 27(4):19–31.

This account of nemawashi was informed by Chapter 8, Case 13, in an online book: Shohei Koike (1996), *Rational Japanese: A Guide to Understanding Ordinary Japanese Behavior* (www2b.biglobe.ne.jp/~shohei/index.htm).

Deconstructive criticism: Robert Kegan and Lisa Laskow Lahey (2001), *How the Way We Talk Can Change the Way We Work* (San Francisco: Jossey-Bass), Chapter 7.

FINDINGS FROM THE FEEDBACK FRONT

This work was carried out as a research and development initiative at the Universidad Jorge Tadeo Lozano in Bogotá, Colombia. We thank the university for its sustained commitment to the program. A full account can be found in Daniel Wilson, David Perkins, Dora Bonnet, Cecilia Miani, and Chris Unger (in preparation), *The Management of Learning.* A brief account can be found in David Perkins and Daniel Wilson (1999), "Bridging the Idea-Action Gap," *Knowledge Directions: The Journal of the Institute for Knowledge Management,* 1:65–77.

CHAPTER 4

WHAT IS INTELLIGENCE?

Dispositional view of intelligence: See, for example, David Perkins and Shari Tishman (2001), "Dispositional Aspects of Intelligence," in S. Messick and J. M. Collis (eds.), *Intelligence and Personality: Bridging the Gap in Theory and Measurement* (Maweh, NJ: Erlbaum), pp. 233–257.

David Perkins, Shari Tishman, Ron Ritchhart, Kiki Donis, and Al Andrade (2000), "Intelligence in the wild: A Dispositional View of Intellectual Traits. *Educational Psychology Review,* 12(3):269–293.

Spearman's analysis of intelligence: Charles Spearman (1904), "General Intelligence, Objectively Defined and Measured," *American Journal of Psychology,* 15:201–293. There are of course many accounts of Spearman, Binet, and the development of concepts of intelligence. For a brief sketch in relation to modern views of intelligence, see David Perkins (1995), *Outsmarting IQ: The Emerging Science of Learnable Intelligence* (New York: Free Press).

Multiple intelligences: Howard Gardner (1983), *Frames of Mind.* (New York: Basic Books).

His more recent reassessment: Howard Gardner (1993), *Multiple Intelligences: The Theory in Practice* (New York: Basic Books).

Sternberg's triarchic theory of intelligence: Robert Sternberg (1985), *Beyond IQ: A Triarchic Theory of Human Intelligence* (New York: Cambridge University Press); (1997), *Successful Intelligence* (New York: Plume); (1999), "The Theory of Successful Intelligence," *Review of General Psychology*, 3:292–316.

My view of intelligence: Perkins (1995), *Outsmarting IQ*.

Limited rationality: Herbert Simon (1957), *Models of Man: Social and Rational* (New York: Wiley).

Hasty, narrow, fuzzy, sprawling: Perkins, *Outsmarting IQ*, Chapter 7.

Mindfulness and mindlessness: Ellen Langer (1989), *Mindfulness* (Menlo Park, CA: Addison-Wesley).

On perspective taking in moral development, see Lawrence Kohlberg (1981), *Essays on Moral Development*, Vol. 1: *The Psychology of Moral Development* (New York: Harper & Row); Carol Gilligan (1982), *In a Different Voice: Psychological Theory and Women's Development* (Cambridge, MA: Harvard University Press).

Emotional intelligence and characteristics of emotional competence: Daniel Goleman (1998), *Working with Emotional Intelligence* (New York: Bantam Books).

Yerkes-Dodson law: R. M. Yerkes and J. D. Dodson (1908), "The Relationship of Strength of Stimulus to Rapidity of Habit Formation," *Journal of Comparative Neurology and Psychology*, 18:459–482.

The Enron scandal and Jeffery Skilling: These few points were drawn from a range of Web sources, including *BBC News Online*, http://news.bbc.co.uk/; *BusinessWeek Online*, www.businessweek.com; *Business 2*, www.business2.com; and *Time*, www.time.com.

CHAPTER 5

WHAT LEADERS DO

Study of good-to-great companies: James Collins (2001), *Good to Great: Why Some Companies Make the Leap and Others Don't* (New York: HarperCollins), pp. 26–27. The quote also appears on Collins's Web site along with other materials outlining his view; www.jimcollins.com.

Transactional versus transformational leadership: Bernard Bass

(1985), *Leadership and Performance beyond Expectations* (New York: Free Press); (1990), "From Transactional to Transformational Leadership: Learning to Share the Vision," *Organizational Dynamics,* 18(3): 19–31.

On facilitative leadership: David Straus (2002), *How to Make Collaboration Work* (San Francisco: Berrett-Koehler); Andrea Ellinger, Karen Watkins, and Robert Bostrom (1999), "Managers as Facilitators of Learning in Learning Organizations," *Human Resource Development Quarterly,* 10(2):105–125; Karen Watkins and Victoria Marsick (1993), *Sculpting the Learning Organization: Lessons in the Art and Science of Systemic Change* (San Francisco: Jossey-Bass); Richard Weaver and John Farrell (1997), *Managers as Facilitators* (San Francisco: Berrett-Koehler).

On charismatic leadership: Alan Bryman (1992), *Charisma and Leadership in Organizations* (London: Sage); Jay Conger and Rabindra Kanungo (1998), *Charismatic Leadership in Organizations* (Thousand Oaks, CA: Sage).

Different authors attach somewhat different meanings to terms such as visionary and charismatic: Badrinarayan Shankar Pawar and Kenneth K. Eastman (1997), "The Nature and Implications of Contextual Influences on Transformational Leadership: A Conceptual Examination," *Academy of Management Review,* 22(1):80–109.

Loci of leadership: Peter Senge, Art Kleiner, Charlotte Roberts, Richard Ross, George Roth, and Bryan Smith (1999), *The Dance of Change: The Challenges to Sustaining Momentum in Learning Organizations* (New York: Doubleday), pp. 565–568.

FOUR FORMS OF LEADERSHIP

Daniel Wilson's analysis of leadership: Daniel Wilson, David Perkins, Dora Bonnet, Cecilia Miani, and Chris Unger (in preparation), *The Management of Learning.*

On psychological safety in cardiac surgery teams: Amy Edmondson, Richard Bohmer, and Gary Pisano (2001), "Speeding Up Team Learning," *Harvard Business Review,* 79(9):125–134.

Shared vision: Peter M. Senge (1990), *The Fifth Discipline: The Art and Practice of the Learning Organization* (New York: Doubleday/Currency), Chapter 11.

Jeffrey Skilling's leadership style: See Wendy Zellner and others

(2002), "Jeff Skilling: Enron's Missing Man," *BusinessWeek Online*, www.businessweek.com, February 11.

The parallel participative organization: Rosabeth Moss Kanter (1983), *The Change Masters* (New York: Simon & Schuster).

The British Airways case: Ronald Heifetz and Donald Laurie (1997), "The Work of Leadership," *Harvard Business Review*, 75(1): 124–134.

Adaptive leadership: Ronald A. Heifetz (1994), *Leadership Without Easy Answers* (Cambridge, MA: Belknap Press).

Leading through abandonment: Wilson, et al., *The Management of Learning*.

LEADERSHIP FOR INTELLIGENCE

Celebrity leaders: Collins, *Good to Great*.

STREETWISE STREET BY STREET

Fred E. Fiedler (1996), "Research on Leadership Selection and Training: One View of the Future," *Administrative Science Quarterly*, 41(2):241–250.

Transformational leadership and organizational structure: Pawar and Eastman, "Nature and Implications of Contextual Influences on Transformational Leadership."

Henry Mintzberg's analysis of organizational structure: Harold Mintzberg (1979), *Structuring of Organizations* (Englewood Cliffs, NJ: Prentice Hall).

Clan mode of governance: A. L. Wilkins and W. G. Ouchi (1983), "Efficient Cultures: Exploring the Relationships between Culture and Organizational Performance," *Administrative Science Quarterly*, 28:468–481.

CHAPTER 6

KING ARTHUR'S ANTS

On distributed systems and the centralist mind-set: Mitchel Resnick (1994), *Turtles, Termites, and Traffic Jams: Explorations in Massively Parallel*

Microworlds (Cambridge, MA: MIT Press), pp. 59–69; (1996), "Beyond the Centralized Mindset," *Journal of the Learning Sciences,* 5(1):1–22.

COMMON SCENTS

Newell's analysis: Alan Newell (1990), *Theories of Cognition* (Cambridge, MA: Harvard University Press).

KNOWLEDGE WEATHER

The problem of follow-through: Jeffrey Pfeffer and Robert Sutton (2000), *The Knowing-Doing Gap: How Smart Companies Turn Knowledge into Action* (Boston: Harvard Business School Press).

Cultures of getting things done: Larry Bossidy and Ram Sharon (2002), *Execution: The Discipline of Getting Things Done* (New York: Crown Business), pp. 16–18.

Project Exodus and other DOD knowledge management initiatives: Tony Kontzer (2002), "U.S. Army Ready to Capture and Build on Information," *Information Week Online,* www.informationweek.com.

British Petroleum's Virtual Teamwork Program: Thomas Davenport and Lawrence Prusak (1998), *Working Knowledge: How Organizations Manage What They Know* (Boston: Harvard Business School Press), pp. 20–24.

The culture-making power of symbolic conduct: Examples from Rosabeth Moss Kanter (1983), *The Change Masters* (New York: Simon & Schuster), pp. 245–246, 298.

WHY SHOULD I BUY THIS?

Alignment with the literature (various sources):

Harold Wilensky (1967), *Organizational Intelligence* (New York: Free Press).

S. Haeckel and R. Nolan. (1993), "Managing by Wire," *Harvard Business Review,* September–October, pp. 122–132.

Chun Wei Choo (1998), *Information Management for the Intelligent Organization* (Medford, NJ: Information Today).

James March (1999), *The Pursuit of Organizational Intelligence* (Oxford, UK: Blackwell).

Michael McMaster (1996), *The Intelligence Advantage* (Woburn, MA: Butterworth-Heinemann).

Yes, But, Rebut

The cult of talent: Malcom Gladwell (2002), "The Talent Myth: Are Smart People Overrated?" *New Yorker*, July 22, pp. 28–33.

Negative structural features: Wilensky, *Organizational Intelligence.*

Segmentalism: Kanter, *The Change Masters.*

The requisite organization: Elliot Jaques (1997), *Requisite Organization: A Total System for Effective Managerial Organization and Managerial Leadership for the 21st Century*, 2nd ed. (Gloucester, MA: Cason Hall).

CHAPTER 7

Three Faces of Coblaboration

On handling meetings well: Michael Doyle and David Straus (1976), *How to Make Meetings Work* (New York: Jove Books).

On groupthink: Irving Janis (1972), *Victims of Groupthink: Psychological Study of Foreign-Policy Decisions and Fiascoes*, 2nd ed. (Boston: Houghton Mifflin); a concise discussion of groupthink along with a critical perspective appears in Em Griffin (1997), *A First Look at Communication*, 3rd ed. (New York: McGraw-Hill), Chapter 18.

What Facilitation Does and Why It Is Not Enough

On facilitation: Doyle and Straus, *How to Make Meetings Work;* David Straus (2002), *How to Make Collaboration Work* (San Francisco: Berrett-Koehler), Chapter 5.

The Good: What Collaboration Means, How It Helps, and When It Helps

Communities of practice: a key source for this concept is Etienne Wenger (1998), *Communities of Practice: Learning, Meaning, and Identity* (New York: Cambridge University Press).

On background conditions for collaboration: J. Richard Hackman (1998), "Why Teams Don't Work," in R. S. Tindale, J. Edwards, and E. J. Posavac (eds.), *Applications of Theory and Research on Groups to Social Issues* (New York: Plenum Press), pp. 245–267.

The Challenger disaster: See, for example, W. H. Starbuck and
F. J. Milliken (1988), "Challenger: Fine-Tuning the Odds until
Something Breaks," *Journal of Management Studies,* 25:319–340.

THE ART OF CITIZENSHIP

Citizenship responsibilities: Doyle and Straus, *How to Make Meetings
Work,* Chapter 8.

Cultures of conversation: Daniel Wilson, David Perkins, Dora
Bonnet, Cecilia Miani, and Chris Unger (in preparation), *The Management of Learning.*

On teams: Jon R. Katzenbach and Douglas K. Smith (1993), *The
Wisdom of Teams: Creating the High-Performance Organization* (Boston:
Harvard Business School Press).

Concept of relational collaboration: Mark Haskins, Jeanne
Liedtka, and John Rosenblum (1998), "Beyond Teams: Toward an
Ethic of Collaboration," *Organizational Dynamics,* 26(4):34–50.

HERE THERE BE DRAGONS

The writing of the Declaration of Independence: This information is
drawn from the Web site of the U.S. National Archives and Records
Administration, www.nara.gov/exhall/charters/declaration/dechist
.html.

CHAPTER 8

CALM AS A CLAM

Creative destruction: Joseph A. Schumpeter (1975; orig. pub. 1942),
Capitalism, Socialism and Democracy (New York: Harper).

THREE WAYS OF SETTLING CONFLICT

Why conflict is inevitable in organizations: Lee Bolman and Terrence
Deal (1991), *Reframing Organizations: Artistry, Choice, and Leadership*
(San Francisco: Jossey-Bass).

THE LOGIC OF TRUST

The fragility of organizations: Richard Farson (1996), *Management of
the Absurd: Paradoxes in Leadership* (New York: Simon & Schuster).

Trust in the Land of Lear

Unexpected expectations: Kenneth Blanchard and Spencer Johnson (1982), *The One Minute Manager.* (New York: Berkeley Books).

The fundamental attribution error: Lee Ross (1977), "The Intuitive Psychologist and His Shortcomings: Distortions in the Attribution Process," in L. Berkowitz (ed.), *Advances in Experimental Social Psychology,* Vol. 10 (New York: Academic Press), pp. 174–220.

Better Conflict through Trust

Frontier visions: James Brian Quinn (1992), *Intelligent Enterprise: A Knowledge and Service Based Paradigm for Industry* (New York: Free Press), pp. 256–260.

Concepts of interdependence: Morton Deutsch (1973), *The Resolution of Conflict* (New Haven, CT: Yale University Press).

Interdependence and constructive versus destructive conflict: Dean Tjosvold (1997), "Conflict within Interdependence: Its Value for Productivity and Individuality," in Carsten De Dreu and Evert Van De Vliert (eds.), *Using Conflict in Organizations* (London: Sage), pp. 23–37.

Language of blame versus contribution: Douglas Stone, Bruce Patton, and Sheila Heen (1999), *Difficult Conversations: How to Discuss What Matters Most* (New York: Penguin).

Negotiation based on interests: Roger Fisher and William Ury (1981), *Getting to Yes: Negotiating Agreement without Giving In* (New York: Penguin).

On trust: Francis Fukuyama (1995), *Trust: Social Virtues and the Creation of Prosperity* (London: Hamish Hamilton).

Antitrust cases: Information from *Business Week Online,* www.businessweek.com, and *USA Today Online,* www.usatoday.com.

Here There Be Superdragons

The Osgood proposal: C. E. Osgood (1959), "Suggestions for Winning the Real War with Communism," *Journal of Conflict Resolution,* 3:295–325.

Enron as a culture gone awry: See the following Web sources: *BBC News Online,* http://news.bbc.co.uk/; *BusinessWeek Online,* www.businessweek.com; *Business 2,* www.business2.com; and *Time,* www.time.com.

CHAPTER 9

Presto Change-o

On the knowing-doing gap: Jeffrey Pfeffer and Robert Sutton (2000), *The Knowing-Doing Gap: How Smart Companies Turn Knowledge into Action* (Boston: Harvard Business School Press).

The idea-action as a hostile environment with unseen threats: Alan Robertson and Graham Abbey (2002), *Clued Up: Working through Politics and Complexity* (London: Pearson), p. 7.

Poetry in Motion

Negotiating from positions as action poetry: Roger Fisher and William Ury (1981), *Getting to Yes: Negotiating Agreement without Giving In* (New York: Penguin).

The One-Eyed Woman

The jungle metaphor: From Robertson and Graham, *Clued Up.*

Pocket Change

On communities of practice: Jean Lave and Etienne Wenger (1991), *Situated Learning: Legitimate Peripheral Participation.* (New York: Cambridge University Press); Etienne Wenger (1998), *Communities of Practice: Learning, Meaning and Identity* (New York: Cambridge University Press).

Study of Xerox technical representatives: Julian Orr (1990), "Sharing Knowledge, Celebrating Identity: Community Memory in a Service Culture," in D. Middleton and D. Edwards (eds.), *Collective Remembering: Memory in Society* (Beverly Hills, CA: Sage).

Exchanging lore through stories: see John Seely Brown and Paul Duguid (2000), "Balancing Act: How to Capture Knowledge without Killing It," *Harvard Business Review,* 78(3):73–79.

As mentioned in Chapter 3: Daniel Wilson, David Perkins, Dora Bonnet, Cecilia Miani, and Chris Unger (in preparation), *The Management of Learning;* David Perkins and Daniel Wilson (1999), "Bridging the Idea-Action Gap," *Knowledge Directions: The Journal of the Institute for Knowledge Management,* 1:65–77.

How Change Takes Flight

The story of robins and titmice: Arie de Geus (1997), *The Living Company: Habits for Survival in a Turbulent Business Environment* (Boston: Harvard Business School Press).

Systems thinking: See Peter Senge (1990), *The Fifth Discipline: The Art and Practice of the Learning Organization* (New York: Doubleday/Currency).

The Dragon Unlearning

Organizational immune system: Edgar Schein (1997), *Organizational Culture and Leadership* (San Francisco: Jossey-Bass).

The Three Arts of Unlearning

Substituting talk for action: Jeffrey Pfeffer & Robert Sutton (2000). *The Knowing-Doing Gap: How Smart Companies Turn Knowledge into Action* (Boston: Harvard Business School Press).

Action projects to get people moving: Perkins and Wilson, "Bridging the Idea-Action Gap"; R. Revans (1980), *Action Learning: New Techniques for Management* (London: Blond & Briggs); Kurt Lewin (1948), *Resolving Social Conflicts* (New York: Harper & Row).

Practice fields: See, for instance, Robert Fulmer, Philip Gibbs, and J. Bernard Keys (1998), "The Second-Generation Learning Organizations: New Tools for Sustaining Competitive Advantage," *Organizational Dynamics,* 27(2):7–20.

Languages of transformation: Robert Kegan and Lisa Lahey (2001), *How the Way We Talk Can Change the Way We Work: Seven Languages of Transformation* (San Francisco: Jossey-Bass).

Single- and double-loop learning: Chris Argyris and Donald Schön (1978), *Organizational Learning: A Theory of Action Perspective* (Reading, MA: Addison-Wesley).

On implementation intentions: Peter M. Gollwitzer (1999), "Implementation Intentions: Strong Effects of Simple Plans," *American Psychologist,* 54:493–503.

Yerkes–Dodson law: R. M. Yerkes and J. D. Dodson (1908), "The Relationship of Strength of Stimulus to Rapidity of Habit Formation," *Journal of Comparative Neurology and Psychology,* 18:459–482.

On the complex impact of stress on performance: See G. R. J. Hockey (1986), "Changes in Operator Efficiency as a Function of Environmental Stress, Fatigue, and Circadian rhythms," in K. R. Boff, L. Kaufman, and J. P. Thomas (eds.), *Handbook of Human Performance,* Vol. 2: *Cognitive Processes and Performance* (Chichester, U.K.: Wiley).

Systemic barriers to change: Andrew Molinsky (1999), "Sanding Down the Edges: Paradoxical Impediments to Organizational Change," *Journal of Applied Behavioral Science,* 35(1):8–24.

Risk and innovation: Sim B. Sitkin (1996), "Learning through Failure," in M. D. Cohen and L. S. Sproull (eds.), *Organizational Learning* (Thousand Oaks, CA: Sage), pp. 541–577.

The problem of polarization: Richard Elmore (1996), "Getting to Scale with Good Educational Practice," *Harvard Educational Review,* 66:1–26.

EPILOG

Quip about democracy: From a speech by Winston Churchill to the House of Commons, November 1947, according to Rhoda Thomas Tripp (compiler) (1970), *The International Thesaurus of Quotations* (New York: Harper & Row), p. 231.

Memes: Richard Dawkins (1976), *The Selfish Gene* (New York: Oxford University Press).

Index

A

AAR. *See* After-action review

Abandonment, 117

Abbey, Graham, 211

Academy of Management Review (periodical), 109

Action poetry, 213, 243

Action projects, 221

Action theories, 213, 243

Active inhibition, 61

Adams, John, 171–172

Adaptive leadership, 101

Administrative Science Quarterly (periodical), 109

After-action review (AAR):
  as communicative feedback, 53–54
  limitations of, 54

Aggressive criticism, 58

Analytical intelligence, 73

Answer-centered leadership:
  Arthur and, 96
  defined and described, 95–97
  limitations of, 97
  from perspective of knowledge processing, 104–106
  from perspective of symbolic conduct, 105–106

Archetypes of interaction:
  defined and described, 29, 123, 246
  and organizational intelligence, 123
  progressive versus regressive, 84, 123–125, 246

Archetypes of negotiation, 33–35

Argyris, Chris, 13, 234

Aristotle, 1

Arthur:
  and answer-centered leadership, 96
  and communicative feedback, 46–50
  and conciliatory feedback, 50–51
  and constructive criticism, 55–56
  and the "Deal," 91
  and deconstructive criticism, 56
  and inquiry-centered leadership, 99
  and leadership, 91, 96, 98, 99, 101
  and negative feedback, 50
  as an organizational consultant, 20
  and problem sharing, 158, 162–165
  as a social theorist, 1–2
  and trust, 178–179
  and unlearning, 227–230
  and vision-centered leadership, 98

Athenian democratic institutions, 5–7

Authoritarianism, 113–114, 117

Autocratic decision-making archetype, 29
Autocratic decision-making process, 30–31

B

Bass, Bernard, 92
BATNA. *See* Best alternative to a negotiated agreement
Behaviorism:
 described, 52
 and one-minute managing, 52
Behaviorist techniques, 52
Berra, Yogi, 44
Best alternative to a negotiated agreement (BATNA), 35
Binet, Alfred, 72
Blame system of conducting disputes, 195
Blanchard, Kenneth, 51
Blinding vision, 117
Bodily kinesthetic intelligence, 73
Bolman, Lee, 180
Bossidy, Larry, 130
Boule (Athenian senate), 5, 6
Boyle, Richard, 132
Bridgestone/Firestone tire recall of 2000, 28
British Airways, 100–101
British Petroleum, 131
Brown, John Seely, 220
Brown, Robert, 150
Brownian motion:
 as coblaboration, 150–151, 153
 defined and described, 150–151
 facilitators and, 153

C

Camp David treaty of 1978, 34
Centralized mind-set, 120
Challenger space shuttle disaster of 1986, 168
Change Masters, The (Kanter), 36, 99–100, 132
Chaotic culture, 114, 117
Charan, Ram, 130
Charismatic leadership, 93, 98
Choo, Chun Wei, 134
Churchill, Winston, 93, 248–249
Citizen Kane (motion picture), 26, 29

Civil resolution of conflict, 181
Clan mode of governance, 110–111
Clued Up (Robertson and Abbey), 211
Coblaboration:
 archetypes of, 149–154
 Brownian motion, 150–151
 downspiraling, 151
 groupthink, 152
Cognitions in the Wild (Hutchins), 9–12
Cognitive oversimplification:
 and individual intelligence, 77–78
 and organizational intelligence, 77–79, 85, 87
 and regressive archetypes, 78
Collaboration, 147–176
 challenges of, 166–168
 circumstances favoring, 157–158
 defined and described, 154–156
 dragon situations, 171–175
 example (Declaration of Independence), 171–172
 see also Problem sharing
Collaborative citizenship, 166–173, 176
Collaborative commitment, 1–2, 20
Collective behavior, 13
Collective decision making, 33–35
Collective nonintelligence (examples):
 King George and American Revolution, 13
 Montezuma and Cortez, 13
 United States and Vietnam Conflict, 13
Collins, James, 92, 103
Command-and-control leadership, 93, 97
Command hierarchy:
 defined and described, 11–12
 example (U.S.S. *Palau* navigational emergency), 9–12
Communicative feedback:
 Arthur and, 46–50
 communicative feedback step-by-step, 47–51
 defined and described, 43, 44
 dragon situations, 64
 implementing, 57–61
 organizational intelligence and, 82
 tacit rules for giving and receiving, 62–63, 67

Communities of practice (COPs), 220–222
    defined and described, 220
    developmental leaders and, 221–222
    knowledge resources and, 220
Conciliatory feedback:
    Arthur and, 50–51
    as conflict avoidance and encourage-
        ment, 44
    defined and described, 42–45
Conflict and conflict resolution:
    archetypes, 181–182
    civil resolution, 181, 182, 184
    consensus resolution, 181, 184
    power resolution, 181–183
    regressive and progressive conflict,
        183–185
Consensus resolution, 181–183
Contact architecture:
    and conversations, 37
    defined and described, 36, 124, 246
    and progressive and regressive interac-
        tions, 146
Contribution system of conducting dis-
    putes, 195
Contrient interdependence, 193–194
Conversations:
    conversations as interactions, 19
    conversations as key component of orga-
        nizations, 17–18, 123
    cultures of conversation, 169–170
Corruption versus trust, 202–203
Creative conflict, 179
Creative destruction, 179
Creative intelligence, 73
Cuban missile crisis of 1962, 17, 23, 33
Culture of command, 114–115, 117
Culture of crisis, 115–116

D
Dawkins, Richard, 250
Deal, the, 91
Deal, Terrance, 180
Decision making:
    autocratic decision making, 29
    four general moves and, 24–25
    four general needs and, 24–25
    good decision-making factors, 26

knowledge processing and, 24
    participative decision making, 30
    procedural knowledge and, 23
Deconstructive criticism:
    Arthur and, 56
    as communicative feedback, 55–57
de Geus, Arie, 223
Dell Computer Corporation, 130
Democracy and democratic institutions:
    in early Athens, 5
    Kleisthenes and, 5
    Socrates on, 6, 248
    Winston Churchill on, 248–249
Design processes:
    sequential design, 24, 26
    simultaneous design, 24, 26
Deutsch, Morton, 193
Developmental leaders, 216–219, 241,
    243
    and archetypes, 241, 243
    and communities of practice, 221
    and law of global impact, 224
    and law of local impact, 241
    marks of, 218–219
    and unlearning, 230–240
Difficult Conversations (Stone, Patton, and
    Heen), 195
Dinosaur paradox, 32–33, 67, 74, 247
Distributed cognition, 19
Domino effect, 82–83, 86, 87
Double-loop learning, 234
Downspiraling:
    as coblaboration, 151, 153
    defined and described, 151
    facilitators and, 153
Doyle, Michael, 150, 169
Dragon situations:
    authoritarian culture and, 114, 117
    challenging climates and, 63, 67
    chaotic culture and, 114–115, 117
    collaboration and, 171–175
    culture of command and, 115, 117
    culture of crisis and, 115–116
    defined, 64
    feedback and, 64–66
    inquiry-centered leadership and,
        113–116

Dragon situations *(Continued)*:
  negative people and, 65–66
  round-table model of organizational
    intelligence and, 145
  savior syndrome and, 117
  stressful circumstances and, 66, 67
  trust and, 200–207
  unlearning and, 225–240
Duguid, John, 220

E
Eastman, Kenneth, 109–112
Edmondson, Amy, 97
Ekklesia (Athenian assembly), 5
Emergence, 126, 127
Emotional oversimplification, 79–81, 85,
  87
Enron scandal of 2001, 83, 99, 136, 206
Execution (Bossidy and Ram), 130
Experiential intelligence, 73
Explanation theories, 212, 243

F
Facilitators and facilitation:
  case study (Harvard Graduate School
    administrators), 89–90
  facilitation and collaboration, 153–154
  facilitative leadership, 93
  facilitators and Brownian motion, 153
  facilitators and downspiraling, 153
  facilitators and groupthink, 153
  facilitators and ho'oponopono, 7, 8
  facilitators versus inhibitors, 89–90,
    94–95
  what facilitation achieves, 152–154
False openness, 101, 117
Farson, Richard, 185
Fast Company (periodical), 209–210
Feedback:
  after-action review (AAR) as feedback,
    53–54
  communicative feedback, 43–44, 46,
    47–51, 57–60
  conciliatory feedback, 42–46
  deconstructive criticism as feedback,
    55–57

  dilemma of feedback, 42
  feedback as fundamental key to perfor-
    mance and learning, 39–67
  feedback from standpoint of knowledge
    processing, 46
  feedback from standpoint of symbolic
    conduct, 47
  feedback in a challenging climate, 65
  negative feedback, 42, 43, 45, 46
  nemawashi as feedback, 54–55
  one-minute praising as feedback, 51–53
  one-minute reprimand as feedback,
    51–53
Feuds, 173–174, 176
Fiedler, Fred, 109
Fifth Discipline, The (Senge), 98, 224–225
Firestone tire recall of 2000, 28
Fisher, Roger, 33, 35
Five-brain backlash, 75–76, 85, 87
Flores, Fernando, 18
Frame breaking (unlearning countermoves):
  bracketing old frames of reference, 232
  double-loop learning and, 234
  establishing clear expectations for action,
    232
  exposing competing commitments,
    233–234
  having a good reason for, 231
  identifying talk-walk discrepancies, 234
  language of transformation and, 233
  practice fields and, 233
  raising consciousness regarding, 231–232
  selecting low-risk projects, 233
  single-loop learning and, 234
Frame defenses (unlearning archetypes),
  226, 227–228, 243
Franklin, Benjamin, 171–172
Fukuyama, Francis, 197, 206

G
Galloping democracy, 172–173, 176
Gardner, Howard, 73
Getting to Yes (Fisher and Ury), 33
Gilligan, Carol, 79
Gladwell, Malcolm, 136
Goleman, Daniel, 80

Gore, Ernesto, 17
Group planning, 24
Groupthink:
    as coblaboration, 150–153
    defined and described, 152
    facilitators and, 153

H

Habit breaking (unlearning countermoves):
    active inhibition, 236
    framing backsliding as normal, 236–237
    implementation intentions and, 235
    planting reminders, 235–236
    raising consciousness, 235
    stress management, 236
    whens, wheres, and hows of, 235
Habit defenses (unlearning archetypes),
    226, 228–229, 243
Hackman, Richard, 157
Harvard Business Review (periodical), 100,
    134
Haskins, Mark, 170–171
Heen, Sheila, 195
Hegel, Georg Wilhelm Friedrich, 180
Heifetz, Ronald, 100
Hierarchies, 12
Hihia (Hawaiian relationship of negative
    entanglement), 8
Ho'oponopono (Hawaiian group therapy
    practice), 7–9, 157
*How the Way We Talk Can Change the Way
    We Work* (Kegan and Lahey), 55
How to Make Collaboration Work (Straus), 153
How to Make Meetings Work (Doyle and
    Straus), 150, 153, 169
Hutchins, Edwin, 9–12, 19

I

Idea-action gap, 129, 210, 213, 240, 243
ImageTech (pseudonym), 18–19, 21,
    29–30, 64
Individual intelligence:
    analytical intelligence, 73
    bodily kinesthetic intelligence, 73
    creative intelligence, 73
    David Perkins theory of, 73

experiential intelligence, 73
    Howard Gardner theory of, 73
    individual intelligence defined and
        described, 71, 133
    interpersonal intelligence, 73
    intrapersonal intelligence, 73
    linguistic intelligence, 73
    logical–mathematical intelligence, 73
    musical intelligence, 73
    neural intelligence, 73
    practical intelligence, 73
    reflective intelligence, 73
    Robert Sternberg theory of, 73
    spatial intelligence, 73
*Information Management for the Intelligent
    Organization* (Choo), 134
Inhibitors:
    case study (Harvard Graduate School
        administrators), 89–90
    defined and described, 89
Inquiry-centered leadership:
    Arthur and, 99
    case study (British Airways), 100–101
    conditions favoring or discouraging,
        111–112
    defined and described, 96, 99–101
    dragon situations and, 113–116
    from perspective of knowledge process-
        ing, 104–106
    from perspective of symbolic conduct,
        105–106
    limitations of, 101
Intelligence, individual. See Individual
    intelligence
Intelligence, organizational. See Organiza-
    tional intelligence
Intelligence Advantage, The (McMaster), 135
Intelligence quotient (IQ):
    Alfred Binet and, 72
    Charles Spearman and, 72
    group IQ versus group size, 76
    Outsmarting IQ (Perkins), 4, 73, 77
Intelligent Enterprise (Quinn), 24–25, 193
Interactions:
    as key ingredient of organizations, 19
    progressive interactions, 20

Interactions *(Continued)*:
  progressive interactions versus regressive
    interactions, 20, 89–90, 144–145, 246
  regressive interactions, 20
Interpersonal intelligence, 73
Interpersonal stress, 109
Intrapersonal intelligence, 73
Intrinsic motivation, 101
IQ. *See* Intelligence quotient

J
Janis, Irving, 152
Jaques, Elliott, 138
Jefferson, Thomas, 171–172
Johnson, Spencer, 51
Johnson & Johnson Tylenol recall of 1982,
  28

K
Kanter, Rosabeth Moss, 36, 99–100, 132,
  138
Katzenbach, Jon, 169–170
Kegan, Robert, 55–57, 233
Kennedy, John F., 17, 23
King Arthur. *See* Arthur
King Lear (Shakespeare), 177–178, 191
Kleisthenes, 5, 248
Knowing-doing gap, 129, 210, 232
Knowing-Doing Gap, The (Pfeffer and Sutton), 210, 232
Knowledge archetypes:
  explicit knowledge, 130
  hard knowledge, 130
  soft knowledge, 130–131
  tacit knowledge, 130–131
Knowledge processes and processing:
  acting on knowledge, 128–130, 240
  communicating knowledge, 128, 240
  generating knowledge, 127, 128, 240
  integrating knowledge, 128–129, 240
  knowledge processing and decision mak-
    ing, 23–26
  knowledge processing and progressive
    versus regressive interactions, 28
  knowledge processing as key component
    of organizational intelligence, 74, 123

knowledge processing defined and
  described, 22
knowledge processing and feedback, 45,
  46
knowledge processing and leadership
  archetypes, 103–106, 246
patterns of knowledge processing, 24
Knowledge weather, 126–132, 247
Kohlberg, Lawrence, 80

L
Ladder of feedback, 47, 57
Lahey, Lisa Laskow, 55–57, 233
Langer, Ellen, 78
Languages of transformation, 233
Laurie, Donald, 100–101
Lave, Jean, 220
Lawnmower paradox, 3, 4, 13, 74, 246
Law of global impact, 224, 241, 243
Law of local impact, 222, 241, 243
Leaders and leadership:
  adaptive leadership, 101
  answer-centered leadership, 95–98
  Arthur and leadership, 91, 101
  charismatic leadership, 93, 98
  command and control leadership, 93
  executive leaders, 94
  facilitative leadership, 93, 101
  inquiry-centered leadership, 95, 96,
    99–101
  leadership by leaving alone, 95, 96,
    101–103
  Leadership for intelligence, 103–106
  leadership trap, 106, 107
  leading through abandonment, 102
  local line leaders, 94
  network leaders, 94
  servant leadership, 101
  smart leadership, 137–138
  stewardship, 101
  transactional leadership, 93
  transformational leadership, 93, 98
  vision-centered leadership, 95–96,
    98–99
Leadership archetypes:
  answer-centered leadership, 95–98

inquiry-centered leadership, 95–96, 99–101

leadership by leaving alone, 95, 96, 101–103

from standpoint of knowledge processing, 104

from standpoint of symbolic conduct, 105

vision-centered leadership, 95–96, 98–99

Leadership by leaving alone:

Arthur and, 101

defined and described, 96, 102–103

limitations of, 102–103

from perspective of knowledge processing, 104–106

from perspective of symbolic conduct, 105–106

Leadership Without Easy Answers (Heifitz), 101

Liedtka, Jeanne, 170–171

Linguistic intelligence, 73

Living Company, The (de Geus), 223

Local line leaders, 94

Logical-mathematical intelligence, 73

Lurking autocracy, 173, 176

M

Magellan, Ferdinand, 245

Majli (Saudi Arabian problem solving discussion process), 17

Management of the Absurd (Farson), 185

March, James, 134–135

March of Folly (Tuchman), 13

Marshall, Colin, 100–101

Marx, Karl, 1

Maturana, Humberto, 18

McMaster, Michael, 135

McNamara, Robert, 17

Mental effort versus physical effort (pooling of), 3, 4, 246

Micromanagement, 117

Mintzberg, Henry, 110

Molinsky, Andrew, 237

Moore, Gordon, 193

Multiheaded animal syndrome, 150

Musical intelligence, 73

My Fair Lady, 191

N

Negative feedback, 42, 43, 45, 46

Negative reinforcement:

behaviorism and, 52

one-minute managing and, 52–53

Negotiation and negotiating:

negotiating from interests, 33, 34

negotiating from positions, 33

Nemawashi (Japanese consensus-building process):

defined and described, 17, 31

as feedback, 54–55

Network leaders, 94

Neural intelligence, 73

New Yorker (periodical), 136

Noyce, Robert, 193

O

One-minute goal setting:

and one-minute praising, 51

and one-minute reprimand, 51

One Minute Manager, The (Blanchard and Johnson), 51

One-minute managing, 53

One-minute praising, 51

One-minute reprimand, 51–52

Organizational Dynamics (periodical), 53

Organizational intelligence:

arguments for, 126, 133–136

cognitive oversimplification and, 77–79, 85, 87

defined and described, 122–126

developmental leaders and, 248

dinosaur paradox and, 74

domino effect and, 82–83, 86, 87

emotional oversimplification and, 79–81, 85, 87

feedback and, 39–67

five-brain backlash and, 75–76, 85, 87

knowledge processing and, 74

lawnmower paradox and, 74

limitations of, 14

power advantage and, 83–84, 86

Organizational intelligence (Continued):
  progressive archetypes and, 247
  regression in the face of stress and,
    81–82, 85
  regressive archetypes and, 247
  role of culture in, 140–143
  round-table model of, 123–124,
    133–140, 246
  symbolic conduct and, 74
  what-why-how question and, 14, 246
Organizational Intelligence (Wilensky), 134
Organizational Learning (Argyris and
    Schön), 13
Organizational structure, 110–111
Organizations:
  conversations as key component of, 17,
    123
  Ernesto Gore and definition of, 17
Orr, Julian, 220
Osgood proposal, 201–202
Othello (Shakespeare), 203–204
Outsmarting IQ (Perkins), 4, 73, 77
Oversimplification, 77–79

P
Paine, Thomas, 1
Palau, U.S.S. See U.S.S. Palau navigational
    emergency
Participative decision-making archetype,
    30, 31
Participative decision-making process, 30–31
Patton, Bruce, 195
Pawar, Badrinarayan, 109–112
People smart:
  defined and described, 20
  and the language of actions, 26
  progressive interactions and, 20
Pfeffer, Jeffrey, 129, 210, 232
Physical effort versus mental effort (pooling
    of), 3, 4, 246
Piaget, Jean, 79
Positive reinforcement:
  behaviorism and, 52
  one-minute managing and, 52
Power advantage, 83–84, 86
Power resolution of conflict, 181–182
Practical intelligence, 73

Practice fields, 233, 234, 238
Problem sharing:
  Arthur and, 158, 162–165
  balancing act of, 165–166
  dividing up the task, 160, 162, 164
  entrusting an individual or small group
    to produce a solution, 159, 162, 163
  generating an initial take, 160, 162,
    164–165
  talking through the problem, 159,
    162–163
  see also Collaboration
Process smart:
  and deciding smart, 22
  defined and described, 20
  and progressive interactions, 20
Progressive archetypes, 35, 38
  organizational intelligence and, 122
Progressive interactions:
  defined and described, 20, 21, 246
  knowledge processing and, 28, 29
  versus regressive interactions, 20, 21, 246
  symbolic conduct and, 28, 29
Project Exodus (U.S. Department of
    Defense), 131
Promotive interdependence, 193
Pryor, Karen, 53
Prytaneis (Athenian executive committee),
    5, 6
Pursuit of Organizational Intelligence, The
    (March), 134–135
Pygmalion principle, 191

Q
Quinn, James Bryan, 24, 26, 193

R
Reflective intelligence, 73
Reframing Organizations (Bolman and Deal),
    180–181
Regression in the face of stress, 81, 85
Regressive archetypes:
  autocratic group decision making, 38
  cognitive oversimplification and, 78
  emotional oversimplification and, 81
  negotiation from positions, 38
  organizational intelligence and, 122

Regressive interactions:
  defined and described, 20, 21, 246
  example (motion picture *Citizen Kane*),
    26, 29
  knowledge processing and, 28, 29
  versus progressive interactions, 20, 21,
    246
  symbolic conduct and, 28, 29
Relational collaboration, 170–171
Resnick, Mitchel, 120
Resolving conflict. *See* Conflict resolu-
  tion
Responsible citizenship, 169
Responsible collaboration, 169
Robertson, Alan, 211
Romeo and Juliet (Shakespeare), 51
Rosenblum, John, 170–171
Ross, Lee, 189
Round table:
  as symbol and facilitator of collaborative
    commitment, 1–2, 20
Round-table model of organizational intel-
  ligence:
  alternatives to, 136–140
  arguments for, 133–136
  dragon situations and, 145
Rusk, Dean, 17

S
Savior syndrome, 117
Schein, Edgar, 28
Schön, Donald, 13, 234
Schumpeter, Joseph, 179
Segmentalism, 37
Senge, Peter, 94, 98, 224
Shaw, George Bernard, 191
Shook, E. Victoria, 7, 195
Simon, Herbert, 77
Simultaneous design process, 37
Single-loop learning, 234
Sitkin, Sim, 238
Skilling, Jeffrey, 83, 99
Skinner, B.F., 52
Smith, Douglas, 169–170
Social loafing, 3
Socrates, 6, 248
Spatial intelligence, 73

Spearman, Charles, 72
Spoilers, 174–176
Star Trek, 69
Stereotyping, 77
Sternberg, Robert, 73
Stone, Douglas, 195
Straus, David, 150, 153, 169
Streetwise (periodical), 107–108, 113
Stress:
  interpersonal stress, 109
  and organizational intelligence, 87
  stress management, 109
Sutton, Robert, 129, 210, 232
Symbolic conduct:
  defined and described, 27
  examples, 28
  versus exchanges of hard knowledge, 132
  and feedback, 45, 47
  and leadership archetypes, 103, 105–106,
    246
  and organizational intelligence, 123
  and participative versus autocratic deci-
    sion making, 32
  and progressive versus regressive interac-
    tions, 28
System breaking (unlearning counter-
    move):
  avoiding missionaries and unbelievers,
    239
  coping with change fatigue, 238–239
  coping with stirring the swamp,
    239–240
  creating a low-risk culture, 237–238
  making time, 238
  practice fields and, 238
  raising consciousness, 237
System defenses (unlearning archetypes),
    226–227, 229–230, 243

T
Team intelligence:
  case study (U.S.S. *Palau* navigational
    emergency), 9–12
  command hierarchy and, 9–12
Telephone (game), 36
Tjosvold, Dean, 194
Transactional leadership, 93, 97

Transformational leadership, 93, 98
Triarchic theory of intelligence, 73
Trust, 185–207
  animosity and trust, 203–205, 208
  Arthur and trust, 178–179
  broken trust, 201–202, 208
  capability and trust, 186
  categorical trust, 188, 189, 195
  commitment and trust, 186
  corruption and trust, 202–203, 208
  dragon situations and trust, 200–207
  how trust works, 185–187
  logic of trust, 187
  Osgood proposal for rebuilding trust, 201–202, 208
  practicality of trust, 185–186
  Pygmalion principle, 191, 208
  reflective trust, 190–191
  trusting in the civil mechanism, 196–200
  trusting in the common vision, 192–196
  trusting only in yourself and yours, 198–199
Trust (Fukuyama), 197
Tuchman, Barbara, 13
Tylenol recall of 1982, 28

U
Unbiased collective judgment, 5–7
Underfacilitation, 101, 117
Unlearning, 225–240
  Arthur and, 227–230
  frame breaking and, 231–234
  frame defenses and, 226, 227–228, 243
  habit breaking and, 234–237
  habit defenses and, 226, 228–229, 243
  system breaking and, 237–240

  system defenses and, 226–227, 229–230, 243
Ury, William, 33, 35
U.S.S. *Palau* navigational emergency, 9–12, 17, 19, 157

V
Virtual Teamwork Program (British Petroleum), 131
Vision-centered leadership:
  Arthur and, 98, 227–230
  defined and described, 95, 98–99
  limitations of, 98–99
  organizational structure and, 109–111
  from perspective of knowledge processing, 104–106
  from perspective of symbolic conduct, 105–106
VisionTech (pseudonym), 18–20, 29–30

W
Watson, John, 52
Wells, Orson, 26
Wenger, Etienne, 220
Wilensky, Harold, 134, 138
Wilson, Alan, 223
Wilson, Daniel, 95, 102, 169
Win–win negotiating solution, 34
Wisdom of Teams, The (Katzenbach and Smith), 169
Working with Emotional Intelligence (Goleman), 80

Y
Yakety yak, 39–40
Yerkes–Dodson law, 81, 236

Printed in the United States
53203LVS00002B/131

9 780471 237723